An Active Service

An Active Service traces the story of a young Sid Dowland from civilian life into the tough environment of the Guards Depot in the 1930s and then on to a Guards Service Battalion in London and pre-war Egypt. The outbreak of war finds Sid taking part in the retreat to Dunkirk and then service in North Africa before volunteering for the SAS. Captured after a disastrous raid in Sardinia, he escapes from the Prisoner of War camp in Italy before making it back to England. The end of the war does not signal peace, as the Guards are sent into action in Palestine and subsequently to the jungles of Malaya, where Sid finds that his SAS experience is in great demand.

This book is a tale of adventure, but will be of interest to anyone studying the Second World War or the early days of the SAS. Most of the historical information is previously unpublished, and much of it is drawn from SAS operation reports in the National Archives and from the war diaries of the Grenadier Guards. The story is accompanied by many previously unseen photographs from private collections, and is brought to life by a series of high quality and accurate drawings depicting the uniforms of the day.

This is an enjoyable human story, but is also an accurate account of military life during the war years, which will be of interest to anyone researching or studying this period.

Richard Dorney, a keen military historian, has served for thirty years in the Grenadier Guards. He is 49 years old, married with three sons, and is currently living in Surrey.

Richard's work with the Regimental Association led him to first come into contact with Sid Dowland, and they became firm friends. It was both Richard and Sid's wish, when the project for this book was first discussed, that all proceeds go to the Grenadier Guards Association, a cause close to both men.

This is Richard's first book, which took over three years of careful research, and heralds the successful completion of a personal challenge.

GW00750444

AN ACTIVE SERVICE

The story of a soldier's life in the
Grenadier Guards, SAS and SBS
1935–1958

by

Richard Dorney

Illustrations by Sean Bolan

Helion & Company Ltd

Helion & Company Limited
26 Willow Road
Solihull
West Midlands
B91 1UE
England
Tel. 0121 705 3393
Fax 0121 711 4075
Email: info@helion.co.uk
Website: www.helion.co.uk

Published by Helion & Company 2005
This paperback reprint 2009

Designed and typeset by Helion & Company Ltd, Solihull, West Midlands
Cover designed by Bookcraft Limited, Stroud, Gloucestershire
Printed by Lightning Source

© Helion & Company Limited 2005, 2009

Cover illustration 'Sardinia' by Sean Bolan

ISBN 978-1-906033-48-4

British Library Cataloguing-in-Publication Data.
A catalogue record for this book is available from the British Library.

For details of other military history titles published by Helion & Company Limited contact
the above address, or visit our website: http://www.helion.co.uk.

We always welcome receiving book proposals from prospective authors.

Contents

Foreword

My first encounter with Sid Dowland was many years ago. He was a well known Grenadier character who appeared at all the regimental gatherings, often proudly wearing his medals including a series of polished stars which indicated that he had served in Europe, Italy and North Africa. There was little to distinguish him from the white haired comrades who regularly paraded alongside him in their blue blazers and grey flannels but his name was regularly mentioned in casual conversation. Over the years I became more involved with my regimental association and I came to realise that Sid was greatly respected. I came to believe that this was purely because he was a very long serving branch secretary but I was later to learn that there was a great deal more to Sid's story.

It was at a lunch hosted by the Surrey Branch of the Grenadier Guards Association that I started to chip away at the 'real story'. Over lunch I chatted to Sid and to others and picked up snippets about the SBS and previously unheard anecdotes. I was intrigued, I knew that he was a Dunkirk veteran and his medals told their own story but there was clearly more to this modest man. For his part Sid offered very little about his service outside of the Grenadier Guards but when pressed mentioned that he had been a prisoner of war although 'not for long because I escaped'. During the fairly short meal I had been fed snippets of information; SAS, SBS, POW, escaped and so on. I was totally hooked and wanted to know the whole story. Sid was infuriatingly casual about the whole thing and spoke throughout as if it was of no interest.

Much later when I questioned some of Sid's friends it became clear that most of them knew very little about his story and they too had been fed little snippets. I had managed to glean that he was a pre- war regular soldier and that in addition to his service with the SAS he had served in no fewer than four of the six war time Battalions of the regiment. My curiosity was fuelled and I realised that this was a story worth recording. I had carried out research on various projects before, particularly on the period of the Great War and had always been struck at how few accounts there were from the enlisted men. Many documents had survived and had been archived but hardly any of these were written by Private soldiers (later Guardsmen). Presumably they were thought irrelevant at the time. Such documents are now vital pieces of history as the last living eye witnesses are now well over a hundered years old. This then, was I suppose a part of my motivation for approaching Sid to see if he would allow me to record his life as a Grenadier.

I had no idea that this project would lead to the production of a book. I thought that a couple of typed pages would be sufficient to record this man's war time service but I had completely misjudged the depth of his story. Over the next two years I came to know Sid well as we sat together in his conservatory. He was so very typical of his generation, uncomplaining, modest and possessing the most incredible talent for understatement. As his story unravelled we talked about other characters, men equally worthy of note by history, men representative of a generation decimated by war. We talked for hours at a time, two Grenadiers of different generations, pausing only to drink our tea provided by Pat, Sid's lady wife. There was no bragging, no great sense of achievement and no expectation that I should be remotely interested in the details of an adventure that took place sixty years ago. It was a true story, one full of adventure and tragedy too. Much of the detail was long forgotten and I was confused on more than one minor detail.

When I started to cross reference, and research the story that Sid had related to me I discovered more details more intrigue and more characters. It was then that it occurred to me that perhaps I could tell the tale through Sid's own eyes. I had discovered a great deal about life as a soldier in the twenty or so years of Sid's service, perhaps it would be of interest to others. I have consequently mentioned as many of the key players as I can. These are not selected by rank but by the frequency that they were mentioned by Sid when he was relating his tale, they are men who will otherwise be forgotten by history. Many officers and warrant officers had faded from his memory but the antics of Jim Kosbab and others were as fresh as if they had occurred yesterday. For this reason I have attempted to record history through the eyes of those at the coalface, the ordinary men rather than the decision makers.

Operation Hawthorns, the raid on Sardinia remained unclear to me until I was able to locate the operation file from the national archives. It was only then that the story made sense. Set out in sixty year old bold type were the names of the SAS men and the detail of what had befallen them. They felt at the time that they had been betrayed by their American interpreter, this fact is clearly recorded in the operation report. Those who survive remain bitter at the conduct of the man who had been attached to 'aid' them. I have not listed the name of the American in this book although it is clearly listed in the report, after sixty years some things are perhaps best left alone.

It is important to remember that Sid and thousands of others fought a powerful enemy that had the upper hand for a large part of the war. The outcome was uncertain for most of the time and when they fought overseas their home was under attack too. I mention this because it may be difficult for those of my generation to relate to this in an age where the enemy is often a 'rogue state' or a terrorist, 'our wars' are very short lived by comparison. The actions that are fought in the second millennium are short in duration, weeks or months rather than years and those at home seem hardly affected or inconvenienced. The whole affair can now be watched live on TV. Compare this to the battles of the last war, relatives often had no clue that large actions had even been fought until long after the event and their loved ones were sometimes away for years. The casualties too are mercifully light, in recent conflicts our total losses have been a fraction of those lost in single actions of the Second World War.

This story is not a regimental history and it is not Sid's biography either, it is a simple true adventure as experienced by many men. Few will have served in as many theatres or in as many units but most will recognise parts of the story that they can identify with. Anyone who has served in the Household Division at any time will recognise parts of this story as being similar to their own. Sid's story is now safely recorded for history, please read it, enjoy it but above all remember that it was his generation that guaranteed our freedom.

Acknowledgements

Recording this story whilst trying to hold down a full time job at the same time has been a major undertaking for me. It would simply not have been possible without the help and encouragement of scores of people who have given up their time to assist me with this project. Most of the historical events that I have described have come directly from the memories of those who were there. Sid Dowland B.E.M. the central character in this story was an unassuming man with a wonderful memory. He was always quick to credit others whilst relating the events that surrounded him and without his accurate descriptions and memory for detail, it would have been impossible to conduct most of the supporting research. As Sid and I sat in his conservatory talking over the events of sixty years ago, we were constantly supplied with tea and coffee by Pat Dowland. Her patience and understanding will live long in my memory as will her continued support of this project and of the Grenadier Guards Association.

The superb illustrations in this book were drawn by Mr Sean Bolan a magnificent military artist who has produced many works for Regiments of the Household Division and others. This project would never have been finished were it not for his constant support and encouragement. Sean's eye for detail and deep interest in Grenadier matters are doubtless due to the attentions of his father Edward. Edward Bolan joined the Grenadier Guards in 1928 and served at Dunkirk in 1940, he later fought in North Africa and Italy where he was seriously wounded. At the age of 90 Edward has a memory that should be the envy of any man half his age, he was a major contributor to the book and I am deeply indebted to him and to Sean.

The list of eye witnesses must be topped by In-Pensioner Dougie Wright M.M. who was himself a pre-war Grenadier and Dunkirk veteran. He joined the SAS with Sid and later saw service in the Mediterranean and Yugoslavia where he worked alongside the partisans with such legendary figures as Major Anders Lassen V.C., M.C. Dougie's recollection of the characters involved and of the detailed events were essential. There could be no sharper eye for detail than that of Len Bozeat M.M. another Grenadier veteran of North Africa and Italy. Len has constantly kept me on my toes where detail is concerned, particularly in relation to the early days of the 6th Battalion Grenadier Guards.

There are Grenadiers all over Great Britain who have sent me snippets of information and even extracts from their own memoirs but I am most grateful to those who have settled in Australasia and America for being so supportive. I must thank Colonel Andrew Duncan L.V.O, M.B.E. who took the time to put me in touch with a number of very helpful contacts. His own work on the Medmenham ranges was most helpful. The Training Battalion at Victoria Barracks Windsor proved to be unexpectedly difficult to research, so the recollections of those who served there were invaluable. Among these men were, Major Warren Freeman-Attwood, Bill Grandfield M.M., Tom Woolcott, Bill Spragg, Ron Rainford, Harry West, John Edwards and Robin Russell. Robin remains a stalwart of the Windsor Branch of the Grenadier Guards Association and his enthusiasm for this book and knowledge of war time Windsor were incredibly helpful.

The Internet has been a vital tool in contacting and researching various details. The Grenadier Guards Association web site has allowed me to contact a wide network of Grenadiers. This would not have been possible without the hard work of Jim White and Derek Money who have been quick to pass on any requests for assistance. The web site now boasts around 400 Grenadiers of all ages who are able to communicate either directly of indirectly with each other. E mail has allowed me to speak to all manner of contributors not least of which was Mr Sid Dowland, known as 'young Sid', a cousin of our central character and a mine of information on the early years.

Many anecdotes were sent to me and I have used several of them in the text but I must particularly thank Harry Mansell, Peter Youdale and Peter Horsefield for their memories of Palestine and Malaya. During my research I have spent many hours in the archives at Regimental Headquarters of the Grenadier Guards in London. The knowledge combined with extreme patience of Mr Alan Kear, Sgt Jupp M.B.E. and of successive Quartermaster Sergeants has made the task an enjoyable one. The advice and assistance of the London District photographer Sgt Harvey have also been greatly appreciated.

None of the research would have been possible without the support of the Regimental Adjutant Lieutenant Colonel C J Seymour whose father is featured in this book. I was able to access the archives at Regimental Headquarters and to reproduce some of he photographs by kind permission of the Lieutenant Colonel Commanding the Grenadier Guards, Colonel E.T. Bolitho O.B.E. The research concerned with the production of this book was conducted by me alone and any errors omissions or inaccuracies are my responsibility. Finally I should thank my wife Sue and the boys for simply putting up with me.

Richard Dorney
July 2004

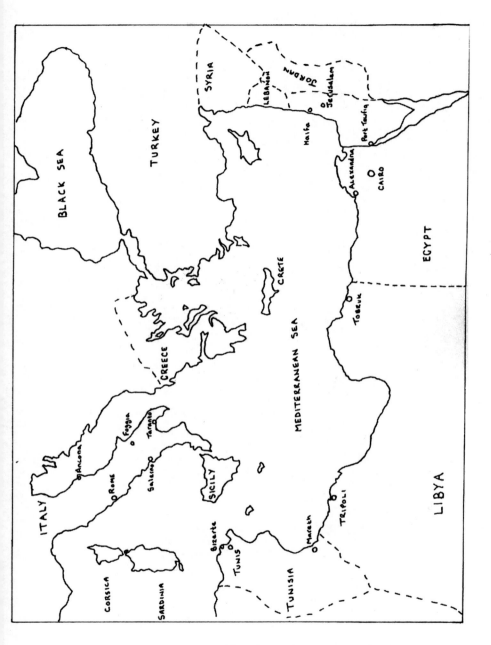

North Africa, Italy and the Middle East - some of the areas covered in the story

'Service is the price we pay for our room on earth'
Rev Tubby Clayton

Chapter 1

Aldershot November 2002

November 11th 2002 was a typically crisp British autumn morning. The crematorium car park was filled by grey-haired men who stood solemnly in groups. Occasionally, newcomers were greeted with warm handshakes and nodding heads. Most of the men were old soldiers, discernable by highly polished shoes, and the blue and red tie of the Brigade of Guards. Their upright postures and rugged faces suggested long service in the army, indeed many were veterans of the Second World War. Their wives too were present, most forming their own groups and conversing quietly. They had come to pay their respects to one of their own, not a famous man, but a great man in his own regimental community. It was appropriate that this was Armistice Day.

The gathering was interrupted by the arrival of the hearse. A Guard of Honour was formed by tall silver-haired men, some proudly wearing the blazer badge of the Grenadier Guards Association. The little chapel was by now filled to overflowing. Mourners pressed into the foyer as the coffin, draped in the union flag, was borne down the aisle. In the congregation, Generals mingled with those who had never experienced promotion from the ranks. Civilians sat alongside decorated men, and serving soldiers stood quietly in respect. On top of the flag-draped coffin rested campaign medals and decorations, suggestive of another time when our country fought for its very survival.

At the end of the service, the last post sounded around the chapel. Sobs could be heard. Tears filled the eyes of the old soldiers who perhaps remembered other fallen comrades. There was a deafening silence, followed by the 'Grenadiers Return', an emotional tune played on drum and flute. It grew fainter, until it tailed off completely. Finally, reveille was sounded, provoking the thought that our old friend had returned to his maker, and to the many comrades who had passed before him.

Although emotional this was not an unusual funeral. The man for whom so many had turned out was, in many ways, unremarkable. He was typical of an unselfish generation that endured hardship without complaint. His military service, although distinguished, was not unique amongst his generation. But devotion to his regiment, and to his comrades, make him very special to those who knew him. Over sixty years of service, both in uniform and to the regimental association, mark Sid Dowland as a great Grenadier. An ex-Prisoner of War, and member of the Special Air Service, who served in four separate Battalions of the regiment he loved, he was a greatly admired and respected man. This book celebrates his service as a Grenadier Guardsman, but it is not his story alone. It is the story of those men who served alongside him, the ordinary men, most of whom will be forgotten by history, whilst the name of their Regiment lives on.

Chapter 2

Dorset

In April 1917, the Great War was well into its third year and King George V was on the throne. At home in England, people were reeling from the dreadful casualty lists which were published daily. It was a difficult time for a child to be born, but on the 15th of that month young Sidney Charles became the latest addition to the Dowland family. It was decided to christen him Sidney in honour of his uncle Sid. He was a Royal Marine who had died on HMS Hampshire, along with Lord Kitchener, when the cruiser struck a mine off the Orkneys in June the previous year. Uncle Sid's death had been a blow to the family. But they had been relatively lucky. Their oldest son, Frank, had been just too young to serve in the war, and the immediate family had escaped loss.

The post war years were very turbulent times. Hardly a family in the country had been untouched by the war, and veterans found that work was scarce. The Dowland children had a happy childhood none the less. The family home was in Poole, and the Dorset countryside proved to be a pleasant environment. Another son, George, had been born a couple of years later, and young Sid now had five brothers and sisters. Sadly, George was left disabled by meningitis, and was not expected to survive past his teenage years. The youngest boys were very close and the two were often found playing together. Happily, George confounded the experts and lived well into his eighties.

A young Sid Dowland with his father circa 1931

Sid's school years were spent in Poole, and he soon found himself following in the sporting footsteps of his older brothers. Frank was an outstanding footballer who could well have been signed by a professional football club, had it not been for his father's objections. Walter Dowland too had a talent for the game, but as a goalkeeper. Sid and George often looked on enthusiastically as their brothers took penalties against each other. Sid proved to be relatively competent with his studies at the Heatherlands School at Parkstone, but the outdoor life was more to his liking. He was expected to follow his brothers into the school football team, and he didn't disappoint, eventually becoming captain. George had been unable to attend school, so Sid spent many evenings at home helping to teach his brother what he himself had learned in the classroom. His school years were generally successful. He also gained a reputation as a good cricketer, but happy childhood soon passed into adult reality and, at the age of fourteen, he left school.

It was 1931, and there were few decent jobs around, but a placement had been arranged for him as an office boy in a local garage. The office environment was not to his liking and he grew to resent being used as a 'dogsbody'. His wages were a paltry five shillings a week, which his father said wouldn't pay to feed him for a day!

His frustration grew, and it wasn't long before he was answering back. Such behaviour was not tolerated from a boy his age and before long, to his father's horror, Sid found himself unemployed. He badly needed work, and when a job came along at Bournemouth central railway station he took it. But a disagreement over working hours soon saw him redundant once again.

This had been an unhappy and frustrating start to his working life. He had not enjoyed either of his jobs since leaving school, so he was greatly relieved when his father announced that he would take him on in the family business. Mr Dowland had run a rustic fencing business in the area for some time, and Sid found that he was much happier working in the open air with his father and his partner. He soon fell into the role of apprentice and mastered the skills of the trade.

In the summer there was a good deal of work available in the gardens of the affluent folk of Dorset. The problem was that demand tailed off in the winter. Britain's economy was in crisis, and the Labour government under Ramsay Macdonald seemed powerless to halt its decline. In late 1932 there were almost three million unemployed. Against these conditions, there was little that Sid's father could do but lay him off until the work returned. He now found himself at the mercy of economic forces and there seemed to be no end in sight to the problem.

When the work was scarce he was able to pursue his passion for football and he soon became a regular in a local team. He made many new friends through this association, and one of them made a great impression. Cyril Scott had left Poole some years earlier, to join the army, and was now home on leave. Scott had joined the Coldstream Guards and had served for three years. Sid was immediately struck by his appearance. He looked fit, athletic and was full of stories from far off lands like Egypt and the Sudan. Sid listened to these exciting stories which seemed a world away from his own rather bleak circumstances.

Over the next few days he couldn't get the idea of joining the army out of his head. Here was an opportunity to escape the cycle of unemployment and uncertainty. He decided to discuss this option with his father, who was rather disappointed. He had hoped that Sid would eventually take over the family business. It was decided that he should stick it out a little longer to see if the situation improved. The prospect of a few years in khaki remained firmly in his mind. When the economy failed to recover he decided to take the plunge, and his father agreed not to stand in his way.

It was with some trepidation that he set out for the army recruiting office in Bournemouth, and was relieved to find himself in the company of a friend when he arrived. Douglas Rickman had found himself in similar circumstances to Sid and had also arrived at the office with the intention of becoming a soldier. The two young men entered together and found themselves being interrogated by a red faced, moustached recruiting sergeant. Sid noticed that he wore the medal ribbons of the Great War on his chest. Neither of the boys had given any serious thought as to which regiment or corps they should join and they enquired about the Royal Engineers. Both young men were over six feet tall, a fact not overlooked by the wily recruiting sergeant.

'Two big tall chaps like you should think about the Guards', he said.

Sid remembered the stories that Cyril Scott had told him about the Desert and he asked if the Guards were due to go overseas.

'The Grenadiers are warned for Egypt', replied the recruiting sergeant. He then proceeded to describe to them the magic of this exotic country. This was just what the boys wanted to hear. No further persuasion was needed, the romance of the pyramids was enough. On 19th July 1935, at the age of eighteen years and three months, Sid, along with his pal Douglas, enlisted in the Grenadier Guards.

Chapter 3

Caterham

For a young man of eighteen who had rarely been out of Dorset, the journey to Surrey was full of anxiety. Douglas had received instructions to report to Caterham on the same day, so the two friends decided to travel together. After they had enlisted they discovered more information about the Grenadier Guards. They were joining a highly disciplined and elite regiment, and they now wondered if they had made the right decision. Some of the old soldiers they had met in Poole laughed loudly when they heard of their decision to join the Guards. 'You don't know what you've let yourselves in for', they said. This reaction did nothing to reduce their feelings of trepidation. When they arrived in Caterham they asked directions to the Guards Depot and were directed to the top of a formidable hill. The man who provided their route added helpfully, 'You'll find it next door to the lunatic asylum'. The pair wondered if this piece of information was significant!

When they arrived at the entrance to the Guards Depot, Sid had a distinct sinking feeling in the pit of his stomach. At the barrack gate a sentry stood rigidly in front of a tall sentry box, a rifle with fixed bayonet firmly held in his right hand. Highly polished, heavy looking boots joined tight layers of khaki cloth which were wrapped neatly around the sentry's lower legs. The creases in the man's trousers looked sharp enough to cut you if touched. A set of shining belt brasses glinted from the white belt around his waist. Before the two had time to take in this scene, they were pounced upon by a previously unseen man dressed in khaki. Rapid staccato sounds exited from a mouth half concealed by a large waxed moustache. In no time the two boys were standing at the Guardroom, once again being interrogated by a frightening Non Commissioned Officer who seemed to have no hair at all at the sides of his head. The boys noted that he wore three chevrons on the upper arms of his tightly buttoned khaki tunic. They were instructed to stand to attention, in spite of the fact that they had not been taught how to, but the desired position was quickly achieved with some strident encouragement.

Their identities established, the two were placed in the hands of the Picquet sentry, who was instructed to take the new arrivals to the receiving room. The young sentry was a recruit himself and had only served a few weeks more than his charges. His lack of seniority however, did not prevent him from marching the two boys off at breakneck speed. Sid and Douglas were alarmed at the young man's apparent enthusiasm for speed marching as he barked out the time amid the clatter of hobnailed boots. Doubtless he felt obliged to demonstrate the fact that he had already experienced this particular pleasure and was in some way superior.

The sentry pointed out certain areas of the barracks as they passed. 'Orderly room', 'Cookhouse', 'Gymnasium', he reported. Sid immediately noticed that the whole barracks seemed to be a hive of activity. Squads of khaki clad recruits marched briskly past. Rifles were struck as though they would break and salutes were practised all over the place. The sound of hobnailed boots on tarmac was everywhere and the high-pitched voices of the drill instructors were resonant. There was a sense of purpose and uniformity that was both obvious and daunting.

The barracks at Caterham had been the home of the Brigade of Guards since the 1870s, and at the time of its construction had been revolutionary. Large Victorian brick structures dominated the landscape, and overlooked a huge barrack square where countless numbers of young men had been turned into Guardsmen. The Brigade of Guards was famous the world over for its strict discipline and high standards. Sid was already starting to feel that this was not going to be easy.

At the receiving room various questions were answered, and signatures were placed on official looking documents. The boys were soon joined by other equally confused and breathless young men. They were all then taken on the route, followed by thousands of recruits before them, to the Quartermaster's store via the cookhouse. The cup of tea that they received was welcome, but it hardly seemed to touch the sides before they were whisked away to be issued with various unfamiliar items of military uniform.

The new recruits left the stores carrying piles of uniform with boots precariously balanced at the top. They were eventually shepherded into a barrack room. Sid surveyed the room that would be his home for the next couple of months. It was bare, but for a few tables and chairs, and a large number of ancient looking iron framed beds which had large lockable boxes stowed neatly underneath. At one end there were a number of brushes and other items, clearly intended for use when cleaning the room. It looked as though this happened frequently, if the shine on the floor and the smell of polish was anything to go by. His living area consisted of one of the rickety beds and two wooden shelves screwed to the wall above. Blankets were piled on top of the thin mattresses, which he soon learned were to be known as 'biscuits'.

He slept well that night and was not surprised to be woken early the next morning by a rather loud, and alarmingly awake, Non Commissioned Officer, who shouted loudly until every man was out of bed. Breakfast was a confusing affair; they spent so long learning how to stamp their feet that there was hardly any time left to eat when they arrived. The following days were spent mainly in the barrack room, under the supervision of the 'Trained Soldier', a Guardsman who had spent time in the Battalions of the Brigade. He was entrusted with teaching the finer points of dress and administration. Although he held no rank, he was addressed as 'Trained Soldier', and conducted himself as if he were a Non Commissioned Officer. As the days went by, more confused young men joined the squad and the barrack room slowly filled up. The recruits spent most of the time dressed in 'Fatigue Order', a sort of denim outfit which was prone to fade rather quickly when washed. It was consequently possible to deduce how much service a man had accrued by the colour of his denims. The lighter the denims, the longer he had been around. Sid's 'Fatigue Order' may not yet have been very faded but it certainly stank of moth-balls.

Before long the Squad was complete and they had all been issued with the necessary equipment. They endured a medical examination where they stood in line in a draughty inspection room, stripped to the waist, their braces hanging lifelessly behind them. An ancient bespectacled doctor briefly studied their white bodies. He tapped a few chests and mumbled something about needing 'sand in their bellies', before he pronounced them all fit to serve in His Majesty's Guards. Some of the recruits later speculated that the doctor probably wouldn't have noticed if one

Lance Sergeant Raikes' squad Caterham 1935 (Sid Dowland standing front right)

of them had a wooden leg. A slightly longer examination took place at the tailors' shop where they were measured for their service dress. They were prodded and turned, pushed and pulled by the depot tailors. They made a series of rapid and bewildering chalk marks on each man, as he stood to attention in his newly issued uniform.

This early administration had taken place under the supervision of their Squad Instructor, Lance Sergeant Bill Raikes. Raikes, a small man and by no means an archetypal Guardsman, had introduced himself to the Squad by teaching them how to stand to attention and how to march. It seemed to Sid that he had done nothing but confirm what he had already been taught. The Squad were marched around the barracks at a seemingly impossible rate and he wondered if someone would drop dead if it continued. They puffed, panted and sweated until their uniforms were soaked, all to the 'yak-yak' of Raikes's voice.

Every day they were taught new drill movements, which became increasingly more complex. Men were often dumped upon their backsides, as their boots slipped out from under them when attempting to turn in one direction, whilst still moving in another. Each error was met with a deafening admonishment from Raikes, who pointed and prodded with his drill cane. Almost everyone was apparently 'idle' and often 'dozy' too. Completely new words entered their vocabularies on an almost daily basis. No one wanted to be described as a 'brahma' even though the exact definition of this particular word was unclear. These seemingly endless hours on the drill square brought the squad together. Failure by one meant failure by all and team-work was the result.

Most of the evenings were spent cleaning and polishing not only their own kit, but the barrack room and ablutions too, this was known as 'swabbing'. Many hours were spent on hands and knees scrubbing floors and polishing copper pipes. It was necessary to learn how to present your equipment in your bed space for inspection. Every item had its own set position on the bed or shelves, and uniformity was essential. Any man whose kit didn't exactly match the remainder of the squad's could watch out. Each morning there seemed to be an inspection where every part of the room was scrutinised. If the Squad failed to meet the required standard they could expect serious reprisals from their 'trained soldier'. He would without hesitation, scream abuse at the offender and throw any object from a boot to a mattress out of the window. They were all issued with a brass 'bed plate' which was stamped with their own name and regimental number. This was to be polished and hung above the bed space. If during an inspection the bed space was found to be in bad order, the bed plate would be removed and the name noted for disciplinary action. It became known as 'losing your name', an experience that would be repeated many times in the coming weeks.

At the end of each day there was a 'shining parade', the purpose of which was to dedicate time to improving the standard of personal equipment whilst learning the regimental history. These parades were conducted in silence, each man sitting astride his bed cleaning his equipment. The 'trained soldier' would ask questions on the history of the regiment, which was formally taught during the training day. A great deal of time was dedicated to dress, as it was considered to be most important for a guardsman to be better turned out than other soldiers at all times. Puttees were wound around the leg eleven times, no more no less and the recruits practised this until it could be achieved effortlessly.

More challenging was the Slade Wallace webbing equipment. This was assembled by means of a series of complicated straps and buckles which had to be fitted carefully to each man. Two large ammunition pouches were attached to the front of the belt by buckles. A greatcoat and cape could be fastened on at the rear by more straps. The equipment was made of leather buff material which had to be whitened with 'blanco', and the numerous brass buckles and studs polished to a high shine. It was impossible for a man to fit the equipment to himself, the help of another being essential to ensure correct assembly.

As if this wasn't bad enough, if the greatcoat and cape were to be attached, they had to be rolled or folded meticulously to exactly the right dimensions. Three or four men would be required to stretch a cape over the table, and to roll it tightly before fastening it to the lower back. A similar process was necessary for the greatcoat. It would culminate in two recruits standing on the folded article, on top of an upturned bench, while other recruits hammered the sides of the now square greatcoat with long handled scrubbers. When the hammering was finished, the greatcoat would be completely square and would meet the exact dimensions laid down. It was then wrapped tightly with leather straps and attached to the webbing. Some found it helpful to add cardboard to 'stiffen' the appearance of the folded greatcoat, but most were too frightened, in case they invoked the wrath of the 'trained soldier'.

It had been a real effort for the squad to meet the exacting standards that Lance Sergeant Raikes had set. Most had managed but one or two found certain skills beyond them. Sid often cleaned the boots of a fellow recruit who was just unable to produce a decent shine. This man would then make amends by helping with some other task that was within his ability. This was the team-work that the army wanted but there was another benefit, great friendships were made. In the hours after the evening shining parade, the squad characters made themselves known. Sid became great friends with a fellow recruit called Wally Durrant, whose musical talents were soon revealed. Wally was often seen hula dancing around the barrack room dressed in an improvised grass skirt to the tune of a ukulele, as the rest of the squad roared with laughter. Wally had also managed to retain a small accordion which he played with gusto. Unfortunately he only knew six tunes and four of these were hymns. Although Durrant was only a year older than Sid, he was not as 'green' as he pretended. He had served as a 'boy' with the 24th London Regiment for over two years and he knew most of the dodges.

The Squad also had a 'Superintending Sergeant' who frequently appeared, usually when things were not going well. Sergeant Betts was a small man but was renowned for the penetration of his voice. The recruits were very wary of him and quickly realised that Raikes answered to him also. When the Squad was being drilled on the square they always worked that bit harder when Betts was around. A company officer would sometimes come out to watch their drill and he would usually be accompanied by the Company Sergeant Major, 'Snapper' Robinson. The officer would generally find some aspect of their drill or turn-out at fault, and would point in their general direction with a leather covered cane. The Company Sergeant Major would immediately spring into life screaming at the squad instructor and indicating an 'idle man' or a 'dozy lot'. The end result would invariably mean the whole squad being marched around the square, at a very demanding speed, until the CSM was satisfied that the point had been made.

In addition to the drill parades and inspections, there was PT every day. At first the recruits spent a lot of time in the gymnasium, vaulting horses and carrying out various exercises. This soon gave way to cross-country running with steadily increasing distances. Sid found that all those hours spent on the football pitch were valuable, as he was able to cope well. Not everyone found it easy, and members of the squad could often been seen vomiting at the side of tracks on the Caterham hills. Extra PT was on the programme for those who were unable to keep up. Sid usually enjoyed these physical periods, but the instructors soon noticed he was rather skinny and that his right leg was slightly bent. This made him appear a little bow-legged and he became the butt of their jokes. Raikes took great pleasure in announcing to the squad that 'Dowland should wear cymbals on the inside of his knees'!

On Saturday mornings there was always a drill parade and the whole depot took part. This was generally known as 'swank parade'. It was conducted by the Regimental Sergeant Major, RSM 'Tibby' Britton, Coldstream Guards. The RSM was considered by most to be God himself. He was a fearsome man with a striking, barrel-like figure and a mighty voice which could be heard all over Caterham. His Drill Sergeants chased around the square at the sound of his voice, zeroing in on any man who had been spotted being idle. Sid noticed that one of these Drill Sergeants was a Grenadier, Drill Sergeant Teece. He was immaculately dressed and looked very tough, but Sid didn't want to be caught looking. The recruits were marched around all four sides of the parade square to the accompaniment of the Corps of Drums. Their saluting was practised as they passed the Adjutant, standing near the RSM. The Adjutant was a rather mystical figure and none of the recruits was sure what he did. They understood however that he was a powerful figure, and not to be upset. They feared his swagger stick being pointed in their direction. This was normally the signal for one of the Drill Sergeants to launch himself into the ranks as if he was going to murder one of them.

The Depot was run on bugle calls, and all recruits were expected to be able to recognise the various tunes and their meaning. During swank parade these calls were sounded by a lone drummer, on the RSM's instructions, and nominated recruits would be expected to identify the relevant call. There were many tunes, so to make the identification a little easier, each call was allocated a little rhyme to assist the non musical in memorising it. The pioneers were summoned to the tune of -

'Pioneers, pioneers, pioneers, there's dog s — t on the square'.

The in-lying Picquet call would follow –

'Dirty dog, dirty dog, you can't go on with a dirty frog'.

There were scores of these rhymes to learn, reveille, cookhouse, mail-call, and so on. Some of the calls were identical, but for the number of final notes played, so it was important to listen carefully. Some of the recruits found this a difficult skill to master, but Sid was rapidly gaining a reputation as a bright young recruit, and he had no such trouble with his bugle calls.

On Sunday there was a Depot church parade and the recruits were marched to the Caterham Garrison church in their companies. Service dress was worn with forage caps and turnout, as always, was expected to be of the highest standard. It seemed to Sid and his pals that the church parade was just another excuse to practise more drill, but once inside the church there was a little respite. The boys usually fought to remain awake, nudging each other in case they were spotted by one of the many Non Commissioned Officers in the church. It may have been the House of God but the padre usually turned a blind eye to the Drill Sergeant violently poking a recruit with his pace stick.

One of the squad members was an Irishman by the name of Ryan, he was a Roman Catholic who of course regularly attended confession before mass. When poor Ryan rejoined the squad, Raikes was always waiting. 'I don't know what you confessed, but I know you owe four extra drills, because it's here in my notebook'. The rest of the squad saw the funny side but poor Ryan didn't. He later earned the dubious honour of becoming the first member of the squad to be locked up. He underwent a period of local detention for some minor indiscretion. The other recruits saw him daily in the distance being drilled by the Police Sergeant. The boys were sympathetic to his plight but grateful that they weren't in his position.

As their training continued, the recruits were introduced to the rifle, the most important part of the Infantryman's equipment. They learned about the .303 Short Magazine Lee Enfield (SMLE) and how it had been used to stop the German advance in 1914. At that time, trained soldiers had been expected to fire fifteen rounds a minute, accurately. The recruits looked forward to firing this perfectly balanced rifle. It was much lighter than they had expected at only eight and a half pounds. Of course shooting was one thing, but the rifle required more drill, until they could march at the slope, present arms, and fix the menacing looking sword bayonet.

Their foot drill was formally tested in the presence of a company officer, and to the relief of the squad, they managed to pass. This was the first hurdle. Failure would have meant remedial training and re-testing a week later. After about five weeks they were again formally tested, this time with the rifle and bayonet. The inspecting officer cast his critical eye over each man, checking his bearing, the standard of his boots, buff equipment, and his position of attention, from the angle of his feet to the position of his rifle. He also asked questions on their regimental history and on the names of various personalities within the Depot, from the Commandant down. Each man was more nervous than ever before. When they performed their rifle drill, they struck the wooden furniture as if to break it. After the recruits passed this inspection they were judged to be capable of carrying out guard duties and they were placed on the duties roll. It wasn't long before Sid found himself receiving other recruits as the Picquet sentry.

There were more inspections to come. Each required an ever more difficult sequence of drill movements to be demonstrated to the inspecting officer. None of them looked forward to the Adjutant's Inspection as they knew this would be a stiff test, and the RSM himself would be present. The thought of the red-faced RSM Britton breathing down their necks was terrifying.

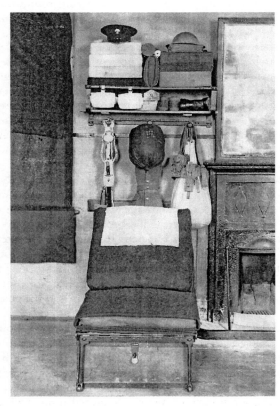

Typical bed space circa 1930's. Note the brass name plate in the centre and the folded greatcoat top shelf centre.

Guardsmen were expected to reach a reasonable standard of education and the whole squad attended 'school' on most days. These education classes were a welcome break from the piercing screams of the drill instructors, although the journey to school invariably turned into a drill session, which would be resumed after lessons ended. Sid gained his 3rd class education certificate with ease, and progressed to the 2nd class certificate. This was important because it meant a pay increase of 6d a day. Those who failed to pass were expected to continue their efforts when they arrived in their respective Battalions. This was always difficult and unpopular due to the lack of time available to study. Happily he was one of the few who managed to pass.

Regimental history was taken extremely seriously and there was much to learn. The origins of the regiment, its battle honours, of which there were many, the names of regimental heroes, were some of the many customs that a Grenadier should know. The Regiment had eleven Victoria Crosses and each recruit was expected to reel off the names of those who had won them, together with the battle in which it had been won. Seven of these had been awarded during the Great War and the exploits of the Guards Division were legendary. In 1918, the King had directed that as a mark of honour, Privates in the Guards Division should be known as Guardsmen in recognition of their great services during the war. It was little wonder that most of the training was still based upon the outdated tactics of the First World War.

Most of the Squad Instructors were too young to have served in the war, but there were plenty of Officers and Senior Sergeants who wore the medal ribbons of 1914-18. Little had changed in the military since the end of the war, and the economic situation meant that this was not a happy time for the army. Defence spending was tight and numbers had been reduced. There was a shortage of ammunition for training, and football rattles were sometimes used to simulate machine-gun fire. Motor transport was virtually non-existent and horse transport was not officially phased out until 1936. The Bren gun and the 3-inch mortar would also not see service until the following year.

Young officers sometimes gave lectures on tactics using a sand box and this would often be followed up by a march into the countryside to train. Sid enjoyed these excursions. They would be played out of barracks by the Corps of Drums, and passers-by sometimes stopped to applaud the soldiers. The route marches, in full kit, were very tiring but essential. The recruits were reminded how the 2nd Battalion of the regiment had retreated from Mons in good order, in 1914, and had lived to fight another day. Good march discipline was very important and it was strictly imposed by the likes of Sergeant Betts. They would all puff out their chests as they returned to barracks, and were met once again by the sound of flute and drum, as the Corps of Drums struck up their stirring tunes.

Time passed quickly, and Sid felt that he had progressed well. He looked forward to the day when he could finally 'pass off' in front of the Commandant. The Barracks routine of course continued and the squad were required to carry out a number of fatigues when it was their turn. One such task was to carry the food from the kitchen to the cookhouse at meal times. The food was transported in large metal containers and it was hard messy work. Those transporting the food were known as 'swabs' and they hated the task.

The Platoon progressed well. One or two 'brahmas' fell by the wayside and were transferred to other regiments, but there was a sense that the remainder would soon be ready to leave. They were fit, and regularly ran long distances around Caterham. They could march for miles with full pack and a rifle. They had fired a few rounds through their rifles but the ammunition shortage had prevented them from becoming marksmen. Each man knew his regimental history and could fold a greatcoat and cape. They had learnt how to wear a tunic and a bearskin cap, and how to carry out ceremonial drill.

The difficult art of sentry drill had been learnt if not mastered by everyone. This entailed the squad working together, in two separate halves, with no words of command or verbal communication. All of their actions were carried out to the sound of rifle butts tapping on the ground or by hand signals as they marched toward each other. When marching in opposite directions it was essential to dig the heels in hard so that they could hear each other and maintain a mirror image of their actions. It took a great deal of time for the squad to master the art, but eventually it came. They waited anxiously for the day to come when the Commandant would inspect them.

The great day finally arrived, in December 1935, when Lance Sergeant Raikes's squad paraded for the Commandant. A new RSM was on parade, this time a Grenadier, RSM Arthur Brand. He was every bit as terrifying as RSM Britton, the recruits had heard that he was known as 'Shagger', but had no intention of repeating this knowledge. The squad marched on and were inspected by the Commandant who seemed to have a huge entourage. He stood before each man, in his riding breeches and highly polished boots, scrutinising each of them in turn. When Sid's turn came he stuck his chest out, raised his chin and was relieved when the Commandant seemed to find no fault with him. There followed a long sequence of drill, until they finally stood in front of the Commandant and waited for the verdict. To their delight he not only approved their performance, but also awarded a 'credit' to the whole squad.

The recruits were relieved and happy to have now earned the right to be called Guardsmen. Twenty-three of them had survived the test and they looked forward to reporting to one of the three Grenadier Battalions. Sid discovered that he was to be posted to the Second Battalion along with Wally Durrant and most of the others. After a short spell on leave he was to report to Chelsea Barracks in London. But the Battalion were being sent to Egypt in the New Year. Excitement buzzed around the squad as they packed up their kit.

Chapter 4

Chelsea Barracks

Most of the young men who accompanied Sid to the Second Battalion Grenadier Guards at Chelsea Barracks, had never been to London before. The Barracks were situated close to Chelsea Bridge, on the river Thames, and a stone's throw from Sloane Square. The hustle and bustle of the city was a far cry from Caterham. Motor vehicles and buses mixed with many forms of horse transport in the busy streets, and bowler hatted city gentlemen could be seen rushing off to work. The Barracks was an imposing sight. It was a large four-storied barrack block. Almost two hundred yards long, it dominated a huge parade square, where squads of guardsmen were frequently drilled. Large crowds often gathered to look on as the famous Brigade of Guards prepared to mount guard on the various Royal Palaces.

Sid's pal Wally Durrant had also been posted to the Second Battalion, and the two were full of anxiety as they entered the barracks. They immediately noticed that the same sense of purpose was present, but the pace of life seemed somewhat slower. Their arrival was treated as a routine affair, which helped to put them at ease, although the tall Non Commissioned Officer who received them at the gate was far from friendly. Several of the new arrivals were admonished for minor points of dress, and they were all marched to the orderly room in quick time. The whole draft attended the Adjutant's Memoranda, a formal parade known simply as 'orders' in the rest of the army. They stood in front of the young officer's oak desk as he warned them of the standards required in the Battalion. Each man was then posted to an individual company. Sid found himself in Number Four Company, where the CSM explained some of the more earthly dangers that could befall a young man in London.

The old Chelsea Barracks

On his first morning in Chelsea, he was able to watch the King's Guard mounting its duties on the barrack square. The various detachments were formed up for inspection by the Adjutant. The Buckingham Palace, St James's Palace, Tower of London, and the Bank of England Detachments were rigorously inspected to the accompaniment of the Regimental Band. Sid looked on as the Colour was marched on parade by the Drill Sergeant, before the assembled troops marched out of barracks with great ceremony. Crowds gathered outside the gates and old soldiers removed their caps as the Colours passed.

Sid thought that this was wonderful and he looked forward to taking part in the ceremony. Unfortunately he soon learned that he would have to wait. Because the Battalion was due to move overseas, the decision had been made not to issue any Home Service Clothing to the new draft. Preparation for the move was well under way but the Battalion continued to find the public duties. The men in Sid's barrack room prepared their equipment for guard in the evenings and he watched with amazement as the experienced guardsmen rolled capes, polished boots and groomed bearskin caps in a seemingly effortless performance. Their kit was of a very high standard but it seemed to take half the time to prepare. All this took place to the accompaniment of the barrack room story-tellers and he soaked up their tales like a sponge.

There were quite a few older Guardsmen, because at this time it was forbidden for men to marry until they were 26 years old. These men were quick to pass on the tricks of the trade to their newly joined apprentices. Sid concentrated on keeping his nose clean and he soon learned who the characters were in the barrack room. Most were friendly and helpful, but there were one or two who were clearly to be avoided, especially when they had taken a drink.

The new draft soon settled into the routine which was almost cushy when compared to Caterham. Walking out was fairly rare for the younger men, but Sid was sometimes granted a short pass, and he looked forward to these occasions. He never lost his enthusiasm for the game of football, and when he was able, he attended games at Fulham and Chelsea.

He was not allowed to wear civilian clothing, which was to be known only as 'Plain Clothes', and would have to present himself for inspection before walking out. In the winter months he had to wear boots, puttees, blue-grey greatcoat and forage cap. At the guard room he was scrutinised by a Non Commissioned Officer before being allowed to leave barracks. It was not at all unusual for guardsmen in their forage caps to mingle with the cloth-capped men on the football terraces, and he soon came to enjoy those excursions.

He was also enjoying the Battalion routine. There was much more time to relax than there had been at the Depot. Sid loved to listen to the old soldiers telling their stories from the Royal Palaces, and it seemed that the Prince of Wales featured heavily in many of them. There were stories of late night encounters with HRH. It was said that he never failed to return a salute, even when it was clear that he had had a 'heavy evening'. The Prince was very popular with the guardsmen and with the public at large. He had served in the regiment in the Great War. Although he had been forbidden from leaving for the front with the First Battalion in 1914, he had later served in France on the Staff. None of them could have imagined that he would be King before the end of the year, and would spark a constitutional crisis.

One evening Sid entered his barrack room to find everyone convulsed with laughter. It took a while to discover the cause of such hilarity, but he eventually heard the story of an unfortunate guardsman on the Bank of England Picquet. In wet weather the Adjutant sometimes allowed the Officer of the Bank Picquet to take the guard to their destination on the underground train. The whole detachment would squeeze themselves on to the tube for the short journey. When they arrived they would form up again, ready to march to the Bank. On the day in question, the detachment formed itself up, and the word of command was given for them to dress by the right. Each man looked sharply off over his right shoulder and shuffled to his left in order to gain the correct 'Arms Distance'. The left hand man shuffled to his left, but unfortunately ran out of ground and toppled down the steps of the ladies' lavatory, landing in a crumpled heap at the bottom. The remainder of the detachment was crying with laughter as the poor man dragged himself back up the stairs, declining the help of some rather concerned ladies. The story spread around Chelsea like wild fire and was greatly embellished each time it was told.

Like many generations of guardsmen, before and since, they regularly encountered the 'In Pensioners' from The Royal Hospital Chelsea. These old soldiers were veterans from the wars of Queen Victoria's reign. They were happy to recount tales of battles in far off lands to the eager ears of the young guardsmen, in exchange for a pint. They were happy to repeat the process in the Sergeants' Mess. The men on guard often saw them weaving their way back to the hospital at the end of the evening.

The turnover amongst the young guardsmen was quite high, with most only serving their minimum engagement. There were few married men, and those that were, tended to be in 'employed' jobs such as storemen and servants. The Police Force was a popular alternative to the Brigade of Guards. Most Constabularies were more than happy to take on these fit, well-disciplined men, and a recommendation from the Commanding Officer was usually enough to guarantee a career in blue.

The preparations for the move to Africa were suddenly interrupted on 20th January 1936. After a series of debilitating attacks of bronchitis, King George V died at Sandringham. Everyone knew that the King was ill, but the nation was none the less shocked and saddened by his death. The Battalion were told very quickly that they were required to take part in the State Funeral of the late King. This was an unexpected turn of events which caused a great flurry of activity in the Battalion Headquarters. The Second Battalion were winding down their ceremonial commitment, ready for the move overseas, so much work would now have to be done to get everyone ready. Sid soon found himself being issued with the home service clothing he thought he would never wear.

Orders were rapidly issued from the Headquarters in Whitehall, and tasks were passed down to the various companies. There would be a small marching Detachment from the Battalion, but most would be required for street lining duties. The Sergeant Major wasted no time, and the guardsmen soon found themselves being drilled relentlessly. It was necessary to learn several new drill movements such as the 'Reverse arms' and 'Rest on Arms Reversed'. This took place under the Sergeant Major, RSM Tom Garnett. Garnett was an experienced Grenadier with

Grenadier Guardsman in winter walking out order c. 1936

an eye for detail. He missed very little and was determined that things should be done correctly. He had enlisted in the Regiment in 1911 as a Drummer Boy, and had been a Drum Major in the Guards Machine Gun Regiment during the war. He had also served as RSM of the Honourable Artillery Company. Garnett was far from daunted by the task at hand, and he drilled the officers and men alike, until satisfied. Sid found that drill in home service clothing was much more uncomfortable than he had imagined.

Preparations for the funeral continued at a rapid pace, and the Grenadier Guards were involved from the very start. As early as 21st January, a party from the King's Company travelled to Sandringham to act as a bearer party for the late Sovereign. The King's body was moved by train to London, and then on to Westminster Hall where there was to be a Lying-in-State before the funeral. At Westminster Hall things had not gone completely to plan. When crossing the cobbles, the cross on the orb of the Imperial State Crown fell off. This was noticed by the Prince of Wales and the cross was subsequently recovered by Lieutenant Huntington. It was then discovered that two pearls were missing, but these were recovered on the gun carriage later. Everyone concerned hoped that things would go a little smoother for the funeral.

On 28th January 1936, Sid marched out of Chelsea Barracks with the rest of the Battalion, to line the streets for the King's funeral. He was aware that this was a very historic occasion. George V had been on the throne since before he was born. There were thousands of people in London and everyone seemed to be dressed in black. The mood was a sombre one. The King was also very well respected in the army. He had seen the country through the ravages of the war, and had been a regular visitor to the troops in France. He had been seriously hurt during one visit, when thrown from his horse, but had insisted on presenting medals from his sick bed. Sid was proud that the King would be borne to his grave by Grenadiers.

This was the first time that he had worn a bearskin cap on a ceremonial parade and he found it hard going. He had been positioned in Friary Court at St James's Palace and could see the many thousands of mourners who were situated behind the street liners. The soldiers all wore their Athol Grey greatcoats and the officers were adorned with black arm-bands. The muzzle of Sid's rifle rested on his boot and his hands were placed on the butt of the reversed weapon as the procession passed. He noticed that the drums were draped in black cloth and that the marching parties had their rifles tucked under their arms with the butt facing forward. Although his own head was lowered in respect, he was able to see the tall men of the King's Company as they passed, with the coffin on a gun carriage. The procession seemed as though it would go on for ever.

There were representatives from many countries, most of which were not obvious to him. The long columns of escorting troops eventually made their way to Paddington station where the King's body was placed on a train for Windsor. As he made his way back to Chelsea Barracks, the funeral in Windsor began. The Company Colour of the King's Company was placed upon the coffin in St George's Chapel, before the final committal of the late Sovereign. Sid was proud of the part that he and the Regiment had played.

When the funeral was over, preparations for the move to Egypt once again began in earnest, but there were other matters to attend to. Firstly, command of the Battalion changed on 1st February. Lieutenant Colonel F.G. Beaumont-Nesbitt MC, handed over to Lieutenant Colonel F.A.M. Browning DSO. The new Commanding Officer was quick to inspect the Battalion. He had been notified that the King himself would be inspecting the Battalion before it departed to Egypt.

The Sergeant Major and the Drill Sergeants seemed to be in their element, as squads of officers were marched around the parade square at all hours of the day. The guardsmen thought that the parades would never end, but they understood that this would be a very big occasion for all concerned. To underline the importance of the event, the Lieutenant Colonel Commanding the Regiment carried out a dress rehearsal at the end of month. He pronounced the Battalion to be in good order, but listed a large number of points to be rectified before the King's inspection.

On 3rd March, King Edward VIII arrived at Chelsea Barracks. This was to be the first and last time that he would review the Second Battalion Grenadier Guards. No one could imagine that his reign would be so brief. The King clearly felt at home with his Grenadiers, and he appeared to know some of the more senior officers well. Sid and the remainder of the guardsmen concentrated on their drill. It was clear that the King knew what to look for, and it would be the ultimate disgrace to be criticised by the Sovereign himself. Their hard work was rewarded. The King complimented the Battalion on its turnout and high standard of drill. He departed

Chelsea, having delivered his best wishes to the Grenadiers for their forthcoming tour in Egypt.

It was necessary for units going overseas to be at full strength, and drafts of men from the First Battalion started to arrive. The guardsmen in the two Battalions had little contact, even though the First Battalion was stationed only a few miles away at Wellington Barracks. The newly arrived Guardsmen inevitably discussed with their new acquaintances the differences between the two Battalions of the same Regiment. Some major differences were discovered. Apparently reveille in the First Battalion was at 06.30 hours, half an hour later than in the Second Battalion. As if this were not bad enough, it was further discovered that the First were permitted to make their beds down at 12.00 hours, when in the Second, this was not allowed until 16.00 hours. These seemingly minor differences were regarded by the guardsmen as a 'bloody swindle'. Such things mattered a great deal to young men whose lives were dictated by the sound of the bugle, but they soon got over it.

In any case, the last laugh was had by the Second Battalion men, because those men joining from the First were not allowed to mix until they had completed three weeks of drill. This was deemed to be necessary because of yet more differences in the way that the two Battalions performed their drill.

As the departure date for Egypt approached, tropical uniforms were issued and the medical staff delivered a series of inoculations. Each man was issued a sun helmet. These were cumbersome and unpopular items with a wide rim which everyone said would prevent them from ever getting a tan. They were unusual because the Royal Cypher was worn at the front of the helmet, instead of the usual brass grenade fired proper. A white plume could be fitted on the left side as if it were a bearskin.

Because of the rather cumbersome nature of the new headdress it was decided that a drill parade should be held to get the men used to the helmets. Sid and his pals paraded as ordered. It was a strange sight indeed to see so many guardsmen dressed in blue winter greatcoats in the middle of London, sporting tropical sun helmets. The guardsmen were not at all concerned at their rather odd appearance, feeling rather cocky at this visible demonstration of their imminent departure to foreign lands. Unfortunately, when the command 'Slope Arms' was given, a good number of these pristine helmets were knocked off of the heads of their owners, causing more than a few red faces. Adjustments were made and the men were soon carrying out their drill to the usual high standard. Sid had the feeling that the Sergeant Major had done this before.

Kit bags and boxes were packed, inspections took place and the barracks was handed over in good order. The Second Battalion Grenadier Guards formed up on the drill Square for its final parade in Chelsea. Their advance party was already sailing for Egypt as the Commanding Officer took his place at the head of the column. He gave the command which would signal the Battalion's departure from their familiar surroundings. The best part of a thousand men marched out of the gates behind the Corps of Drums. A large number of civilians had gathered to say farewell. Girlfriends sobbed, and old soldiers stood to attention, as the Grenadiers passed on their way to Waterloo station.

The train journey to Southampton was a fairly short one, but Sid was aware of a great sense of excitement amongst the young men. The dockside was a hive of activity. Civilians mingled with khaki clad troops who were carrying all manner of equipment up the gang plank of a large troopship, called the 'MS Cameronia'. A band was playing in the background, and he was delighted to find his mother and sister waiting with many other families. Relatives were allowed to come aboard the Cameronia to say their farewells, and Wally Durrant introduced his mother to Sid's. The two ladies became involved in a jolly conversation and seemed to be getting on rather well. It wasn't long before there were hugs, kisses, and more than a few tears, as the relatives were ushered down the gang-plank having said their good-byes. The band played as the Cameronia slipped her moorings and eased away from the quay. Hundreds of young men lined the gunwales, waving to families as the band became more distant. It was a sad moment, but there was no time to dwell on it, as the Sergeants soon started to direct the men towards their accommodation.

The wives and children of the married men were also aboard the Cameronia, although they were accommodated in a separate part of the ship. The married men were mainly the Battalion seniors, such as the Sergeant Major and the older officers, but there were a number of guardsmen with long service who had brought their families along. A ship's guard was mounted straight away, and the men on duty were required to patrol the decks wearing PT shoes. When patrolling the ship the guardsmen tried to stay away from the married families' area, as this was thought to be a rather undesirable place to visit.

The conditions below decks were very cramped and the troops slept in hammocks. These were rolled and packed away each morning before the accommodation was rigorously inspected. Roll Call was held on deck as if the Battalion were still in barracks, the only difference being the gym shoes worn by everyone. At meal times the food was served in the troop decks, and the 'swabs' brought the rations round in large metal containers. The cramped conditions, and the constant drone of the ship's engines, led to many cases of sea-sickness. Moving around the troop decks at night was a challenging experience, as they were invariably packed with sick guardsmen. The journey to Egypt took eight days. Keeping nearly a thousand men occupied for this amount of time, in such cramped conditions, took a degree of imagination. There was regular PT, and deck games were organised between the various platoons. Unfortunately none of this convinced Wally that they weren't turning into sardines.

At night some of the old soldiers could be heard telling their desert tales, stories of disease, heat and dishonest Arabs. Most of the men had never been overseas and they listened with awe to the exotic descriptions of Alexandria and Cairo. These were delivered by the few older men who had served in other Grenadier Battalions. There were even a few who had accompanied the Battalion to Turkey during the crisis of 1922.

Life aboard the Cameronia rapidly became unpleasant. Mediterranean heat did nothing to ease the living conditions, so it was a great relief when the shores of Africa finally came into view. Everyone was eager for a first sight of Egypt. As the ship drew closer, the desert shores became clearer and palm trees could be distinguished. The colourful scene was everything that Sid had expected, and he excitedly took in every detail as they sailed into the port of Alexandria. It was 18th March 1936.

Chapter 5

Alexandria

The newly arrived men were surprised to see the Corps of Drums of the Third Battalion on the Quayside. They were dressed in service dress, complete with their grenadier forage caps, and were playing all those familiar marches just as if they were in central London. Drum Major Tankard directed the whole performance with great aplomb, and local Egyptians politely clapped each rendition. It didn't take long for the battalion to disembark, as the troops were only too pleased to get back on dry land. Kit was unloaded and packed on to the waiting transport, and the companies were formed up for the march to their new quarters at Mustapha Barracks.

Alexandria had long been known as the jewel in the Mediterranean and the guardsmen took in the sights, sounds and smells of their exciting new home. This was Egypt's second city and the country's major port. It had been built on the orders of Alexander the Great and had immortalized his name. It had been the site of the Great Library, and the Lighthouse, one of the Seven Wonders of the World. Mark Anthony, Julius Caesar, Cleopatra and Octavian had all frequented the ancient City. In addition to the Egyptians, there was a large European community. Many of them had turned out to welcome the Second Grenadiers as they marched into barracks. The troops were shown to their accommodation and each man claimed his new bed space. The old iron bed frames were familiar, but a large mosquito net hung over each bed, a reminder of the deadly insect borne diseases that

The Corps of Drums of the 3rd Battalion Grenadier Guards welcome the Second Battalion to Egypt, Alexandria 18th March 1936

Grenadiers dressed for Guard Duty, Alexandria

existed in the country. The barrack rooms were large and spacious. If you were lucky there was a spectacular view of the Mediterranean Sea. This all looked great to Sid. Once the day's fatigues had been completed, he was able to join his pals at the window, to watch the sun set over the sea.

The following days were filled with routine tasks. There were stores to be unpacked and carried to their final destinations, and of course there were various inspections to ensure that things were all in order. Each morning began with PT on the parade square, this was designed to help the men acclimatise, and it was usually good fun. By late morning the sun was overhead. The heat was often unbearable. The troops soon learned to keep themselves protected from the desert sun.

It was often possible to go for a swim in the 'Med'. It was reached by means of a tunnel underneath the Coronation Coast Road and was only a very short walk. The beach was divided so that the married families had their own section, as it was thought to be inappropriate for the single men to mix with them. Sid wasn't at all bothered, this was the life he had hoped for when he joined, and so far it was great. The young men could hardly wait until they were granted a pass to 'walk out' into the town. They had heard so much, and wanted to feel the atmosphere of this African city.

The Guards Brigade in Egypt was divided between Alexandria and Cairo. It was generally felt that 'Alex' was the better posting of the two. There were several other units in the town too, notably an armoured car unit and, of course, a large contingent of Royal Military Police. For the time being, the men were kept busy in barracks with the many routine tasks that had to be completed. Naturally, it wasn't long before the drill parades started. The value of the sun helmets was now understood. It didn't take long for the desert heat to take its toll on an unprotected man.

A break from training Eygpt 1936

They were all fairly sensible about exposure to the heat. Sunburn would inevitably lead to loss of name and none of them wanted that. The Grenadier athletes, at least, managed to demonstrate that they had acclimatised by winning the Alexandria area athletics competition, only a month after arriving in Egypt. The General Officer Commanding British troops in Egypt, Lieutenant General Sir George Weir, inspected the Second Battalion on 24th April. He had recently reviewed the departing Third Battalion, and was pleased to see that their fellow Grenadiers were in equally good order.

Sid and pal clean their kit in the Egyptian sun

Sentry duty in the desert

Not long after arrival, when the guardsmen in Number Four Company were reading the daily detail, there was a paragraph stating that Officers' Servants were required, and volunteers should report to the CSM. A good deal of a guardsman's pay was spent on cleaning kit, such as shoe polish, but officers' servants were granted an allowance by their employing officer, and consequently were seen as a source of cleaning material. Someone had to be found, the opportunity couldn't be missed. The thought of volunteering did not enter Sid's head, but the detail also stated that all applicants had to have passed their second class education certificate, and he fitted the bill exactly. He was promptly frog-marched to the Company Office by his Platoon, to 'Volunteer'.

Guardsman Dowland was accepted for the post, and was detailed to look after 2Lt Geoffrey Gwyer. His officer proved to be a likeable man and a very good young officer. He soon developed a good relationship with Gwyer and rapidly came to respect him. It was now necessary to prepare Mr Gwyer's kit for all of the Battalion parades, in addition to his own. There could be no slacking, as the Adjutant would soon notice any aspect of an officer's appearance that was below the required standard. This could lead to 'extra Picquets' for the officer, and would inevitably draw attention to Sid, which could result in 'loss of name'.

Before long a routine was established and the Second Battalion settled in well. Sid also learned to enjoy this new environment, and it wasn't long before he was selected to represent the company at football. His talent was recognised, and he was soon playing for the battalion against the other units in Egypt. Life was good, and he was able to enjoy the perks that being an officer's servant brought. There were even 'Dhobi Wallahs' in the barracks who laundered the men's kit for a shilling a week, although khaki drill uniforms, sheets and mosquito nets were sixpence extra. As a servant he was often required to wear a suit, paid for by his officer. When he wanted to walk out he was required to 'apply' on the Company Commander's Memoranda. Major Hargreaves looked him over before granting his application.

Alexandria held many delights for the young men. There were countless cafés and refreshment stops, and more than one establishment of ill repute. There was a cinema which proved very popular, and on one occasion Sid was witness to scores of Guardsmen reliving the 'Charge of the Light Brigade'. As Errol Flynn charged the Russian guns on the screen, the guardsmen stood on their seats waving imaginary sabres over their heads. Many of the men were a little the worse for wear from drink, and Sid thought that the scene was hilarious.

The Battalion was required to provide manpower to the Military Police for town patrols, and he was occasionally detailed for this job. He didn't mind because he enjoyed being out in the town. There was always something to see, and he regarded it all as great experience. These patrols often encountered men who had over indulged and they were frequently placed in arrest, but this was mainly for their own protection. There were many unscrupulous individuals in the Egyptian streets who would take advantage of a European whose senses were dulled by drink.

Working in the Officers' Mess gave him the opportunity to view the Battalion's Officers from a different perspective. He now realised that the young Subalterns and Ensigns were terrified of the Adjutant. It seemed that they were subject to just as much discipline as the guardsmen, although it was administered in a very different way. The excesses of the young officers were ruthlessly punished by the award of extra duties. Some of the Second Lieutenants seemed to be forever on duty, because there seemed to be no shortage of distractions for a young officer in Alexandria. Sid got to know most of the officers well, many of whom were not much older than him. Mr Gwyer and his friends, Second Lieutenants Seymour and Trotter, were no strangers to the Adjutant's memoranda.

The servants often exchanged stories about the exploits of their officers. One of Sid's friends told the story of a Major who had berated his servant for being late arriving in the mess. The officer had complained that he had been unable to go to bed because his servant had failed to lay out his pyjamas! None of them believed the story, but it was a good tale all the same, and it did the rounds like all good tales. Some of the servants had worked for the same officer for years. Others had changed officers, but had remained as servants because they enjoyed the perks. These men were quick to exploit any opportunity that presented itself and were keen to pass on their dodges to Sid. Each servant was required to maintain a book showing all allowances paid to him, and all purchases made on behalf of his employing officer. The book was formally shown on the Adjutant's Memoranda. This was to ensure that the servant was being paid on time, and that all business was above board. The old hands ensured that things were seen to be above board by maintaining a second illicit book. Neither the employing officer nor the Adjutant would see both books. Sid couldn't contemplate such action, he was far too junior, and respected his officer who always treated him fairly.

When the battalion had settled itself in Alexandria, manoeuvres were organised in order to introduce everyone to the harsh desert conditions. Motor transport was still scarce so the battalion marched into the hot interior. Sid noticed the

A brief halt to manoeuvres, Egypt 1936

change in the air, gone was the fresh sea breeze only to be replaced by a hot wind. Water discipline was rigorously enforced, and any man caught drinking from his canteen without orders would be in serious trouble. The guardsmen carried their small packs with their essential equipment and their rifles were slung. Forage caps were worn, as were service dress jackets, but khaki drill shorts replaced trousers. Puttees were rolled around their stockings which made the legs hot and itchy. It was very tough going at the beginning.

When the battalion camped, large marquee type tents were erected for essential administration and feeding. There was generally a large tent each for the Officers and Sergeants, and one or two for the guardsmen. Smaller Bell Tents were put up in neat rows for the men to sleep in, and they were always a welcome sight at the end of a hard day's marching. A central area was usually cleared and this would become the Parade Square. The guardsmen often joked that the first part of the camp to be sited was the latrine, and everything else followed. After the Duty Drummer had blown reveille in the morning, the battalion would wash and shave using the tiny water ration and would parade for breakfast. Roll Call was held as if the Battalion was still at Chelsea, with the full Corps of Drums at the front of the parade. The constant stamping of feet naturally created huge dust clouds which was an irritation, particularly when it settled on the recently cleaned rifles.

The companies took part in various 'schemes' all aimed at improving their ability to operate in the desert. Route marches were often thirty miles or more, no joke in the blistering desert sun. As a servant, Sid was also required to act as the Platoon Runner. This meant that he had to 'double away' to other Platoons or Companies, in order to deliver messages from Mr Gwyer. This was exhausting work and his platoon had often moved off by the time that he returned, so he would have to run to catch them up. The battalion rapidly adapted to their new environment. They were very soon fit and bronzed just like the Third Battalion that they had replaced.

A Guard of Honour found by the second Battalion Grenadier Guards, Alexandria

In the summer of 1936 the King's Birthday Parade was held. This was repeated in British colonies all over the Empire. Egypt was no exception. RSM Garnett, assisted by Drill Sergeants Bridges and Chatterton, put the Battalion through its paces as if the parade were to take place on Horse Guards. It was exhausting work under the Egyptian sun and men often succumbed to the heat.

The Adjutant supervised the Officers' drill to ensure that they were at a good standard before the Commanding Officer joined the Parade. Lt Colonel Frederick 'Boy' Browning was a fiercely Regimental Officer, with an eye for detail, and he demanded high standards. Browning had won the DSO during the Great War and had also been an Olympic hurdler. His officers were in awe of him. It was no surprise, during one of these rehearsals, when the Commanding officer expressed his displeasure at the standard of officers' sword drill and ordered that the movement be repeated until it was correct. Whilst this was taking place the guardsmen stood to attention with their rifles at the present. The heat was too much for Sid and he felt as though he was about to pass out. He was spotted by a Sergeant and wheeled away into the shade. He was told that he was idle and he was put in the report.

Justice was swift, and he soon found himself on the Adjutant's Memoranda charged with falling out from a parade. The Adjutant asked if he had been into the town on the previous evening and Sid replied that he had, not the most prudent reply under the circumstances. He received a serious dressing down and was confined to barracks (CB) for seven days. In the event, the Trooping of the Colour passed off successfully. It was held on the polo ground of the Alexandria sporting club on the 23rd June and the salute was taken by the Consul General. On the same day, in London, the King's Company found the escort for the Birthday Parade. Everyone seemed to be most satisfied and there were various social gatherings that evening. The Commanding Officer's wife often attracted some attention at these events. She was the novelist Daphne du Maurier.

Lt Col FAM Browning, Commanding Officer of the Second Battalion Grenadier Guards accompanies a dignatory during the inspection of a Guard of Honour

There were many other ceremonial duties, and Guards of Honour were frequently mounted for visiting dignitaries and senior officers. All of this was routine for a Foot Guards Battalion and Sid took part in a good number of parades. It was the Second Battalion who were tasked to parade on the occasion of the departure of the High Commissioner the following month, and Sid was included in the Guard of Honour. He didn't particularly enjoy these occasions, or the preparatory drill that was necessary, but he was still enjoying army life. Back in England the political situation was no better. There was still a shortage of jobs, and the Jarrow Hunger Marches were under way. He felt that he had made the right decision to join the army.

Hygiene was a constant problem and disease was always a concern. Sid took care to ensure that his mosquito net was correctly draped around his bed at night. The old iron bed frames were frequently taken out of the barrack rooms for 'debugging'. A smoke dispenser or blow torch was used to expel any unwelcome inhabitants from the hollow frames. Dysentery was a major problem, and most people were affected to one degree or another at various times. Malaria was the biggest fear, and the troops took their medication daily to prevent them falling ill. Despite the rigorous standards of hygiene, men still became sick and were confined to the hospital. Occasionally disease triumphed and someone died. The battalion always received the news with great sadness and every effort was made to provide a full military funeral. The whole battalion would parade for the service on these occasions, which acted as a constant reminder of the dangers that Egypt could present. Unfortunately, there were a number of deaths. Each man was laid to rest in the Military Cemetery by a Grenadier Bearer Party.

On 10th December news reached Egypt that King Edward VIII had renounced the throne of England in favour of his brother the Duke of York, who was to become King George VI. Edward was now to be known as the Duke of Windsor. This was shocking and unexpected news. It was the talk of the barracks. Everyone seemed to have an opinion about the situation and it was debated endlessly. The routine continued, regardless of the news from England, and the boxing championships went ahead as planned. Boxing was one of the most popular sports at the time and the competitions were always keenly attended. At the end of November, the battalion did very well at the Egyptian Command championships, and everyone was looking forward to the battalion event. No one was surprised when Guardsman Harris retained his heavyweight title, but the hero of the evening was Boy Hudson who was victorious in the Flyweight category. The enthusiasm of the troops was again fuelled when the Grenadiers beat the Irish Guards team in January.

Brigade Manoeuvres were held in the spring, and Sid once again found himself running up and down the rocky hillsides. The culmination of the exercise saw the Grenadiers repulse a heavy tank attack, against expectation. The Commanding Officer was delighted that his Battalion had proved themselves to be so capable and it was decided that a nearby hill be renamed to mark the event. Point 271 near Eweibid Station was re-titled 'Grenadier Hill'. The troops marched back to their barracks well satisfied with themselves.

In England preparations were under way for the coronation of King George VI who had succeeded his brother after the abdication. It was decided that a large celebration was required in 'Alex'. This was to be organised by the British community in Alexandria and would be held at the Smouta City race course on 12th May, to coincide with the coronation. For their part, the Second Battalion were to give a demonstration of drill as it was carried out in 1743. The troops were required to wear period costume, and a large number of suitable uniforms were acquired. These were topped by Mitre caps, and each man carried a large replica musket. Sid was a little distressed, because both he and his officer were required to take part. Each tunic had around twenty brass buttons that required cleaning, and it was very time consuming.

A military funeral Egypt 1936

Guardsman in marching order c. 1937

As rehearsals got under way Sid along with several other men, was detailed to throw a firework during the performance. On set commands the men had to march to the front, light their fireworks, and throw them at exactly the right time. On several occasions things went wrong, as the fireworks failed to light or went out, and the Sergeant Major became increasingly agitated. Several attempts were made until things seemed to be going to plan.

On the final occasion Sid who had previously had no difficulty with his pyrotechnic was the only man unable to light the firework. The Sergeant Major was furious. There were shouts of 'brahma' and 'idle man', along with a few other helpful expletives, and he was thrown off the parade.

Shortly afterwards he once again stood to attention in front of an officer's desk to explain his conduct. Major Hargreaves was unimpressed by his lack of proficiency with pyrotechnics. He asked the CSM how Dowland usually did. The CSM was quick to reply that Sid didn't often get into trouble, and furthermore he had scored three goals for the company football team in a recent competition. This piece of information was clearly quite irrelevant but it seemed to do the trick, and he escaped with a dressing down from his Company Commander. His football skills had helped him again.

There was more time to practise Skill at Arms in Egypt and his shooting improved. He was sent to an old Egyptian army barracks at Dekalia just outside Alexandria, in order to qualify for his Skill at Arms Badge. To achieve this, it was necessary to reach the required standard in both rifle and Lewis Gun. If you had been selected as a Machine Gunner, the Vickers Gun had to be mastered. The Lewis Gun was completely new to most of the students but they found their first introduction to automatic fire agreeable. The Lewis was capable of firing 550 rounds per minute, from drum magazines mounted on top of the gun, and Sid enjoyed the experience immensely. Although he passed the required tests and gained his Lewis Gun Badge, this was not a happy time as he was unfortunate to enough to fall ill with dysentery.

His condition rapidly worsened and he was transferred to the San Stefano Military Hospital for treatment. The standard remedy in such cases was to swallow 'Medical Salts' four times a day. Not surprisingly he lost a great deal of weight and remained in hospital for three weeks. There were soldiers from all over Egypt in the large wards but his favourite character was a rather rotund Scottish sailor, who sported a huge beard. The hospital was run according to strict military routine. The ward was administered by an RAMC Warrant Officer, who took an instant dislike to the rather un-soldier-like beard. Instructions for the demise of the excess hair were soon issued to the unimpressed Scot, who responded by informing all and sundry that in the Royal Navy he was perfectly entitled to grow a beard. The dispute continued with both sides vigorously fighting their corners to the delight of the other patients. The occupants of the ward, of course sided with the rebellious sailor, who was still holding out with his facial hair intact when Sid was discharged.

The desert manoeuvres continued at regular intervals and the Second Grenadiers soon developed a reputation as a fit and formidable Battalion. Camps were set up at exotic sounding locations such as 'Sidi Bisr', but they were little more than pieces of desert when the men arrived. The troops got used to the environment and became very competent. Fortunately the Brigade Commander was more than happy with their performance.

Sid was able to continue his education and managed to pass his 1st Class certificate. This was quite rare for a young Guardsman. There were a good many senior ranks and even Warrant Officers who had not passed. Sid kept his latest qualification under wraps in case he ended up in hot water with a resentful NCO. He was also lucky enough to attend a driving course, when his officer was away, which he also passed.

There was no real opportunity for a guardsman to take leave in England, so periods of local leave were organised. He travelled to Palestine with a number of pals on one of these leave periods. They were accommodated in another British army barracks and were able to visit Jerusalem with its famous sites. He visited Cairo on many occasions and often took camel rides into the desert to marvel at the pyramids.

Life in Alexandria was good. There were plenty of duties to be done and of course the exhausting desert manoeuvres, but there were ample attractions in town when off duty. Unfortunately the seedier establishments drew a regular crowd from the Battalion. One morning the troops were unexpectedly paraded to be addressed by the Commanding Officer. There had apparently been a recent increase in the number of venereal disease cases in the Battalion. Lt Colonel Browning told the assembled battalion that he was disgusted and that such a situation would not be tolerated. He further told the men that the first Company to reach ten cases would be confined to Barracks. There was much debate about the situation and a good few jokes circulated after the announcement. Unfortunately for Number Four Company they managed to reach ten cases and were immediately gated. The irony of the situation was that the men who had managed to bring these circumstances about were in no position to walk out anyway. It was a long week for the company but they survived and thankfully the number of men reporting sick soon fell away.

Time had rolled on and the Battalion's tour in Egypt would soon be drawing to a close. Everyone was looking forward to seeing their loved ones in England again, and to sampling the ale in London's pubs. Officers' Servants usually accompanied their officers on posting, and Sid was informed that when they returned to London Mr Gwyer would be moving to the First Battalion. This was a surprise and it would mean leaving all his pals in the Second Battalion but he clearly had no choice. That evening he sought the opinion of the men he knew who had served in the First, and he was reassured when they were all quite positive about the prospect. He was further comforted when he learned that the First Battalion were to be posted to Bermuda. He looked forward to a spot of leave, and had a rather pleasant vision of blue seas and white beaches in the back of his mind. Most of the young men were as yet oblivious to the events that were taking place in Europe, although Sid often listened to the officers debating the complicated politics of the continent. The Spanish civil war was raging. Madrid was being regularly bombed by German and Italian aircraft, but few people realised how significant this would be for them in the future.

The end of the tour soon came around and although there was great eagerness to get back to England, no one was looking forward to the long, cramped voyage home. One of the last Battalion parades in Egypt was a Divine service to dedicate a memorial tablet to the memory of Guardsmen CH Stevenson and J Holdstock. Both had died in hospital during the tour. Sid didn't know either of the men personally, but it was a very sad occasion for everyone. In December 1937 the Battalion was relieved by the 3rd Battalion Coldstream Guards. The Grenadiers

An accomodation block, Mustapha Barracks, Alexandria 1936

marched out of Mustapha Barracks for the last time. The Drums played at the Dockside as the troops and families boarded the H.T. Dunera bound for England. A number of the more senior Guardsmen had married girls that they had met in Alexandria, most were of European descent, and quite a few came from the large Greek community. The waving crowds were soon a distant memory as the ship eased out into the Mediterranean. The routine on the return journey was much the same as it had been almost two years earlier and the voyage was relatively uneventful. After what seemed an eternity, England's misty shores finally came into view and everyone clambered on deck for a reminder of Great Britain's chill winter winds. It was 14th December 1937.

Chapter 6

Back to Blighty

There was a frustrating 24 hours when the ship was anchored off Southampton for reasons that no one seemed to understand, but eventually the Battalion was disembarked. There were the usual delays and roll calls before the Companies boarded two trains for London. At Waterloo Station they once again formed up, this time with the Regimental Band. The Commanding Officer stepped them off with great ceremony, for their new quarters at H.M. Tower of London. There were great crowds of people on their route. Some had turned out especially to welcome the Grenadiers, but most had just stopped what they were doing to watch the great procession pass.

It had been decided that the Battalion would exercise its ancient right to 'March through the city of London with bayonets fixed, drums beating and colours flying'. The Battalion halted at the entrance to the city and was granted permission to enter. The Lord Major of London took the salute at the Mansion house and welcomed the Grenadiers back to London. Shortly after, the troops marched into the ancient fortress of the Tower of London.

Sid had never visited the Tower before and he marvelled at the ancient buildings, and at the Yeomen Warders with their huge grey moustaches and strange uniforms. He was informed that several of them were ex Regimental Sergeant Majors who would be quick to report any slackness. A fierce looking man with grey whiskers was pointed out to him, 'he's an ex Sergeant Major', he was told. Sid looked at the many rows of medals on the man's chest and decided that it would be prudent to give him a wide berth. It didn't take long for the Second Grenadiers to settle in, this was familiar ground and quite a few men had served here before.

Sid decided not to get settled, as he would soon be off to the First Battalion which was now based at Chelsea Barracks, just a couple of short miles away. The Battalion routine continued as if there had been no move at all, and Sid was in the Tower just long enough to receive three extra drills for being found with a kink in the peak of his forage cap. He was reminded of the differences between the Battalions when he attended the Commanding Officer's Memoranda prior to leaving the Second. The Sergeant Major ranted at a group of men who had been drafted from the First, they had attended Memoranda in a different order of dress from that which was customary in the Second Battalion. 'Get off, get off and don't bring your First Battalion tricks here', he screamed. Sid wondered if a similar reception awaited him at Chelsea Barracks.

As he left the Tower of London, his pals were being sent on leave, a half battalion at a time. He felt a little deflated at not being able to go back to Dorset and his family for a while. He felt sure that he would be granted leave when he arrived in the First Battalion. It was a short journey to Chelsea and he knew the streets around his new home very well. Almost as soon as he arrived at Chelsea Barracks, he was told to parade for the Adjutant's Memoranda. When the parade was placed in open order, Sid without thinking carried out the timing he had been taught in the Second Battalion. He was quickly pounced upon and told to wake his ideas up, 'He was in the First Battalion now'.

When he was finally marched in front of the Adjutant, he was asked if he had been granted any leave in the Second Battalion. Sid replied that he had not, fully expecting the Adjutant to take steps to rectify the situation. The response was not at all what he had hoped to hear. 'Well that should have been sorted out in the Second Battalion, not here', said the Adjutant. Sid was more deflated than ever, he felt as though he was a recruit joining the battalion, just as he had done two years ago. It wasn't all bad though, there were a number of young officers who had also travelled from the Tower of London, and Sid was pleased that he at least knew someone. He guessed that most of them had volunteered with the prospect of a tour in Bermuda in mind.

The First Battalion were still engaged in carrying out the public duties in London and Sid set about preparing his officer's uniforms. There was a lot more kit to be cleaned than he had been used to in Egypt, and he spent a good deal of time working in the officers' mess. He accompanied Mr Gwyer when he mounted Guard at the Royal Palaces and soon found that life was fairly pleasant, as he was afforded more freedom than he would have had as a Duty Guardsman. Things took a distinct turn for the better when his officer was sent on a PT course. Sid was not required to accompany him and his application to take his outstanding leave was granted.

He set out for Dorset full of anticipation. It had been two years since he had seen any of his family, although they had written to him regularly. When he arrived in Poole he quickly found that all was not well. His father was seriously ill with pneumonia and the whole family were gravely concerned. Sadly his father died two days later. It was a terrible blow, but he was grateful that he had been able to see him before he died. The rest of his leave was rather subdued and of course there were reminders of a pleasant childhood all around. It was a tough time and his leave soon came to an end. With a heavy heart he caught the train back to London and reported back to Chelsea Barracks on time.

In the following months he settled into a routine with his officer. Much of the time was spent just as it had been before he left for Africa. His military duties were broken by visits to football matches and he came to know London very well. He thought that he could identify which part of the capital a girl came from just by listening to her accent. Servants were often entrusted with their officers' motor cars, but the Transport Officer had refused to endorse his UK driving licence unless he re-took his test. Resourceful as ever, Sid got around the problem with the help of a friendly Post Office official who issued him with a visitor's driving permit. In the weeks that followed he drove Gwyer's car into the Royal Palaces on many occasions. The Sentries would always give the car a cheeky present arms, even though they knew full well who the occupants were. The Servants raised their bowler hats to acknowledge their fellow Guardsmen, it was all good fun.

As 1938 progressed Sid got to know the First Battalion's Officers very well and he became accustomed to their ways. One day he was at St James' Palace when he bumped into a fellow guardsman who was shaking his head in disbelief. 'I've seen it all now', he said. The guardsman went on to explain how he had delivered a telegram to one of the officers. The telegram brought the wonderful news that the officer's wife had delivered a baby son. 'I've just 'erd him on the phone; 'e's only been an put 'im down for the Regiment already!' This was of course a long standing custom in the regiment, but the young guardsman was incredulous. The child was indeed registered for the regiment and was subsequently commissioned, rising to the rank of Colonel, a very useful registration indeed.

Sid was enjoying life in London, particularly the perks that being an officer's servant brought. He was an experienced man now and was trusted. His officer was able to sign leave passes for him and he took full advantage of the situation whenever he could. Everyone was by now aware of the developing situation in Germany and the newspapers reported the details of each outrage committed by the Nazis. The British Government had finally woken up to the threat that Germany posed, and a programme of rearmament was under way. But years of under investment in defence could not be righted overnight. It was becoming increasingly obvious that war clouds were once again forming over Europe. One MP was quoted in the press as suggesting that the Brigade of Guards should be sent to Germany with pick helves, to 'sort out' the Nazi Bullies. It was a ridiculous suggestion and was not well received by either the officers or the men.

Guardsman in home service, guard order c. 1938-39

In September 1938, Neville Chamberlain returned from Munich declaring that there would be 'Peace in our time'. Few people were fooled and many were outraged by Chamberlain's behaviour. Winston Churchill in particular was very critical of such appeasement. It seemed that many officers shared Churchill's view and the political situation was widely discussed in the various messes. A crisis was looming, and there was a great deal of speculation about what might happen.

The rising tension in Europe meant that the pace of life within the Battalion was stepped up. There was a preliminary stand-to during the Munich crisis and there was some concern about air raids. Elements of the Battalion were sent to help the local council authorities with the construction of air-raid shelters and defences. It was a welcome opportunity for the guardsmen to mix with the civilian population, but the work was hard, and the novelty soon wore off. A considerable amount of time was spent in the London Parks, digging slit trenches and shelters which would be well used in the months to come, although no one realised it at the time

Training was also stepped up and the Battalion travelled to Pirbright for manoeuvres. There was still a drastic shortage of equipment and wooden Bren guns were used to make up the shortfall for training. Although rearmament was now under way, army doctrine had not caught up with the modern battlefield. During one exercise, Sid's Company was actually charged by a troop from the Household Cavalry, complete with snorting horses and drawn sabres. The whole episode was reminiscent of Waterloo and the Guardsmen thought that it was ridiculous. There was unfortunately one casualty during the manoeuvres when a Guardsman was hit on the head by a wooden 3-inch mortar! The poor fellow was never allowed to forget the incident.

There were endless route marches through the Surrey and Hampshire countryside which although tiring were quite enjoyable. The distances were no trouble to Sid after his time in the Egyptian heat. The young guardsmen were well aware of what was going on. The general mood in the country was one of anger and apprehension. Few in the battalion doubted that war was coming. Indeed there were still some seniors who had served in the Great War. One such veteran was the Sgt Major. RSM Cyril Sheather had joined the Regiment in March 1917 and had seen action with the 3rd Battalion. He had actually served in France from 1914 with the Royal Sussex Regiment, but had been discharged in 1916 because he had given a false age on enlistment. One wonders what must have been going through the minds of such veterans in 1939.

Meanwhile, Lt Gwyer had been appointed as the Battalion Signal Officer. This meant that Sid was now cross-posted from Number Four Company to Headquarter's Company. Gwyer was sent to Catterick in Yorkshire on a Signals Course and Sid accompanied him. This was a very steady number, as whilst his officer was attending instruction during the day, Sid was left alone with Joe, Gwyer's pet labrador. All this was a welcome distraction from the war preparations going on in London and they both made the most of it. Occasionally Gwyer attended the races and Sid would tag along too. He was sometimes given a pound and told to place a bet for himself. Enjoyable as it was, he knew that it couldn't last and any thoughts he had of Bermuda were now long forgotten.

War preparations continued into the New Year, but routine took over. The same sense of urgency was no longer felt in the army until March 1939. When Hitler finally marched into Prague, public anger exploded. Chamberlain was forced to make a commitment to defend Poland in the event of a German invasion. Everyone studied the newspapers and listened to the wireless for the latest developments in Europe. Things continued to deteriorate and on 31st August, 3,000 reservists were recalled and the army was finally put on a war footing. Mobilization began on 1st September, this was known as 'Z' day and the rifle companies were immediately sent into billets at Henley Park. On 3rd September the Nazis finally invaded Poland. Sid joined many others huddled around a wireless to hear the Prime Minister's fateful declaration that, 'This country is now at war with Germany'.

The First and Second Battalions mobilised at Pirbright in the 7th Guards Brigade, in the 3rd Division, commanded by General Montgomery. The Battalions were now comprised of about 60% serving soldiers and 40% reservists. A large number of these reservists were married men who had left their families at short notice. They were naturally somewhat older than the average soldier and many had seen service in Egypt. The men were not happy at having to leave their loved ones but they were none the less committed to the task at hand. 24 hours' leave was granted to allow the men to put their affairs in order. Drummer Boys and under age soldiers were immediately posted to the Training Battalion which had formed at Windsor. The character of the reservists was a little different to that of the serving Guardsmen. On one occasion a CSM referred to the troops as 'a bunch of bloody sheep' and they immediately responded by bleating loudly. Such behaviour would not have been tolerated in a peace-time battalion, and Sid found it all quite amusing. Things were going to be different now.

Training and preparation went on at a furious pace. The troops were issued anti-gas clothing and a service bayonet. Bren gun courses were held for the reservists and everyone was brought up to date with his inoculations. General Montgomery inspected the whole Brigade on 4th September and the King himself visited Pirbright camp on the 12th. Sid was impressed at the interest the King showed in what was going on. Ammunition was issued to the troops and all personal kit was by now packed. Each man had made a will and all medals had been sent to RHQ for safe keeping. There were a number of air raid alerts but each proved to be a false alarm, as did the various sightings of German parachutists.

Lt Gwyer had been put in charge of the advance party for a Battalion move to the Divisional Concentration Area. Sid travelled with him but had no idea where they were headed. During the journey it became clear that their destination was somewhere in the west country, and he wondered if he would be close to home. Eventually the Convoy arrived in Yeovil, and Mr Gwyer set about finding suitable locations for billets and headquarters. The Battalion Headquarters was sighted in the Liberal Hall, in Middle Street, but Sid was more impressed with the location chosen for the Signal Platoon. A skittle alley at the back of a pub had been selected and the Guardsmen thought that this was most convenient. Sid suspected that this fact had not been overlooked by his officer when the location had been chosen.

Lt Gwyer was tasked to find more billets and the search took Sid closer to home. When his officer was suitably occupied, he decided to visit some relatives who lived nearby, to say his goodbyes. By now it was apparent that the Battalion was probably heading to France. It was a brief visit and he was grateful for the opportunity to see the family. Mr Gwyer didn't seem to mind when he returned and all was well.

By now the countryside was full of soldiers. Military vehicles were parked in farm yards and under trees because of the perceived air threat. The main body of the Battalion had travelled by train from Brookwood station, and were dispersed to their Company billets. The Second Battalion was close by at Sherbourne and Sid occasionally caught sight of some of his old pals. The following days were occupied by a 'Divisional Scheme' and the men of 7th Guards Brigade were moved around the countryside in response to a swiftly moving makeshift enemy. The Guardsmen were surprised when the King came to visit once again on the 19th and on this occasion he inspected the King's Company.

When the manoeuvres ended on the 20th, Sid and the other Guardsmen were instructed to pack up their kit and to load it on to the transport. He knew from his officer that orders had been received, but these were 'most secret' and no one was permitted to know what was going on at this stage. Speculation as always was rife and most people thought that they would be moving to France very soon. Lt Gwyer called the Signal Platoon together for a briefing and he told the men that 'they would soon be going to sort out the Germans'. This speech was very well received by the men and their speculation about the move was fuelled when the Battalion transport departed on the 23rd.

Routine preparations were continued and a Battalion church service was held at St John the Baptist's church in Yeovil. During it the Battalion Chaplain, Captain Griffiths, addressed over five hundred men. Standards of course had to be maintained and an Adjutants Drill Parade was held in the Newton Park. This was less than popular with the guardsmen, so there was relief when the Battalion was placed on one hour's notice to move. Finally they boarded the train for Southampton on 29th September 1939.

Chapter 7

The British Expeditionary Force

At Southampton the Battalion had boarded the MS Royal Daffodil for the short voyage to Cherbourg and she eventually docked at 07.30 the following day. Most of the troops had never been to France and there was a good deal of conversation about the meaning of various French phrases. Most of these phrases would have been hugely offensive to the local population if they had been repeated. Once they disembarked, the Battalion was formed up for the march to the railhead, where they boarded an ancient French train. Sid and his friends found themselves squashed into a carriage for the journey toward the Belgian frontier. Ominously the horse- boxes being towed by the train were marked '8 horses or forty men' just as they had been for a previous Expeditionary Force in 1914.

During the long and uncomfortable train journey, the First Battalion found itself stationary for long periods without explanation. The wooden benches in the carriages were incredibly uncomfortable and the men spent much of the time standing, to rest their aching backsides. On one occasion, their train stopped alongside another series of almost identical carriages and boxes. Word quickly spread that squashed into this train was the Second Battalion Grenadier Guards. It didn't take long for Sid to locate some of his old mates from Number Four Company.

Miraculously he found himself in conversation with Guardsman Hooley who had shared the next bed space in Mustapha Barracks. Hooley had married a local girl and Sid was pleased to hear that she had settled in England. There followed many enquiries about friends, Battalion personalities and life in the First Battalion. The Guardsmen were able to swap stories and to pass on the latest rumours about their eventual destinations. Sid learned that the Third Battalion in the 1st Guards Brigade had arrived in France a week earlier. The unexpected reunion was unfortunately cut short when the trains eventually started to move off. Last minute cheers and shouts of good luck were exchanged as the aged locomotives creaked, and strained slowly apart.

The Battalion was briefly billeted in barns and out-buildings near the village of Neuvillalais where company training was conducted. Sid learned that they were soon to move forward into a concentration area near the Belgian Frontier. Almost immediately they were again crammed into a train for the journey to Lesquins. When they disembarked, the troops were surrounded by enthusiastic civilians who sang 'Tipperary' and 'Pack up your troubles'. It was nice to be welcome but there were those in the Battalion who had experienced this before. As they marched through the cobbled streets the young men noticed large letters daubed on the walls and were told that the translation meant 'They shall not pass'. It was stirring stuff but most of the troops just wanted to reach the concentration area so that they could rest. After a brief spell in billets on the outskirts of Lille, the Battalion finally reached the small French village of Annappes. It was 13th October and this was to be home for a considerable time.

Number Four Company had taken over a sector of the frontier from a French Regiment the day before, and a number of French soldiers were still in the area. They were a surly looking bunch, ill shaven and scruffy, the Guardsmen were unimpressed by their allies. The Frenchmen did not appear to be too keen on the English either. The allied defensive line ran along the eastern border of France. The BEF was deployed along the frontier to the north of the Maginot Line, which the French believed to be impregnable. For the most part the BEF was separated from any contact with the enemy by neutral Belgium, and so set about constructing a defensive line on the border. This defensive line was known as the 'Gort Line' after General 'Fatboy' Gort VC, the Commander in Chief, ex commanding officer of the First Battalion and a very famous Grenadier officer.

The First Battalion's sector of the line ran near the border village of Willems and the Companies took turns in the line. The troops soon discovered that digging in this area was no easy task, just as a generation of Grenadiers had discovered 25 years earlier. The water table was high and the trenches soon filled with water. The winter of 1939/40 was severe, with very heavy rain, and the ground soon turned to thick mud. It became necessary to build the defensive positions above ground, and the Quartermaster set about buying defence stores from local sources. Timber was very useful to shore up the positions, but the Guardsmen were forbidden to chop down fruit trees or to take wood from the houses nearby. It was exhausting work in the cold and the rain, but fortunately most of the men were able to march back to their billets in Annappes, leaving the unfortunate duty company to spend a miserable night in the line.

Accommodation was found wherever possible and the troops were billeted with French families in farm-houses, estaminets or small cafés, and barns. The unlucky ones were allocated derelict buildings in which to make themselves as comfortable as they could. Everyone did their best to organise their equipment into the small amount of space available. There was a feeling that they could be there for a while. Each evening dripping clothing and equipment was hung up to dry wherever practicable. Most of the male population was missing from the villages as they had marched away to defend the homeland. The Grenadiers soon developed a good relationship with the remaining French inhabitants who were willing to provide simple meals at a small cost. The estaminets were kept busy and the local wine was well sampled by all ranks, who were grateful for this small luxury.

The Officers were accommodated in an old chateau at the edge of the village and most of the servants found space in the back rooms. It was cramped but better than some of the living conditions that Sid had seen in the village. There were frequent alerts and false alarms. Fifth Columnists were talked of constantly and there was a general mistrust of the Belgians, although he was unsure why. When the Battalion arrived at the frontier there had been a great sense of urgency, but as the defensive positions neared completion, and the companies' turn in the line came around again, routine took over. There was no sign of a German advance and the weather was now making life very uncomfortable for the troops on the frontier.

When the men were out of the line there was plenty of training to be done and of course the inevitable route marches. Marching on the cobbled roads was hard on the feet and lots of the guardsmen suffered with blisters. From time to time sport was organised, and the football matches against the other Battalions of the Brigade were very popular. When Coldstream opposition was encountered, Sid spotted his old friend Cyril Scott. The two spent a long time talking about people they knew in Poole before Scott departed with the remaining Coldstream spectators. When the opportunity presented itself, the Adjutant held a drill parade. The guardsmen hated these events, particularly those who had come out of the line and had to prepare themselves for inspection.

The local estaminets were well used by the Guardsmen when they were not engaged in training or in the line. The troops were happy to part with a few francs for a plate of chips or a couple of glasses of wine. The Military Police patrolled the villages and the towns, and were quick to challenge anyone who was thought to have 'over indulged'. It was forbidden to consume rum and the MPs kept a keen eye out for likely offenders. When the troops had money they much preferred to purchase a meal in the village, than to eat the unpopular army rations. Some of the West Country boys were very adept at poaching. They would often return to the billets with rabbits and game birds hanging from their belts. Although such behaviour was never sanctioned, some of the catch often found its way into the officers' mess, courtesy of the servants.

Sid was sometimes required to accompany his officer on patrols, both in and out of the line, and they often returned soaked to the skin and covered in mud. During one patrol, the two found themselves in a bog and as they tried to find their way around, Sid became stuck fast up to his thighs. The more he tried to free himself the deeper he sank. He gratefully accepted his officer's outstretched hand when it was offered. Unfortunately this did little to help with his rescue. After a considerable time spent tugging, grunting and heaving, their joint efforts eventually extricated him from the glue-like mud. They now looked more like swamp monsters than an officer's patrol, but they completed the evening's activities none the less.

The experience was wretched for those men who were stuck on sentry duty, in the freezing cold, with no warm barrack room to return to and a pile of wet kit to dry out. Of course there was to be no erosion of standards. Rifles and ammunition had to be kept immaculately clean and the deep sticky mud was no excuse for a slovenly appearance. In November, in the absence of any German assault, the decision was taken to allow the line to be held by a skeleton force, with the remainder of the duty Company in billets just behind. This decision was welcomed by the troops who were sick of the freezing nights in the trenches. Concerts were organised in Annapes and a group even managed to visit Vimy Ridge, scene of fierce fighting in the First World War. On Armistice Day the Battalion found a Guard of Honour in Paris. In these circumstances it was difficult to believe that the Nazis were about to attack, and the troops freezing on the frontier became increasingly frustrated.

Most of the men were able to listen to the wireless from time to time and the latest news was passed around by word of mouth. The infamous 'Lord Haw Haw' was now broadcasting regularly and his bulletins were met by mocking Guardsmen who recognised the Nazi propaganda for what it was. One rainy evening, the listeners were amazed to hear 'Haw Haw' mention the Brigade of Guards on the Belgian Frontier. He went on to tell the world that, 'The Guards are in bad order, with poor uniforms and dirty boots'. The guardsmen were angry that their reputation was being attacked and not a little concerned at the enemy's knowledge of their location. The broadcasts must have struck a raw nerve at Headquarters too, as about a week later the troops were issued with new battle-dress clothing.

As November gave way to December, a series of morale boosting visits were organised. On the 6th the whole of 7th Guards Brigade marched passed King George VI in the morning sunshine. The King later took lunch with the officers and Sid was selected to wait on the party with some of the other Servants. He felt that it was a great privilege to be so close to his Sovereign, and he was very impressed that the King had left the security of London to visit the troops. After all, the German Army couldn't be that far away. The King was clearly following in the footsteps of his father, who had been a regular visitor to the army in France during the last war. Forty-two officers sat down to lunch and the Servants also noted the presence of the Duke of Gloucester.

The Prime Minister also came to France and although he didn't visit the Battalion his presence was designed to demonstrate solidarity. Unfortunately, none of these visits did much to cheer up those in the line who were trying to keep warm. Training continued and a rapid road move was practised to a river line south of St Pol. The Battalion were required to seize and hold the line against an enemy attack. Most of the guardsmen couldn't understand the logic behind this tactic. After all they had spent three months building a defensive position. Sid and his pals knew very little of the Commander in Chief's plans and it was assumed by everyone that the defensive position they had spent so much time preparing would be occupied for a hard fought battle. In fact, the Gort line was one of a number of options that had been considered. Its major disadvantage was that by the time the Germans reached the British positions, Belgium would already have fallen. Plan D, was for the BEF to move forward into Belgium to the River Dyle where they would again prepare defences to meet the German advance.

As Christmas approached the decision was taken to allow the troops to take leave in England. This would have to be strictly controlled with a small part of the Battalion strength away at any one time. Sid was thrilled to learn that he had been selected to return home in mid-December. When the eagerly awaited day arrived, he boarded the truck from Annappes. He took all his essential equipment with him, rifle, helmet, ammunition, gas mask and all the other accoutrements that he would require if war came during his leave. He was accompanied by his pal Alan Short, another guardsman from the Signal Platoon. The two had decided that they would spend their leave together and that it would be split between Poole, and Alan's home in Gloucester.

Once they arrived in England the two pals made their way to Gloucester first. They were well received in the pubs when people realised that they had just returned from France, and they were very happy to accept the many free pints that they were handed. The atmosphere in England had changed since they had been away. There were air raid shelters all over the place and the 'blackout' was in force. There were ridiculous rumours circulating. The two friends heard that the BEF would soon be coming home; that the British, French and Germans were going to attack the Russians; and even that margarine was now being supplemented with fat from cats! Although most of the rumours were ridiculous, most people seemed to be resigned to the fact that the Germans were not going to be stopped without a fight. After a couple of days in Gloucester, most of it spent in the pubs, Sid and

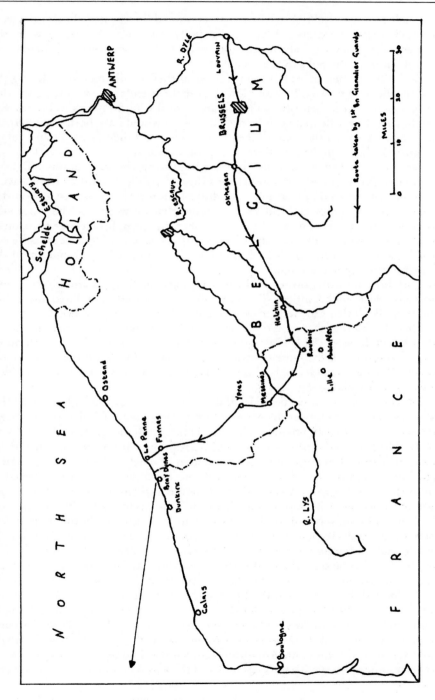

The Withdrawal to Dunkirk, May 1940

Alan made their way to Poole where the process was duly repeated. Their rifles were deposited behind the kitchen door at Sid's family home, for safe keeping when the two went out. They were always careful to check that they were still there upon their return from the pubs in the evening.

Both Guardsmen managed to visit most of their family members during the week but the time flew by. It wasn't long before the friends were removing the rust that had gathered on their rifles in preparation for the journey back to France. Sid thought that if his rifle had been inspected now he would have been in deep trouble. The pals boarded the train to the docks having said their farewells and before they knew it they were back with the battalion in Annappes.

Not much had changed whilst they had been away, the weather was still freezing and the Germans had not appeared. As the two pals had returned from leave it was no surprise when they were taken for duty. They were both warned for guard at an ammunition dump, and Sid was dismayed that he would be there over the Christmas period. There were some happy memories from his recent excursion to England, but on Christmas day these were insufficient to mask the fact that he was sitting at a desk in a shabby French building. He couldn't help wondering if the Germans were doing the same.

Very little information reached the troops and he listened attentively to any comments made by his officer. The Guardsmen were well disciplined and confident, they all felt that the Germans would come, but no one knew how or when. It was generally felt that they would put up a 'good show' and stop the advance just as the BEF had done in 1914. No one really had any idea of the German armoured strength, but some of the more knowledgeable men could reel off the names of the more notable German Generals, this was in contrast to the majority, who couldn't name many British Generals.

Sid was now able to speak a fair bit of French and knew the villagers well. He had made many friends over the winter but was cautious about what he discussed. Talk of spies persisted and there was a general mistrust of the locals. As 1939 passed into 1940 the routine continued without interruption. Most of the men had managed to take some leave at home, and the system of relief in the line was unrelenting. There were many more route marches and battalion personalities started to change through necessity. A new Adjutant arrived and Sid discovered that certain Warrant Officers had been placed in charge of Platoons to assist with the shortage of officers. A fighting patrol had been formed under Captain Thorne. It consisted of a Sergeant and 20 men. Sid wondered what task they would be given but he never found out because they were working directly under 7th Brigade.

On the 17th January the landscape turned white as eight inches of snow fell. This continued into February and March. Each time the snow melted, the countryside flooded, bringing back the thick sticky mud. It was the worst winter for many years and the troops became sick of sitting around freezing. It had been six months since they had arrived in France and there was no real sign of the Germans. People were frustrated, Chamberlain had referred to this period as the 'Twilight War'. Across the Atlantic, the Americans called it the 'Phoney War'. Even so there had been some contact with the Germans and the Royal Navy had seen some fierce action.

A Bren Gun crew, France c. 1940

The atmosphere in the BEF changed again in April when the news filtered through that the Germans had attacked Norway. There was a buzz of excitement around the Signal Platoon and everyone wondered if this was it. In the following days, Norway was steadily overwhelmed, followed by the collapse of Denmark in only four hours. The Battalion was expecting the Germans to advance into Belgium at any time and once more there were many false alarms. The Belgians, together with the Dutch, were eager not to provoke the Germans and so maintained their neutrality, even though everyone in the BEF seemed sure that an attack was imminent. The atmosphere was once again tense and the sense of urgency had returned.

All eyes were on the frontier and the troops in the line watched carefully for any sign of enemy activity. On 10 May 1940, at 05.30 hrs, the Blitzkrieg began. Holland and Belgium were ruthlessly attacked from the air as the massive armoured columns drove forward. The ferocity of the German attack shocked everyone. Word reached the Battalion and a general 'stand to' was called. There was a great deal of excitement and not a little apprehension amongst the guardsmen. Amid great confusion it was announced that the Battalion was to move into Belgium. Companies and Platoons rushed to pack up their kit ready for the move. Non-essential kit was loaded on to the transport and was overseen by the CQMS, who squeezed a miraculous quantity of stores on to his single 15 cwt truck. There was bewilderment when the men realised that their pre-prepared positions, which had been resolutely guarded all through the winter, were to be abandoned without a fight. At this particular moment the Commander in Chief, who had issued the orders, was probably almost as unpopular as the invading German forces. Fortunately some additional motor transport was sent to move the Grenadiers, so at least they wouldn't have to march the whole way to the new position.

Chapter 8

The Road to Dunkirk

Sid was unaware of the Battalion's destination at this point and although his pals in the Signals Platoon were curious, they had no real understanding of the Belgian geography. The strange sounding names meant nothing to them, although most had a rough idea where Brussels was situated. In fact the Commanding Officer had been ordered to take up defensive positions in Louvain, where they were to meet the German advance astride the river Dyle. As the convoy of trucks moved eastwards they met an ever-increasing flow of refugees heading west. There were people of all ages, young and old, struggling with whatever possessions they could transport. They were a pitiful sight and brought home the reality of what lay ahead to the British troops. As the columns progressed on the road to Brussels so the flow of refugees seemed more desperate. The evening of 11th May was spent in a village 5 miles east of the Belgian capital. The Battalion completed its move into Louvain on foot the following morning.

When Sid and the remainder of the Signal Platoon arrived in the ancient Belgian town there was a great deal of confusion. The Belgians were already there in their hastily prepared positions, which did not conform to what Colonel Prescott had in mind for the Grenadiers. The Belgians refused to give up or to move any of their positions, and the Commanding Officer was forced to make the best of a bad job.

Eventually a makeshift defensive line was established with the 1st Coldstream Guards on the left and the 2nd Grenadiers in reserve. There were a number of bridges in place over the river Dyle and the Engineers prepared these for demolition. There seemed to be a constant flow of refugees and demoralised Belgian troops coming over the river, but worryingly not many of the troops seemed to be stopping on the west bank.

The Grenadiers set about digging trenches and fortifying the buildings against the expected German assault. A small tunnel was found under a main road which was selected as a suitable location for the Battalion Headquarters. Blankets were hung over the entrances to conceal them from the air and to stop the light being seen during the night. Sid and the other guardsmen set about filling sand-bags and laying land line to the rifle companies in their various positions. As he found his way around the streets Sid couldn't help thinking what a pleasant little town this must have been only two days ago. One of his mates had told him that it was famous for its beer but there would be no time for that now.

Drill Sergeant Teece and Sergeant Major Sheather were constantly near the headquarters. They chased the guardsmen around and made sure that all of the defensive positions were up to scratch. Sid remembered the first time he had seen Teece on the parade square at Caterham. It seemed like a million years ago. Their activities were interrupted by the drone of aero engines and everyone searched the sky for the source of this noise. It was some way off but they soon saw a German Messerschmitt. It appeared to be chasing another small plane which was identified as an unarmed British Lysander. The slower British plane stood no chance. The

German fighter swooped like an angry bee and the RAF plane fell from the skies. The Messerschmitt disappeared into the distance leaving a thick black plume of smoke rising from the horizon, as a reminder that the Luftwaffe had established air superiority over Belgium. The young guardsmen watched, in silence, until the Drill Sergeant's voice snapped them back into action.

It didn't take long for the enemy to commence its ground assault. The first attacks into the town were probably only fighting patrols and were successfully beaten off. To the dismay of the Grenadiers, the Belgians started to withdraw almost immediately, and the Battalion was forced to move some of its positions in order to stabilise the line. As the guardsmen looked on, scores of Belgian soldiers crossed the river and kept moving west. There was nothing to be done but to hold fast, it was a very unnerving time. Before long the German mortars and artillery started to search the Grenadier positions and the guardsmen squatted in their trenches for protection. The crump of artillery shells and the whine of the deadly shrapnel were terrifying. Sid squatted inside the tunnel and hoped for the best. Not knowing what was going on outside and being unable to hit back at the enemy made things even more frightening.

During one of these bombardments an enemy shell landed almost at the entrance to the Battalion Headquarters tunnel. A deafening bang shook everyone to the core. There was alarm and confusion as shrapnel slammed against the sandbagged entrance and thick black smoke drifted inside. Sid was quick to see that someone had been hit and was lying on his back near the entrance. Several of the Signal Platoon rushed to help and he saw that it was his friend 'Dixie' Dean who had been hit. Dixie's steel helmet had a large hole where it had been penetrated by a shell splinter and judging by the amount of blood, he was seriously hurt. The guardsmen helped to patch up the gravely injured man before he was placed on a stretcher and carried away to the Regimental aid post. The incident reminded everyone just how vulnerable they were to the white hot shrapnel and it was a major incentive for them to stay under cover at all times. Dixie was never seen again, although the Platoon later heard that he had survived his injuries. Sid was able to hear the reports of casualties coming in from the companies, and who were getting most of the attention from the German mortars. He heard that Lieutenant Seymour had also been wounded. Seymour had been in Egypt with him and had come to the First Battalion at the same time. He hoped that the young officer wasn't seriously hurt.

As the German activity in Louvain increased, heavy rifle and machine gun fire was exchanged and enemy soldiers could be seen in the buildings. Although he couldn't see from his position, Sid could hear the small arms fire echoing through the streets. There was now a serious threat that the Germans might be able to seize a bridge in- tact and the decision was taken to blow the remaining structures. He watched as the Engineers blew one of the bridges. There was a terrific explosion which threw the bridge into the air. Unfortunately a Belgian truck tried to rush across at this moment and met the same fate as the old bridge. The vehicle disappeared into the Dyle as rubble splashed into the water all around.

It was obvious that the Germans were getting stronger on the other side of the river and the sniper fire increased. The Battalion was holding comfortably but no one knew what was happening elsewhere. Although they were very concerned about their uncertain position there was nothing that the guardsmen could do but stay under cover and stay alert. They slept when they could and snatched a meal here and there. In an adjacent field, one of Sid's pals had spotted a lone cow and being a farm boy he noticed that the cow needed milking. The sight of this khaki clad farmer complete with steel helmet, squirting fresh milk into a mess tin in the middle of a battle raised many a laugh in the Signal Platoon. But the fresh milk went down well in their tea as they discussed their uncertain situation.

What no one in the Battalion knew at this stage was that the BEF had taken the bait and the German Army Group 'A' had already attacked to the South through Luxembourg and between the Maginot and Dyle lines. Not only had a fast moving enemy already outflanked them, but they were also in real danger of being completely cut off. Holland was overrun too and was about to surrender. The Belgians were now under severe pressure from the German advance. In the command post Sid heard that the Coldstream were under heavy attack on the left and that they had counter attacked to drive the enemy back.

At around 5.30pm on 16th May, word was received that the Battalion was to pull back. As the troops knew nothing of the German breakthrough to the south, this news came as a surprise because the Battalion had been steeling itself for a tough fight in Louvain. There was initial confusion, but the orders were soon passed down the chain that a withdrawal was to be carried out to the west of Brussels. Rumour, as always, was rife and word had also reached the battalion that the Dutch to the north had given in. There was no panic and the withdrawal was conducted in an orderly and disciplined fashion. The forward Companies continued to engage the Germans as they thinned out and moved steadily rearward. Sid was able to see his comrades using the available cover to mask their withdrawal.

The enemy artillery was now searching the roads leading from Louvain. The Grenadiers were forced to avoid the areas that were attracting the most attention from the German guns. They were grateful for the cover that the darkness provided, although the fires in Louvain lit the night sky as they headed away. After several hours of marching, which had been interrupted by frequent spells squatting in ditches as protection from enemy artillery, the Battalion halted. The First Grenadiers and the Coldstream had extricated themselves in good order, in an operation that had been covered by the Second Battalion, and it was now necessary to cover their withdrawal too.

The Platoon dug shell scrapes for protection but no one thought they would be in this position for long. They were by now exhausted, there hadn't been much sleep during the last week, and their first taste of war had also taken its toll. There was a great deal of anxiety at the close proximity of the Germans and at the uncertainty of the situation. It was obvious even to the guardsmen that things were not going well. They slept as they could, but this respite was short lived. Orders were received to move off, and the march toward Brussels continued. Some of the men were furious. They couldn't understand why they were being ordered to retreat, they had not yet got to grips with the enemy, and they wanted to repay the Nazis for the heavy bombardment they had endured.

As day-break came there was no sign of an imminent German pursuit, although the guns could still be heard, and the smoke from the burning towns and villages to the east could be plainly seen. There was now an added threat because

Guardsman in fighting order c. 1940

during the daylight hours they were at the mercy of enemy aircraft. A wary eye was kept on the sky at all times. When the Battalion eventually reached Brussels, Sid was delighted to find himself in a park which was full of British trucks. There was no time to be lost and the troops were quickly detailed to the vehicles which had been sent to ferry them further west. Bren guns were set up on top of the trucks and some of the lorries were already moving as he gratefully clambered aboard.

As the engine sparked into life there was a sudden shout of alarm which was rapidly joined by other voices, 'aircraft!' This one word was enough to spark everyone into action. Troops threw themselves over the sides of the vehicles in an effort to distance themselves from the obvious targets. The roar of aero engines was now getting louder and someone had started firing a Bren gun into the air. Sid followed his mates and leapt from the rear of the vehicle, but a loose rivet on the top of his helmet became entangled in a camouflage net and he was suspended from the top of his head like a desperate puppet. Just as panic was about to set in, his head freed itself from the still suspended helmet and he sprinted for cover.

The scream from the diving Stuka bombers was deafening and several bombs fell close by. He felt the concussion as each bomb struck and he folded his arms over his head for protection. The attack ended as suddenly as it had begun. When the Guardsmen emerged from cover the scene was one of chaos. Thick oily smoke hung over the park and some of the trucks were alight. Wounded men were being helped and NCOs shouted instructions to the men. There was no time to be lost and the remaining vehicles were boarded as soon as possible. Some of the wounded were treated on the back of the trucks, as they pulled out of the park and on to the cobbled street which would take them away from the Belgian capital.

Their progress through the human tide of refugees was painfully slow and getting slower all the time. It was necessary to negotiate abandoned vehicles and burning trucks frequently. It became obvious that to try and continue the withdrawal in trucks was hopeless. The roads were packed with refugees using every imaginable type of transport. The Battalion's vehicles were eventually abandoned in ditches at the sides of the roads and the engines were left running in order to seize the motors.

Two days after their withdrawal from Louvain, the First Battalion crossed the river Dendre at Okhegen. They had travelled almost 30 miles. The Second Battalion were in place here and as soon as their sister Battalion was across the river the bridges were blown. There had been some trouble with snipers. Word was that these were fifth columnists, as a result no civilians were to be trusted. The men were tired and frustrated, they couldn't understand why they were not being allowed to stand and fight.

Orders were further received that the withdrawal was to continue. A week had passed since the invasion of Belgium, and still there was no news of the overall situation. Had the young Guardsmen known that to the south, General Guderian's Panzers were now advancing at the rate of 65 kilometres a day, they may have been even more anxious. By 19th May, they had crossed the river Escaut at Helchin. There had been numerous air attacks. The Luftwaffe pilots had not been at all deterred from their murderous task by the presence of so many refugees. The bodies of civilians now littered the roadside and the constant westward flow of humanity continued.

Refugees and soldiers were intermingled. There were many small groups of men who had become separated from their units, some of these latched on to the Grenadiers. There were French, Belgian and British troops in the columns, and some had lost their discipline. Snipers continued to cause problems and when they were caught out of uniform they were shot. The second Battalion had been compelled to shoot a large number of snipers dressed in civilian clothes.

When the silhouette of an enemy aircraft was spotted a warning shout went up, and the Battalion sprinted for whatever cover was available. Those who were able, returned fire, but they were ineffective against the fast flying Messerschmitt and Junkers aeroplanes. The guardsmen were forced to squat or crouch in ditches as the canon shells ripped into the ground around them. It was terrifying, but there was nothing they could do to prevent the attacks. When the aero engines became distant again, the weary men forced themselves to their feet, and continued the march in long columns either side of the road. There were invariably casualties during these attacks. On one occasion Sid noticed that an old friend of his from Number Four Company had been hit. Lance Corporal Nicholas Van Schalkwyk was obviously dead and there was nothing that anyone could do. It was another terrible shock. He was saddened that Nicholas would now rest in a grave far from his South African home.

By now, the lack of sleep was affecting many of the troops. There were wounded men to be carried and water was getting short. There was great relief on reaching Roubaix because there was time for rest. The Battalion spent three days in the area of the town, and were made responsible for a series of canal bridges. 7th

Guards Brigade had remained in good order. They had kept ahead of the advancing Germans, and had carried out each of the tasks they had been set during the withdrawal. Some of the men thought that the BEF was going to make its stand here and most were relieved. The withdrawal had been exhausting, and now that they had snatched some sleep they would punish their German attackers. Part of the Signal Platoon found themselves in a large factory complex on the edge of the town. Various inspections were carried out, feet were looked at by the Platoon officers, and rifles were also inspected.

The troops were cleaning their rifles when suddenly a shot rang out. People dived for cover expecting another fifth columnist, but it soon became apparent that the shot had been fired from the Commanding Officer's Servant's rifle. Irate Non Commissioned Officers quickly pounced on the 'Guilty Man'. 'Do you always bloody do that?' one of them screamed. 'Only on my birthday!' came the cheeky reply. Given their recent circumstances, this remark somehow seemed to cut through the tension and everyone collapsed with laughter. The mischievous guardsman had rightly surmised that his mistake did not have the same impact, given what they had recently been through.

Bread and cheese was distributed to the men, and Sid managed to locate a small garden, where he found spring onions growing. He quickly pulled a few from the ground to supplement his rations. As he was doing so, he was suddenly reminded of his mother's garden back in Poole. He felt very homesick, and wished he was back in Dorset rather than in France, faced with a very bleak future. He realised his mind was wandering and decided to pull himself together. He would get himself out of this, if he kept alert. The brief respite in Roubaix had been a godsend. The Battalion used the opportunity to reorganise itself. The wounded were treated, ammunition was redistributed and several missing men were relocated. There had been time to catch some sleep and to get some food. The Battalion moved off again on 26th May, once again in a westerly direction. There were rumblings of discontent from those who thought they should stand and fight, but they soon fell into the routine of marching.

The roads and tracks were still crowded, but the percentage of British troops seemed to have increased. There were hardly any vehicles moving now, in fact it seemed as if every vehicle in the BEF had been abandoned by the roadside. Some of these had been set alight, to prevent them from falling into enemy hands. Others had been hit by shells. The Brigade was now heading for the line of the Ypres-Comines canal. The road from Roubaix to Ypres was under heavy fire. For long periods the Battalion was forced to halt, because of the effective enemy artillery.

On one occasion a barrage suddenly started and Sid, caught in the open, dashed for cover. He dived for the doorway of a small house, the frame gave way and he fell headlong into the house. When he looked up to survey his surroundings, he saw that he was not alone. There, crouching on the floor amid the falling plaster, was an elderly man who was being protected by his young daughter. Sid was struck by the oddness of the scene. She was clearly a brave young girl, but when their eyes met he saw only sympathy. He was touched that someone should feel sorry for him, when they were probably in even more dire circumstances. There was no conversation. When the artillery subsided he darted back outside to rejoin the others.

The bedraggled and exhausted men were only able to move when the German guns were punishing some other unfortunate group. There had been a number of casualties since they had left Roubaix, including the Commanding Officer. Lt Colonel Prescott had been injured by a shell splinter and was now unable to walk. As they neared the town of Ypres, the top of St Martin's cathedral was plainly visible. It was a reminder to everyone who passed, that the last BEF had perished in the surrounding fields.

Most of the Battalion were aware that they were getting ever closer to the sea, and everyone thought that sooner or later they would have to make a final stand. Word was passed that they were heading for Dunkirk. Sid imagined that this would be where they would fight, with their backs to the sea.

The Belgian army finally capitulated on 28th May, but they had bought the BEF a little time. The British troops were now effectively trapped inside an ever decreasing perimeter. The Luftwaffe bombers could be plainly seen over Dunkirk. As the Grenadiers trudged ever westward, Sid was suddenly stopped by a Corporal from another regiment. He appeared to be in charge of about ten men, and was heading in the opposite direction to the hundreds of troops on the road. 'Which way to Dunkirk, mate?' he asked. Sid replied it was in the direction that the rest of the army was headed, towards the gunfire and plumes of smoke on the horizon. The corporal thanked him and then headed off in the opposite direction to Dunkirk. Sid thought about calling him back, but then thought better of it.

The following day, the Brigade was ordered to take up positions in the town of Furnes, just a few miles to the north east of Dunkirk. At the headquarters of the BEF, Lord Gort had realised that the situation was untenable. Across the channel, Admiral Bertram Ramsay was putting together Operation Dynamo, the planned evacuation of the BEF from France. The Second Battalion was already in Furnes when their sister Battalion arrived. The troops set about defending the outskirts of the town from German attacks. It was now vital that the Dunkirk perimeter held for as long as possible. The troops on the edge of town were already in contact with the German lead elements, so everyone set about preparing their defences straight away. The Signal Platoon had established the Command Post in a cellar. Drill Sergeant Teece was hastily checking that telephone wires were protected, and that the Battalion Headquarters was correctly defended.

Explosions from enemy mortars could be heard in other parts of the town, but suddenly there was a deafening roar nearby as the first lethal bombs rained upon the new First Battalion positions. Everyone dived for cover; they had learned how deadly the Nazi mortars were. Dirt and chunks of masonry rained down on Sid as he hugged the ground and hoped that none of the bombs had his name on them. The barrage was short lived. As soon as it stopped the troops emerged from their cover to continue with their important tasks. Sid immediately noticed a number of men crouching over a prostrate figure. He wondered who had become a casualty this time. He soon discovered that the unfortunate man was Drill Sergeant Teece. He had been struck by a shell splinter and killed instantly. There was a terrible realisation that no one was immune. Sid had subconsciously assumed that Drill Sergeants couldn't be casualties, and he was shocked at the death of this influential character. Teece came from a Grenadier family. His father, Jabez Teece, had been the Sergeant Major of the Battalion, and had served as the Quartermaster for most of the Great War. There was no time to dwell on the loss. The guardsmen were reminded of the close proximity of the enemy by the sound of small arms fire.

The Second Battalion was holding the centre of the town. Runners passed between the command posts, stretcher-bearers moved to and fro with casualties, and Sid bumped into some of his old pals. There were brief conversations about recent experiences. He learned the shocking news that Lieutenant Colonel Lloyd, the Commanding Officer of his old Battalion, along with Captain Jeffreys and Major Pakenham, had been shot dead by a sniper. The situation was becoming more fragile all the time. The Germans made frequent attempts to gain a foothold in the town, and parties from the various Battalions in the Brigade dislodged them with repeated counter attacks. The artillery was increasing, and he thought that the small arms fire was becoming more intense and closer as the hours passed. There were plenty of enemy aircraft in the skies above, but thankfully most of the air attacks seemed to be concentrated over Dunkirk. Everyone was aware that the situation was desperate, but there was a determination that the Germans would not take the town, as long as it was defended by Grenadiers. Each attempt by the Germans to cross the canal, and gain a foothold in the town, was beaten back. Sid found himself firing into buildings where German activity had been seen, but it was impossible to tell if he had hit anyone, because of the darkness that had descended over the town.

He lost track of the time. They had been in Furnes for a couple of days and there had been no chance to sleep. The Germans were far too close for anyone to be able to relax. The Dunkirk perimeter was fast shrinking, and the Grenadiers were eventually ordered to withdraw. Deception was vitally important. If the Germans discovered that a withdrawal was underway it could spell disaster. The rifle companies abandoned their positions on the north bank of the canal at 02.30 hours. Sid watched the curious spectacle of scores of guardsmen passing him, sandbags wrapped around their feet to mask the sound of their boots on the cobbles. He too had wrapped hessian around his boots, and took his place in one of the silently moving files as it passed.

He had not seen his officer for some time. At first he thought that Mr Gwyer must be busy, but as the time passed by he became more concerned. He heard a rumour that Gwyer had been hit, but there was no way to confirm this. As the hours passed he concluded that it must be true. On the outskirts of the town a number of trucks were waiting, and most of the Battalion managed to mount these. There was some intermittent shelling, but there were no casualties. The Germans had obviously not realised that the Grenadier positions had been vacated. As the convoy approached the village of La Panne, the shelling became heavier, and it was decided that it would be safer to strike off across country towards the beaches. The plan had by now been communicated to the troops. They were to be lifted from the beaches around Dunkirk and transported back to England. Sid thought that this was going to be madness. The beaches were within artillery range, the Luftwaffe ruled the skies and the Germans were snapping at their heels. He didn't see how it could be done. On the other hand there didn't seem to be many other options.

As dawn broke, most of the Battalion had reached the beaches between Bray Dunes and La Panne. It was 1st June. As Sid surveyed the scene he realised that the situation was even more desperate than he had imagined. As far as the eye could see there were abandoned vehicles, some were still smoking. He could see thousands of men, many huddled in groups among the dunes for protection. There were a lot of bodies on the beach. A long row of 15 cwt vehicles was parked nose to tail, extending into the sea. He imagined that someone had tried to form an improvised jetty, but there were no boats near it. In fact, judging by the state of the vehicles, it had become a target for enemy aircraft. Thick oily smoke drifted across the beach, and the smell of cordite and petrol hung in the air.

Standing off shore there were many small boats, and he could see larger ships further out. There were long snakes of men wading out into the sea, where smaller boats seemed to be ferrying them out to the waiting ships. But the whole operation seemed to be painfully slow. Men were horribly exposed as they waited, sometimes for hours. No one seemed to be in charge, but there was a strange order to the chaos around him. 7th Guards Brigade was to take its place among the waiting troops, but in the darkness and confusion the various units had become separated, and intermingled with the masses on the beach. Some companies and platoons had struck out for Dunkirk, hoping that there would be a better chance of being picked up. Those who were left on the beach, near Sid, decided to find some protection until an opportunity came along for them to escape. They had just arrived, and it was clear that some of the men around them had been there for several days.

Now that daylight had returned, it brought with it the Luftwaffe. The scream from the air brakes of the Stukas was even more terrifying than before, because this was the end of the road. There was no where else to go. The troops were defenceless, but for a few Bren guns, and the anti-aircraft guns on some of the ships offshore. Enemy fighters screamed along the beach, strafing as they went, and desperate men ran back up the sand in search of shelter. There was little or no organisation. The troops became dispersed in the dunes, where they sought cover from the frequent air attacks. Some Non Commissioned Officers tried in vain to keep the men together, and Sid clearly heard someone shouting for the Guards to 'form up in threes'. Understandably, there was little response from the men to what seemed like a suicidal order, and it was soon dropped.

Sid and his mates decided that their best chance of survival was to 'dig in', and they sighted their shelter next to the inner wheels of an abandoned truck. Unfortunately. they didn't have any entrenching tools, so having scraped a small depression with their hands, Sid went in search of a shovel. Some of the Quartermaster's party was sighted close by, and he could see that RQMS Archie Douglas had been digging his own shelter with an ancient Belgian spade. Sid asked if he could borrow the spade and it was grudgingly surrendered to him. He gained the distinct impression that he would have been made to sign for it, if the RQMS had been in possession of the relevant paperwork.

He returned to the abandoned truck, where he and his mates took turns with the shovel to spoon away the sand. When the trench was finished they were grateful for the protection that it afforded. The bombs that fell on the beach were less effective in the sand, but they were none the less terrifying to the young guardsmen in their freshly dug hole. A 'Tommy Cooker' was acquired and the inevitable 'brew' was made. It was a strange feeling, to be calmly drinking tea as the German planes screamed overhead. Fortunately, the air attacks were not constant and it was possible to move around between attacks.

As they became used to the situation, the men started to explore the beach for signs of other Grenadiers, and for a route out to the waiting ships. During one of these excursions Sid and one of his mates were caught in the open as a Messerschmitt dived. They sprinted for the protection of a beached paddle-steamer. The two had been eating their ration of bully beef. Once they were safe behind the steel hull of the ship, they tucked in once more. Heavy cannon shells thudded against the ship as the two wolfed down their food. A sergeant sheltering near them looked on with disgust. 'If you two can eat at a time like this, then you're a pair of bloody hogs'! he said.

As they were returning to the relative security of their small trench, they noticed the body of the CQMS. He had been shot through the eye and instantly killed. There seemed to be little or no order to the queuing on the beach, so Sid went in search of something they could use to float themselves out to sea. He was walking in the dunes just behind his position when, incredibly, he stumbled across an old rowing boat. He quickly surveyed the boat to see if it was possible to repair any damage, and to make his find seaworthy. To his absolute amazement he could find no serious damage or holes. Surely it was too good to be true! He double-checked and still it seemed serviceable. He quickly looked around to see who else had seen the boat. There was no one. He had to move fast, before his discovery was snatched away by another group. He sprinted back to the trench and rounded up a party of Grenadiers. The little group raced to follow Sid back to the boat, not daring to believe that his claim could be true.

Once the others confirmed his observations, it was decided that they should get the boat down to the water as quickly as they could. There was a break in the air raids, and there were some small ships standing not too far off the shore. About twenty Grenadiers gathered around the boat, they all seemed to be from Headquarters Company. Sid noticed the Battalion Intelligence Sergeant, several members of the Signal Platoon, as well as the RQMS and Captain 'Johnnie' Walker, the Quartermaster. Walker was a former Sergeant Major of the Battalion, an appointment he had held for seven years and another veteran of the Great War. He looked around the group suspiciously, probably because he was wearing a money belt containing the Battalion's pay!

The rowing boat was dragged into the water, and once that they saw that it stayed afloat, the little group clambered aboard. Several of the men slid a round into the breech of their rifles to show that they meant business. They could not afford to have their boat capsized by any of the panicking men around them. Although the guardsmen had maintained their discipline, some of those on the beach had abandoned their arms and equipment. They would get no sympathy from the Grenadiers. Sid had positioned himself at the front of the little boat and was using his rifle as an oar. Voices from behind shouted for him to slow down. He was paddling too fast! Under the circumstances he couldn't see how it was possible to paddle too fast!

The beaches slowly slipped away and it was possible to look back and survey the scene once more. Long snakes of men were chest deep in water, waiting for a means to escape the beaches. A thick cloud of black smoke hung menacingly over the whole scene. The beaches were a mass of abandoned equipment and desperate troops. In the water, some men were swimming out to sea, others clung to whatever they could find, hoping to be picked up.

The group was heading towards a paddle steamer. They prayed that it would not turn away, or be hit by a bomb before they arrived. After what seemed an age, they finally came alongside the iron hull of the steamer. Sid could hear pom-pom guns firing into the air. He couldn't make out her name, but he was grateful that she had made the voyage across the channel to help. There were Royal Navy sailors on the decks. They shouted down to the Grenadiers to climb up the scramble nets, which had been thrown over the side, to help the desperate troops to escape the beaches. The little boat was packed with soldiers already and the sailors were keen to head for home once she was full. They told the Grenadiers to leave the rowing boat. It was an awkward climb, particularly as they were all still wearing webbing and steel helmets, with their rifles slung across their backs. As they reached the rail they were hauled over by the sailors who shouted for them to get below as they would soon be heading off. They were told to leave their rifles on the deck so that they could move more freely in the confined spaces of the old steamer. Being separated from their rifles was not something that came easily, particularly after the last week or so, but they understood the logic and did as they were told.

As they squeezed themselves below, more troops were being hauled onto the already crowded decks of the steamer. The first thing Sid noticed, when they had found space below, was a man, naked apart from a gas cape. He was covered in black oil and was dripping wet. He had clearly found the desperate situation too much and was hysterical. The Intelligence Sergeant told Sid to 'get a grip of him', so he did his best to calm the soldier by reasoning with him. He thought that he recognised the man from the Second Battalion, but there was no way of telling in his current state. The noise and vibrations from the pom-poms could still be heard, and there was an occasional thud as another bomb exploded in the sea. They were relieved to be off the beaches, but they were not safe yet. Sid was terrified that if they were hit it would be impossible to get back on deck before the ship sank. How ironic it would be if he met the same fate as his uncle.

Before long, the tired men heard the ship's engines spark into life and they were thankful to know that they were heading for England. Everyone prayed that their good fortune would hold and that the Luftwaffe would not find them. Cheese and biscuits were passed around and the Grenadiers tucked in, although more from nervous reaction than from hunger. Gradually the sounds of war from outside were replaced by the steady rumble of the ship's engines as she headed for the coast of England and safety.

Chapter 9

England Threatened

The battered little steamer eventually put into Sheerness, where she off-loaded her exhausted passengers. It was wonderful to be back on English soil, but there was no elation. A quick glance around at the wounded and exhausted men was enough to remind them all that the future was still very uncertain. Many of the men aboard had discarded all of their equipment, and many were without rifles. This was in contrast to the guardsmen, who not only had their arms but their complete marching order. One of Sid's companions had been a Bisley shot before the war and he treasured his rifle. He made a dash for the decks where the weapons had been deposited, in order to ensure that his prized possession wasn't mixed up. Sid, resourceful as ever, decided to join him. His own rifle had a terrible barrel and he thought it was time to exchange it. He quickly selected a better looking Lee Enfield and left his own in its place. He rightly surmised that the checking of rifle numbers would not be a priority in the coming days. These were hardly the actions of demoralised men.

On the quayside the Grenadiers reassembled as a group, they stood out from the dishevelled masses around them because of their appearance. Although no shoulder flashes were worn, everyone knew that they were the Guards. Half-dressed, unshaven men with blackened faces were everywhere, but the group of tall men with arms and equipment were conspicuous. There were a good number of French soldiers some of whom looked as though they were badly injured. Mugs of tea were handed around as the wounded were cared for, and the authorities attempted to process the hundreds of troops that had been constantly arriving. Unknown to the little party, this scene was being replayed all along the south coast.

Once the troops had been identified and processed, the authorities were keen to move men on from the Channel ports as quickly as possible. Before long, the First Battalion men joined hundreds of others on a train bound for Birmingham. It was the first time that anyone had had the time to relax, or to reflect on the events that had led to the beaches of Dunkirk. Most were completely exhausted and soon fell into a deep sleep. Sid was among them.

When the train reached Birmingham its occupants were sent to a newly built housing estate at Kings Standing. These houses would be home for the next few days so that the mixed groups of soldiers could be reorganised. A lot of time was simply spent sleeping or reorganising their kit. Sid was pleased to find that his new rifle did indeed have a better barrel than his old one, and he wondered if it would be fired again in the near future. On the second day at their temporary home the troops were paraded for a lecture. A Scottish officer, who was apparently the senior man present, addressed them. He told the assembled troops that he wouldn't go over the experiences of the last few weeks, he said simply, 'I think you are all bloody marvellous'! He went on to explain that they were to be split up, and sent back to their regiments which were to be reformed. He ended by saying, 'We will reform, and we will go back and kick those bastards right out of it'!

It was just what they wanted to hear and the troops all cheered loudly. It was a memorable moment. They all knew that the Germans had decisively beaten the allies in France, but there was comfort in the fact that they had escaped from under the very noses of their attackers, and had lived to fight another day. There was no mistaking the mood. It was one of defiance, and determination to have another crack at the Germans. Sid was well aware that, despite their defiant attitude, it was going to be a long time before Great Britain was in a position to attack the enemy.

The evacuation from Dunkirk had been miraculous. Over 338,000 British and French troops had been evacuated from the beaches, and the operation had been repeated all along the French coast. In the days that followed many more men escaped to England where they were rapidly dispersed around the country. Reorganisation of the scattered units was no easy task, but once the groups of men were located they were sent back to their reforming units. The 1st Battalion was once again billeted in the West Country and Sid was pleased to be back on familiar ground. There was something comforting about the sight of the sentries, and people going about the Battalion routine as though nothing had happened. The Division was concentrated around Frome, and the Battalion was billeted in barns, outbuildings and tents. It was great to see so many familiar faces, most of which he had not seen since Louvain. He learned that Lt Gwyer was still listed as missing, along with a large number of other men.

Shortly after his arrival in the West Country the first batch of 200 men was granted 48 hours' leave. It was very welcome, but passed by in a flash, and he was soon back in the country billets. New equipment had already started to arrive and

Churchill on the South coast, viewing the opposition!

groups of men were also being drafted in as replacements. There were still a lot of men missing and rumours circulated about their fate. There were many tales of heroism. RSM Sheather was listed as missing too, some said he had been seen embarking troops at the Dunkirk mole, others said that he had given up his place on a boat to a young Guardsman saying, 'Take my place son, I've done this before'. RSM Sheather was in fact killed in action on 1st June.

The following weeks were taken up with administration and training. On 14th June the King once again inspected 7th Guards Brigade. They were battered and bruised, but had already reformed into a fighting unit. There were gaps in their ranks. Colonel Prescott was on leave recovering from his injuries, and the Second Battalion too, had a new Commanding Officer. Drill Sergeant Harrison was appointed as the Sergeant Major of the First Battalion, but Sid couldn't help wondering about the fate of his officer. Many men who had been listed as missing had turned up in hospital, and he hoped that many more Grenadiers would be located in the days ahead. Despite the losses, there was great pride that all three Battalions of the regiment had left France in good order, and with their equipment. They had maintained the Grenadier reputation for discipline and steadiness under fire. The Third Battalion in particular had been badly mauled, but had given the Germans a very bloody nose during the fighting along the Escaut canal. Another Victoria Cross would soon be added to the regimental tally. This one was earned by Lcpl Harry Nicholls, who was sadly also listed as missing from his Battalion.

As an officer's servant with no officer, Sid was somewhat under employed, so he was detailed to look after the Senior Major and soon adapted to the new routine. One day he was informed that Lieutenant Gwyer was not only alive, but that he was recuperating in a hospital at Epsom. Sid was delighted. He felt that he should visit as soon as he could, to ensure that his officer was being well looked after. Permission was granted and he set off for Epsom.

When he arrived at the hospital it took some time to locate his officer. There were many such men, all being treated for wounds as a result of the recent fighting. Gwyer had been seriously wounded in the leg. and was not in good shape. He was surrounded by pulleys, weights and string, but remained as defiant as ever. The two were pleased to see each other. After exchanging pleasantries, Sid suggested that it was unlikely that his officer would return to active duty because of his injuries. He said that he thought that they would find him a job somewhere. Gwyer was outraged. 'Find me a job, I'll be back in a service Battalion!' he raged. Sid was left in no doubt of this young officer's determination to return to the Battalion. He decided that it was best not to raise the issue again, although he secretly thought that this would be their last meeting for a very long time.

The threat of invasion was now ever present. The Battalion was sent to the Littlehampton area to assist with the construction of coastal defences. Wiring parties were formed, and it was necessary to clear civilians from the many beach huts. The Battle of Britain was well under way. There were frequent air raid warnings and reports of enemy parachutists, most of which proved false.

Invasion fever was rife. On one occasion, Grenadiers were mistakenly fired upon by the Middlesex Regiment, who mistook them for invading Germans. Fortunately no one was injured. Preparations for the invasion continued apace, and the Battalion returned to the West Country at the end of July. As time passed, the

Battalion was properly reformed and reinforced with drafts of fresh men. Sid settled into the routine of training, which was similar to that which had been undertaken before the BEF deployed to France. There were of course differences. No-one was under any illusion about the German strength in armour, or of their numerical superiority in the air, and a tank hunting platoon was formed.

The evening black-out, and the air raid sirens were a constant reminder of the threat that lay across the channel. The route marches and manoeuvres went on, spurred by the threat of invasion. When the men were not training they were allowed the occasional pass into Frome. This was a welcome break from routine, and Sid was able to watch the latest news in the local cinema. Winston Churchill had succeeded Chamberlain and his defiant speeches were relayed almost daily. In the evenings the guardsmen were sometimes able to let their hair down in the pubs.

During a short spell away from training, Sid and one of his pals were having a cup of tea in a local café. Their polished brass Grenades were clearly visible in their caps. A couple of Sergeants in the Royal Artillery, who were seated at an adjacent table, engaged them in conversation. One of the NCOs suddenly said, 'Bloody Guards, only any good for marching up and down'. The two guardsmen were outraged. Sid's pal leapt to his feet, with the intention of physically extracting an apology from the offending man. Sid suddenly had a vision of a court martial where two guardsmen were jailed for strangling a sergeant in public. The NCOs were on their feet too, realising their imminent peril, and pleading that they were only joking. Sid was standing now. The situation was only calmed when one of the NCOs declared that he had been at Dunkirk, and had seen the Guards with all their equipment, and that he admired their discipline. An apology was accepted, and no more was said. But the two Grenadiers later commented that the Gunners had been closer to death in the cafe than they had been in France.

From time to time there would be the odd 'drama' with other regiments, or worse the Military Police. They were ever present in the towns where troops were billeted. One infamous 'drama merchant' was Guardsman James Kosbab or 'Kossie' to his pals. Kosbab was well known to Sid from his pre-war days, and from his recent time in Number Three Company. Before the war, Kossie's disciplinary record had been appalling and he was regarded as something of a nuisance by the Battalion seniors. He had however confounded everyone, and proved himself to be a first class soldier. On the night of 14th May, his position had been attacked by a German patrol. He displayed great heroism, in going out and bringing in the wounded Lieutenant Seymour at considerable risk to himself. Seymour was recuperating in hospital. Jim Kosbab was subsequently to be awarded the Military Medal for bravery. However, he didn't know of the award until some time later.

Unfortunately, the recent fighting in France had done nothing to calm his character. It was a safe bet that if there was trouble in the town, Kossie would be involved. He was well known for his love of brawling, and apparent lack of concern for the consequences if caught. After one particular episode in Frome, which involved the theft of a military policeman's cap, and a subsequent assault, Kosbab naturally came under suspicion. His fellow conspirators, from Number Three Company, were found guilty and sentenced to a period of detention. The case against Kosbab however was not proven on this occasion. But on hearing of his comrades' plight he felt compelled to confess! This well known Battalion character

RSM 'Snapper' Robinson presides at an athletics meeting, Windsor, 1941

was doubtless a thorn in the side of those responsible for administering discipline, but his antics were keenly followed by the junior element of the Battalion.

After some weeks, and to his surprise, Sid was summoned for the Commanding Officer's memoranda. He had no idea why he was required. To his amazement, he was informed by the Commanding Officer that Mr Gwyer was now out of hospital, and that he was to join his officer in Windsor, at the Training Battalion. There was no discussion, and he soon found himself in transit to Berkshire. Although he was not keen to leave his Battalion, which was now in the Swanage area, he was excited at the prospect of new surroundings. The threat of imminent invasion had passed, and the routine of route marches was becoming rather tedious.

Through obvious necessity the army had swelled in numbers and a fourth Battalion was raised in October 1940. This new Battalion would later be joined by the fifth and sixth Battalions. The Training Battalion had been formed in Victoria Barracks, Windsor, just before the outbreak of war. Its role was to receive guardsmen from the depot and to prepare them for service in the field Battalions of the Regiment. Given the current shortage of manpower, this was a task that was undertaken with some urgency. When he arrived at Victoria Barracks, Sid was reminded of his time at the Guards Depot at Caterham. The Windsor Barracks were rather smaller, consisting of large Barrack blocks built around a central green, incorporating a married quarters block and, of course, the Barrack square. The British Army had occupied this site since 1795, but the current buildings were mainly of Edwardian design.

The pace of life inside looked a little quicker than the Battalion routine he had become used to. The Parade Square seemed to be full of men marching up and down. These Squads were commanded by eager young Non Commissioned Officers, who gave the impression of being in competition with each other. There appeared to be lots of weapon training taking place too. Groups of soldiers were spaced out around the perimeter of the camp. They were lying behind Bren guns, or kneeling to strip or assemble the mechanisms of their weapons. He noted that the Officers' mess was a large building at one end of the Camp, and he assumed that Mr Gwyer was already installed there.

Soon after his arrival he was ordered to attend the Commanding Officer's Memoranda. He was inspected by the Drill Sergeant, as though he had just arrived from Caterham, and was placed in the correct order, as part of a very long queue. Eventually the Sergeant Major arrived and surveyed the waiting line of men. Several names were taken before he reached Sid's place in the line. The RSM was familiar. He was none other than 'Snapper Robinson', his old CSM from the depot. The Sergeant Major appeared to recognise him, but said nothing.

Very soon the queue was moving as successive men were marched into the Orderly Room at a rapid pace. His turn arrived and he found himself facing the door to the Commanding Officer's office. There was a piercing scream from inside and the Picquet Corporal flung open the door. There was a blur as the preceding Guardsman exited the room, and Sid was brought to attention by the Drill Sergeant. 'One Guardsman ordered to attend Sir'! said the Drill Sergeant. From inside, the Sergeant Major gave the commands to 'quick march', 'mark time' and 'halt'. Sid now stood in front of Lt Colonel G M Cornish OBE, MC, Commanding Officer of the Training Battalion. He was welcomed to Windsor and was assigned to the specialist company. Before he knew what had happened, the process was reversed and he too was flying through the door in the opposite direction.

Lt Gwyer was the new Signals Officer and Sid soon found his way to the Signal Platoon lines. The Specialist Company looked after those Platoons that had undergone additional training in specific skills, such as mortars or signals. He was shown to his accommodation in one of the daunting barrack blocks. A long room housed 30 men who slept in three-tiered bunks. The room looked spotless and the atmosphere was a little too reminiscent of the Guards Depot for his liking. Not all of the Companies were accommodated within the barracks. Number One Company was billeted in the Royal Mews at the nearby Windsor Castle, and was responsible for the security of the ancient fortress. Slit trenches had been dug around the inner and outer wards, from which fire could be brought to bear on any Germans threatening the royal family. The security of the King was taken very seriously. Even the corridors of the castle were patrolled by armed Grenadiers. If attacked, a party of men was detailed to escort the royal family to a waiting aircraft at Smiths Lawn.

Troops were also accommodated at the Etonian Country Club near the Thames. Tents were erected on the lawns, and even the boat-house was used as accommodation. Billets were in short supply, and many buildings in the streets of Windsor were utilised by the army. At one time, the Training Battalion had over three thousand men on strength. Half of them had been billeted at Kempton Park race course, but had been moved to Wellington Barracks when a Grenadier Holding Battalion was formed. The race course was now being used as an internment centre. In addition to training the recruits from the depot, there were various security duties, and Guards to be mounted. Until recently, the Battalion had been responsible for all of the bridges on the river Thames between Kew and Maidenhead. Various RAF headquarters locations were also guarded, as were the aerodromes at Heathrow, Hendon, Langley, Hanworth and Smiths Lawn.

With all this activity going on, the Training Battalion was a very busy place and troops were constantly marching to and from barracks for one thing or another. It was not at all unusual to see squads of soldiers marching through the streets. A favourite scheme of many instructors was to 'double' the tired recruits up the formidable hill on Thames Street, in front of the Castle. The more sadistic Non Commissioned Officers sometimes ordered 'Gas Alert'! and watched as the unfortunate recruits struggled for breath in their respirators. The gasping guardsmen stumbled over the medieval cobbles and up the steep hill, oblivious to the appalled civilians looking on.

There were many familiar faces in the Battalion. Sid learned that 'Snapper' had apparently replaced another of his Sergeant Majors. Tommy Garnett had been commissioned into the Second Battalion. There were other personalities from the Second Battalion, such as CSM Nicklin who he knew well. He wasted no time in snaring him for the football team.

Mr Gwyer was delighted to see him once again. Sid was pleased to note that his officer appeared to have recovered from his injuries fairly well, although he now walked with a pronounced limp. There were specialist courses running constantly, in all manner of subjects, and he was soon detailed for a Signals course.

Many hours were spent in the classroom learning the skills that were required of a signaller. Semaphore was still being taught, although most of the Guardsmen could see no practical use for it on the recently experienced modern battlefield. 'Flag bashing' was practised endlessly, and those who had returned from Dunkirk made light of it. The thought of waving flags at each other from hill-tops as the Panzers advanced was silly. Morse code seemed to the students to be far more useful and was taken more seriously. The field telephone and exchange were also to be mastered, before Sid was eventually qualified as a signaller.

There followed various tactics courses, and one day he found himself being taught bayonet fighting by a young and inexperienced Lance Sergeant instructor. 'I don't know what the bloody Germans will make of you!' the young NCO shouted sarcastically at Sid. 'Well, at least I have been close enough to see one!' he replied indignantly. The NCO was suitably embarrassed and Sid was not subjected to any further jibes.

For an experienced guardsman the routine in Windsor was a steady one, and there was plenty of opportunity to walk out. The Barracks was conveniently situated in the Town, a stone's throw from Windsor Castle, and within easy reach of the local hostelries. Sid soon became a regular darts player at a pub known locally as the 'Donkey House'. The pub was by the riverside, close to the railway station and its nickname was taken from the 'Donkeys' which were used to turn the trains in days gone by. He soon got to know many of the locals, including Albert Kerseley an official at the Naval Ordnance buildings in Slough. Sid's friendship with Kerseley was significant because, after a few weeks, the older man introduced his daughter, Pat. The two hit it off immediately, even though Sid was a little shy. Before long they were meeting two or three times a week.

There were still restrictions because the threat of air raids remained high, but a happy routine was established. The couple visited the cinema, pubs and took walks in the Great Park, where Sid sometimes changed their route to avoid some of the many squads training there. He was soon introduced to Pat's two young sons, David and Brian, and the trio seemed to get on well from the outset. The air raid sirens often sounded. On one occasion, there was some excitement when a German fighter was brought down, close to the Agricultural Show Grounds in the Park. Its Luftwaffe pilot was captured at gun-point as he stepped down from the damaged machine. The Me 109 was displayed in the town, for the population to see that the Germans were vulnerable. Even Princess Elizabeth was taken to see the wreckage before it was moved.

Guardsmen had to be correctly turned out, even when courting, as there were many officers in the town and surrounding area. Compliments were to be paid, even when in the company of a lady. Troops in the town were always alert for the sound of the bugle. That was the method by which soldiers were to be recalled to barracks in the event of an emergency. The Sergeant Major personally briefed all drafts arriving in Windsor, and he recited a little rhyme to emphasise the point-

'Whenever you're out in Windsor or Slough,
when the bugle call you hear,
Get back to camp as fast as you know how'!

It was hardly award winning poetry, but it was to stick in the minds of some of the men sixty years later.

Sid regularly played football, and he made new friends from all sorts of backgrounds. One of his team-mates, George Milligan, had played for Everton, and Sid marvelled at his football skills. It wasn't long before he met another old pal, none other than Wally Durrant. Wally was now a Regimental Cook. He had left the army in July 1939, only to be mobilised, and now found himself in Windsor. Wally's employment didn't last long. He was found in improper possession of a packet of tea, a serious offence when rationing was in place. He was punished and returned to duty, but he remained a good friend. He still possessed the same sense of humour and his musical talents were in great demand. It seemed to Sid that his pal still hadn't increased his musical repertoire, but he was great fun all the same.

Wally's recent misdemeanour had not endeared him to the Quartermaster, Major Beard. No one wanted to be in the Quartermaster's bad books. Randolph 'Tabby' Beard was a legendary figure who had been in the regiment since 1906. He had won the DCM and MM during the Great War and was a holder of the MSM and MBE also. He was the Sergeant Major of the Second Battalion for seven years, before being commissioned and subsequently retiring from the army. In 1939 at the age of 50 he had re-enlisted to serve his regiment once again. Everyone in the Training Battalion was understandably in awe of the great man, so Wally and Sid made a conscious effort to keep out of his way.

Alan Short also turned up in the Training Battalion and there were some happy evenings spent in the Berkshire pubs. All things considered, life wasn't too bad after the experiences of Dunkirk. There was plenty of sport, regular football matches and also boxing. The main feature of the gymnasium was a boxing ring which saw very good use. A good number of pugilists had honed their skills there, including Jack Doyle, an Irish Guardsman and pre-war British Heavyweight Champion.

Of course, there were drawbacks. After all it was a Training Unit, and as such the routine was somewhat more formal than in a service Battalion. The peaks in their service dress caps were not allowed to be cut as harshly as in the Battalion. Peaks were fitted by the tailors' shop and were stamped on the inside in a manner that prevented the owner from altering them. Because of the severe equipment shortages, it was difficult to exchange any clothing items. Socks had to be darned rather than exchanged and if the owner thought that he would just put up with the holes, he could think again. There were regular 'show parades' on which different items would be inspected by the Non Commissioned Officers. A familiar sight was ranks of guardsmen wearing their socks on their hands, in order that the darning could be checked. Their denims were in a pitiful state, having been used many times over. They were faded, patched and very scruffy. Sid often compared their denims with those of the Household Cavalry who were posted nearby. The Cavalrymen always seemed to have immaculate denims and he wondered how this could be.

Boots could be repaired in Victoria Barracks by the Battalion Cobblers. The boot repair team was headed by 'Shoey Jenkins', a Grenadier veteran of the Great War who had transferred to the Welsh Guards when they were formed in 1915. Sid had many conversations with the agreeable Welshman, who often spoke of his experiences in the trenches. In spite of the formal routine, there were many happy months spent in Windsor, but it was too good to last. Mr Gwyer one day announced that they were to be posted to the sixth Battalion which was forming in Caterham. It was late 1941 and Sid was to change Battalions yet again.

Chapter 10

The Sixth Battalion

There was a large draft of men leaving Windsor with Sid, and he was again excited at the prospect of a new challenge. Rumour had it that the sixth Battalion was to be posted overseas. In all probability it would be to the middle East, or North Africa, where Rommel's Afrika Korps was driving back Wavell's Desert Rats.

Sid's draft arrived in Caterham along with groups who had been despatched from other Battalions. As an officer's servant he managed to avoid a good deal of the initial chaos because he was making sure that Mr Gwyer was correctly administered. Although the large Victorian barrack blocks were as he remembered them, the Depot had changed. There were a lot more troops in training and of course many of them had been moved in order to allow the newest Grenadier Battalion to establish itself. A large number of wooden huts had been erected around the periphery of the barracks and these had been filled by the recruits. The 6th Battalion men were now setting up house in the old barrack blocks.

The Sixth Battalion had been formed at reveille on 18th October 1941, and the nucleus had been provided from the holding Battalion at Chelsea Barracks. A large draft, including Sid, had been sent from the Training Battalion. The remaining numbers, probably about 40% of the total strength, was sent from the other Battalions of the Regiment. Equipment was in short supply, very little had been issued on the formation of the Battalion and most of the stores were on loan.

He was posted to Number Four Company which was commanded by Major Sir Thomas 'Tom' Butler and administered by CSM Warburton. There were plenty of old faces from the First and Second Battalions and Sid felt quite at home. The Battalion was commanded by Lt Colonel AFL Clive, an experienced officer who had also survived the experience of Dunkirk, winning the MC in the process. Clive faced a formidable challenge in training a whole Battalion from scratch and having it ready to deploy overseas. The Sergeant Major, Wilf Cutts a Derbyshire man and an ex-miner, rapidly set about knocking the Battalion into shape. The Commanding Officer was not impressed with the calibre of some of the men he had been sent. Many had come from London, and so far, had spent the war guarding government buildings and other key points. Some of those from the training Battalion were rather green and only about 250 of the new Battalion had war experience. To make matters worse, the Sergeant Major suspected that the service battalions had used this opportunity to get rid of some of their less desirable men.

There were regular swank parades, to ensure that standards did not slip, while the Battalion was training hard for war. Sid soon became accustomed to the sound of the Sergeant Major's voice. He also learned that the Sergeant Major had acquired the nickname of 'Salamander' although he couldn't discover why. The troops soon found out that they were to be designated as Motorized Infantry and there was great enthusiasm for their new role. Their training was to be vastly different to that conducted before Dunkirk. Painful lessons had been learned in France. The British army had changed its doctrine, from the static defensive lines of Flanders, to the fast moving armoured warfare created by the Germans. Tactical training was a priority, and the emphasis was placed on rapid movement, with heavy weapons now integrated into the Battalion in greater numbers. There was always time for the familiar route marches and no one escaped the long slogs through the countryside, Sid was amazed that Mr Gwyer was able to hold his own despite his limp. Gwyer had been 'Mentioned in Despatches' in France, and Sid was full of admiration for his young Officer.

Many of the Non Commissioned Officers were pre-war men. Lots more had come from the depot where they had been instructors, so it didn't take long for the Battalion to start to take shape. Once they were settled and organised, short leave passes were granted, and a routine was established. Sid discovered that Caterham wasn't a bad place and of course he was sometimes able to see Pat. The Battalion was granted seven days' leave per quarter, and one 48 hour pass per month. But he was often able to get his officer to sign an extra pass.

Sid soon discovered that the infamous Jim Kosbab had been posted in from the First Battalion, and assumed that this was probably due to some atrocity committed in the west-country. He later learned that Kossie had served 56 days in detention, earlier in the year, and had been released just in time to travel to Buckingham Palace to receive his MM from the King.

It wasn't long before Jim had established his normal routine of crime followed by punishment. It was during one period of confinement to barracks that Kosbab decided to break up the boredom of the barrack room by shooting at the carved stone sign on the adjacent barrack block. It seems that the word 'Coldstream' was sufficiently inflammatory to cause him to fire several rounds at it. The bullets thudded into the stonework, severely damaging the carved letters, before ricocheting off in all directions. Naturally there was a good degree of concern in barracks when it was discovered that an anonymous sniper was shooting out of one of the windows. Kossie was soon apprehended by a nervous barrack guard, retribution was swift and the 'Caterham Sniper' soon received his first punishment in the Sixth Battalion.

The training regime in the Sixth Battalion was more intense than most of the men had experienced before. Just about anyone who could not drive was sent away on a course to learn how. There were schemes and exercises held all over Surrey, Hampshire, Berkshire, and even Yorkshire. On one occasion, elements of the Battalion attacked the RAF base at Biggin Hill. The scheme was designed to test the security of the base but no one had told the RAF. The Grenadiers emerged as the clear victors but the RAF defenders seemed totally confused as to the reason for the assault by British troops.

Even though the Battle of Britain had been won, the skies were still watched for enemy parachutists, and the Sixth Battalion was called out in response to one particular scare. They were deployed at the railway stations along the metropolitan line, where they checked the identity papers of all civilians, male and female alike. This rather heavy handed tactic was not well received by the commuters, even in war time, and no Nazi spies were located. The Guardsmen were slowly adapting to their mechanised role. Their vehicles had arrived in batches and a great deal of movement had been completed around the south of England, in spite of the shortage of fuel. They had practised their tactics on Salisbury plain, and elsewhere, and many slit trenches had been dug. These trenches were a great source of irritation to regiments of the line when they took them over. Most of the guardsmen were over 6ft tall and when the trenches were occupied by infantrymen, most were unable to see over the parapet!

Meanwhile, Wally Durrant's musical talents had been recognised. He was able to play a few tunes on the organ, and when the padre approached the Drill Sergeant for a man who might be able to play in church on a Sunday, Wally was duly detailed. Unfortunately, what the padre did not know was that Wally still only knew four hymns. The new organist had been told to 'shut up and get on with it' by the Drill Sergeant, so he was forced to use his initiative. On Sunday mornings he would sneak into church unseen by the padre and would remove the hymn numbers that had been displayed, replacing them with the numbers of the four hymns that he could play. On the first occasion the Padre was completely bamboozled, but became increasingly suspicious as the weeks went by. The junior element in the congregation had great sport waiting for the Padre's reactions each week and giggles had to be suppressed.

As Christmas 1941 approached, it became apparent that the Battalion would not be going overseas until the New Year at the earliest. Sid was regarded as an experienced and useful man. He was able to drive, he was a qualified signaller and had passed his education certificates, so he was a natural choice as the Company Commander's driver on exercise. He enjoyed this task, and was able to see what was going on from a different perspective. It was certainly better than digging slit trenches, and the sixth Battalion were doing plenty of that.

He was lucky enough to be sent home for a short spell of Christmas leave, and he wondered if this would be the last Christmas in England for some time. A great deal had happened since Dunkirk. The Battle of Britain had been won and the threat of invasion had receded. The war in Africa had raged and the siege of Tobruk had been reported in the newspapers. There were many other events that the troops had followed with interest. The Germans had invaded Russia on 22nd June, but most significantly, the Americans had been attacked at Pearl Harbour on Sunday 7th December and Hitler had later declared war on the United States. The troops wondered what effect America's entry into the war would have.

Sid had now also learned that the Second Battalion was to convert to the armoured role, and that his old pals in the First Battalion were training as motorized Infantry too. Although he enjoyed his Christmas leave, he couldn't help wondering what 1942 would bring. As always his leave seemed to fly by, and he was soon back in Caterham. In the new year the training seemed to become more intense and rumour was rife about the Battalion's future destination. Most thought that they would be heading to North Africa, but there were many other options. Speculation was further fuelled when a pile of Hessian wrapped boxes were spotted outside the Quartermaster's store. Each of these boxes was stamped with a black polar bear and rumour circulated that the Battalion was bound for Russia.

Sid's position of trust enabled him to borrow Mr Gwyer's car, and he was able to make a few 'special trips'. Sid, accompanied by Wally, occasionally made his way to Wally's house at the Elephant and Castle, where his pal's girlfriend would be collected in style. Petrol was, of course, in short supply but there were 'ways and means'. The guardsmen made the most of this period because it was felt that they

Princess Elizabeth inspects a Grenadier colour, having been appointed colonel of the
regiment at age 16, April 1942

would soon be departing for foreign shores. In January, the Battalion was formally
warned for overseas service and embarkation leave was granted. The men spent
their 'last' leave at home shaking hands and saying their goodbyes. Once they arrived back they discovered that the order had been cancelled, and they would be
staying in Caterham a little longer. They were warned for overseas service several
times, only to find that the order had been rescinded when they returned from
their embarkation leave. Inevitably, some of the men became complacent, and
started to over stay these 'final' leave periods.

In April 1942 a Royal review of the Regiment was held at Windsor, and the
Sixth Battalion sent a representative party. They joined those from the other Battalions and marched past Princess Elizabeth, who at the age of sixteen, had succeeded the Duke of Connaught as the Colonel of the regiment. In May, the King
and Queen inspected the newest of the Grenadier Battalions at Caterham, and Sid
was once again impressed at the interest displayed by his sovereign. He thought
that the young Princess Elizabeth was radiant, and they all agreed that she was a
popular choice as their Colonel.

In between the periods away training, and the various preparations for their
departure overseas, the Guardsmen managed to find plenty of time to visit the local
pubs in the Caterham area. These popular excursions inevitably led to more
'drama'. On one occasion, a group of well-known Battalion characters found

themselves in Caterham. The expiry time on their passes was fast approaching and the not inconsiderable hill between themselves and the barracks was still to be negotiated. None of the group was in a fit state to climb the hill before the deadline, and the only answer was to take a bus. As luck would have it, a bus promptly appeared and was waved down by the jolly group. The bus halted, and the conductor leant out to tell the guardsmen that unfortunately the vehicle was full, and that they would have to wait for the next bus. This was not an acceptable solution to a group of young men whose inhibitions had been abridged by drink. The conductor was pulled from the bus and deposited on the pavement. His place was taken by one of the group who felt that his ability to confidently ring the bell would also enable him to fool the driver. The giggling party piled aboard, ignoring the protesting passengers. The bell was rung and the bus chugged away, leaving the unfortunate conductor standing on the pavement shaking his fist.

The merry group of hijackers arrived safely back at the barracks, having made several stops to let off passengers. They cheekily said goodnight to the surprised driver, and left the abandoned bus outside, with angry, now stranded passengers, spilling from the motionless vehicle. A major confrontation ensued at the barrack gate, until the crowd was eventually joined by a red-faced panting conductor, and their journey was eventually resumed. The following morning there was a major investigation and the Battalion was paraded. The Military Police arrived with the indignant bus conductor. The culprits were duly identified and were promptly punished. Such minor distractions were inevitable amongst soldiers training for war. No doubt they were embarrassing for the Commanding Officer, and irritating for the Sergeant Major, but in the barrack rooms they caused great hilarity.

In late May yet another order for Foreign Service was received. It was a Saturday night after lights out, and the whole of Caterham was in darkness. The duty Drummer had 'blown' for the Sergeants in Waiting and they were met by the Sergeant Major. 'Salamander' held a flashlight and he read aloud a warning order. It stated that the Battalion would be embarking on Monday morning. The Sergeants in Waiting were told that this was to remain a secret and no one was to be told. The plan was that, after church parade on Sunday, the gates would be locked. Everyone would be confined to barracks, and only then would the Battalion be formally told of their planned departure.

The routine on Sunday was normal and it appeared that no one was any the wiser. The roll was called and the Battalion proceeded to church. It was only afterwards that the news was broken. There was a buzz of excitement and some of the cynics said that it was another false alarm and that it would be cancelled in due course. They were proved wrong. On Monday morning the Battalion marched out of Caterham barracks, their destination known only to a few seniors. A fair crowd had assembled at the gates. There were many well-wishers and a good few wives, girlfriends and children. But the emotion of the moment didn't interfere with the Commanding Officer's sight. He spotted a couple of slovenly Canadian soldiers and Sergeant Bolan was sent to sort them out. They were made to stand to attention as the Battalion passed.

Sid had already departed the barracks. He accompanied his officer, who was now Second in Command of Number Four Company, and also Officer in charge of the road party. As Sid drove north, the rest of the Battalion boarded a train at

Caterham. On the outskirts of London they changed direction on a turn-table and some of the men entered into conversation with the railway workers. To their amazement the civilians informed them that they were heading for Liverpool and that they would be sailing for the Middle East. It was a great joke, civilians telling the military what was going on. The story spread and everyone had a good laugh about it, of course no one knew if it was true or not.

When Sid arrived in Liverpool he found himself boarding a troopship called the H.T Strathmore, an ex P&O liner of 23,000 tons. The advance party was to receive the bulk of the Battalion. Much work was done to organise accommodation, the loading of stores, and the baggage. The Sixth Battalion eventually arrived and boarded the Strathmore on 16th June 1942. By now everyone had realised that this was it, they would not be returning to Caterham this time. There was some trouble accounting for all of the men. Some had been missed from the manifest, but there were others who had overstayed their leave, not realising that the Battalion had been warned for embarkation yet again.

Among those missing was none other than Jim Kosbab. Kosbab had been listed as AWOL in Caterham, but the Commanding Officer had received a telegram, addressed to him personally. The telegram had been sent from East Mosely, it was simple and a little too familiar. 'Caught a slow train, know you are more than ever in my thoughts at this time. Kosbab'

It was typical of his character that he couldn't resist this cheeky message. Work went on to settle the troops into their accommodation. But this was interrupted by

Guardsman on board ship c. 1942

the arrival of Kosbab. He was marched alongside the ship, escorted by two burly MPs. A great commotion was caused when some of the guardsmen cheered the arrival of the infamous absentee, who was clearly in close arrest. Kossie appeared as cheerful as ever, as he kept step with his hefty escorts. Support was shouted from the decks before the assembly was broken up by NCOs who were, presumably, acting on orders to silence any encouragement for the prisoner.

The guardsmen debated what punishment Kosbab would be awarded for his impertinence. Colonel Clive doubtless had a dilemma, as Kosbab was a good soldier, and every man was needed in the desert. The Commanding Officer was no fool and he knew that the worst possible punishment for this maverick would be to leave him behind. In the event it was decided that Kosbab would remain with the Battalion, albeit undergoing punishment. Kossie's latest deviation from the accepted standard of behaviour had been a minor distraction, and the preparations for departure continued unhindered. The officers were allocated cabins, and the other ranks settled into the troop decks where their hammocks were hung. On board the ship there were many troops from other regiments, corps, and a large number of RAF personnel.

Finally, the Strathmore sailed away from Liverpool, most of her passengers still unsure as to the final destination of the 6th Battalion Grenadier Guards. The privileged few were aware that they were to join 3rd Battalion Coldstream Guards and the 2nd Battalion Scots Guards, in 201st Guards Brigade in the Middle East. These two Battalions had been fighting in the desert for some time, and were to be reinforced by the 'fresh' Grenadiers from England.

The Strathmore steamed north from Liverpool accompanied by the HMT Empress of Australia. Both ships had troops packed in below their decks like sardines. They eventually dropped anchor in the Clyde, amid thick mist. As always, the men could not be left to idle below decks, and the days were split into training periods so that the skills learnt in Caterham would not be forgotten. PT was carried out daily from 07.00 to 07.30 and 'Boat Stations' were called in the mornings. After two days in the Clyde the Strathmore eventually put out to sea, escorted by a small destroyer for the journey around the North Irish coast. There was a great deal of apprehension below decks. Everyone knew that German U-Boats could be lurking below the surface of the cold Atlantic. They all felt terribly vulnerable, not being part of a large protected convoy.

Day after day, the ships headed West across the Atlantic toward America, and eventually reached a rendezvous with a larger convoy. When the guardsmen looked out to sea in the morning there was a small armada around them. There were ships everywhere, and they were greatly relieved to see more Royal Navy vessels there to protect them. It had been a very unnerving time. There had been little or no protection from an enemy torpedo, and most of the troops feared being trapped below decks on a sinking troopship.

The little flotilla continued west, growing ever closer to the United States, until suddenly turning south, and re-crossing the Atlantic in the direction of West Africa. Not all of the ships accompanying them were headed for the Middle East. Some were packed with reinforcements for the war in the Far East, and they were later to part company. The long route was taken to avoid the most dangerous areas of the Ocean, where U-boats could cause havoc among the lightly armed troopships. Even so, there had been some anti submarine activity and depth charges had been heard.

As they headed south the weather became warmer and the Battalion were told to wear their tropical uniforms for the first time. Many activities were organised on board the ship. There were impromptu concerts and competitions of all kinds in addition to the usual deck games. A 'Brains Trust' was arranged. This was a kind of all ranks quiz and the chairman was to be Captain Gwyer. The competition was held in a light-hearted manner and was greatly enjoyed. About halfway through the quiz the chairman asked, 'What type of creature is a salamander? There was a pause as the significance of the question sank in. Suddenly an anonymous voice from the back shouted, 'It's a scaly reptile!' The room erupted into laughter, with the exception of a few senior sergeants' mess members who tried, without success, to identify the heckler. Sid suspected that there was more than coincidence at work, particularly when he noticed the smile on Captain Gwyer's face.

The curiosity of some of the men came to the fore once again. The less experienced were curious about the desert environment. Their eager questions were answered by the 'old hands', whose number now included Sid. On 2nd July the Strathmore steamed into Freetown harbour in West Africa. The many hundreds of troops on board were relieved to see dry land again. There was something reassuring about being in an enclosed harbour. There were several Royal Navy Destroyers moored in the port and the Strathmore passed very close to them. The Sailors, seeing so many soldiers lining the gunwales, shouted across to them, 'Where have you lot been evacuated from now?' The guardsmen replied in kind, 'So this is where you have been hiding!'

The good-natured banter continued until the Stathmore finally docked. It was immediately surrounded by 'bum boats', tiny native canoes filled with half naked locals selling their wares. Bananas and exotic fruits were held up for inspection, and buckets were lowered containing coins which were swapped for the fruit. Coins were tossed over the sides, most missing the boats and disappearing below the oily water, only to be pursued by diving children. Many of the guardsmen decided that it was much better sport to have the natives dive for the coins. No sooner had the youngsters surfaced, than a hail of coins plopped into the water around them, sending them once more in pursuit of the pennies.

There was a great deal of disappointment when it was announced that the Battalion would not be disembarking in Freetown. This was to be a quick stop, long enough to refuel and to take on essential supplies only. Sid dearly wanted to explore the green African shores rather than spend more time aboard the cramped troopship but it wasn't to be. A handful of senior officers were able to make it ashore but everyone else remained aboard the ship. The time was put to good use, as always, and a boxing tournament was organised against the RAF. Boxing was always popular and predictably the Grenadiers made short work of their opponents.

The stop-over was short lived and the little convoy soon steamed towards the open sea once again. As the troopship approached the mouth of the river, the rusting masts of several sunken vessels reminded them that they were still in considerable danger. The shores became distant and the ships were joined by a Sunderland flying boat. It was to provide additional protection on the next leg of their long journey to the Middle East.

A Guard of Honour found by the 6th Battalion Grenadier Guards, Durban, July 1942

The Grenadiers were to be at sea for another fortnight before they were to see civilisation again. The cramped conditions below decks tested tempers and the troops were usually occupied when they were in the open air. It was a great boost to morale when it was announced that the ship would soon put into Durban, in South Africa, where the troops were to disembark. The Strathmore's heading took them and the rest of the convoy around the cape, passing from the Atlantic into the Indian Ocean in the process. This was a well-established war-time shipping route and it was normal to put into Durban for supplies. They had been aboard the Strathmore for over five weeks and no one was sorry to walk down the gangplank for the last time into the South African sun on 20th July.

Before they disembarked, the troops were surprised to see a woman dressed all in white on the quayside. She wore a long flowing gown complemented by a brilliant white parasol and topped by a red 'Gainsborough' style hat. She also carried a huge megaphone as she strode along the dock. The megaphone was a clear indication that she intended to sing and the troops were intrigued. Before long she came to a halt and adopted a suitably operatic pose for her very large audience. The South Africans on the quayside had clearly seen the performance before but they seemed keen to hear their white lady again. As she started to sing the reason became obvious, her voice was marvellous, clearly that of a trained singer. She sang various popular tunes, ballads, operatic themes, and her voice positively boomed around the docks. The guardsmen joined in. There were several accomplished singers in the Battalion, and their voices complemented the white lady very well.

It was a wonderful welcome and morale was high. The sound of merry singing echoed around the South African port. The troops had been issued some rations to tide them over which included one small orange per man. Some of the troops decided to eat their oranges before they disembarked and a shower of orange peel was soon descending on the White Lady. This irreverent display was quickly halted by the NCOs and fortunately no one seemed to notice. The White Lady continued to sing as the Battalion disembarked from the Strathmore.

The assembled companies formed up with the Corps of Drums at their head, Colonel Archer Clive was mounted on a magnificent charger and he looked very satisfied. RSM Cutts gave a series of commands; the Battalion was turned to its right and stepped off behind the Drums and their very proud Commanding Officer. The Sergeant Major had warned the Battalion that they were to be on their best behaviour as they passed through the streets. The guardsmen were surprised at the very warm welcome that they got from the locals, people clapped and cheered as they marched by. They later learned that the enthusiasm of the South Africans was at least in part due to relief that the Guards were in town. An Australian unit had preceded them and chaos had apparently reigned.

The Grenadiers eventually arrived at their temporary billets in the Mansfield Road School. As the Commanding Officer watched the Battalion pass through the gates, he looked as proud as Punch, and many of the Grenadiers realised what a fine Battalion the Sixth had become since their formation only eight months earlier. They were to be in Durban until a ship could be freed to transport them on. The troops made themselves at home in the various rooms at the school and a routine was soon established. There was a Barrack Guard which mounted daily, fatigues were found, and various duty personnel patrolled the billets.

After a few days word was received that the Battalion was to provide a large contingent of men to guard and supervise the transfer of German prisoners of war. The troops were loaded onto transport and driven to the docks where they formed a large circle between two ships. The German POWs marched down the gangplank from one ship around the circle and eventually onto the second ship. The Grenadiers stood with fixed bayonets in case there was any trouble. This was the first time that most of the men had seen the enemy up close. The Germans were Afrika Korps men who had spent many months fighting in the desert sun. They were bronzed and fit looking, they wore smart looking uniforms with tiny shorts and fancy boots, and they all wore the Afrika Korps desert cap at a slant. The prisoners surveyed the Grenadiers contemptuously as they passed, each man maintained the correct step and kept his chin arrogantly raised. By contrast the young Englishmen felt rather inferior in their baggy ill fitting tropical uniforms, they were pasty, sunburned and most had yet to see action. Fortunately there were plenty of hard-nosed NCOs about the place, many of whom had been at Dunkirk and they had little respect for the Germans and were not shy at demonstrating this.

In the evening a ship's guard was found to ensure that the Germans behaved themselves. They were issued revolvers as these were more practical in the confines of the prison ship. The Guard mounted without incident, but during the night a tragic accident occurred when Guardsman Richardson was shot dead. Everyone was shocked by this sudden and unexpected fatality, but it served as a timely reminder of the dangerous business they were in. A full military funeral was held for the unfortunate guardsman and he was laid to rest in a nearby cemetery. The locals turned out in force to pay their respects as the Corps of Drums passed by playing a solemn march.

The guardsmen were permitted to walk out and they were made welcome wherever they went. Many were invited into the homes of the South African civilians and regularly took meals with them. The local police were apparently under-manned and the guardsmen were detailed to carry out police duties in support of them. Some were even offered jobs, although they were in no position to accept them. The Corps of Drums beat the retreat in Smiths Square to the appreciation of the townsfolk. The Battalion received praise in the newspapers when guardsmen helped to avert disaster in a local theatre when the curtains caught light during a performance.

The local girls also seemed appreciative of the presence of so many tall smart young men in their city. There were of course plenty of parades, and the odd route march, to keep the men at the right standard of training. During one 'scheme' Number Four Company were crossing a pineapple field in extended order. This proved to be a mistake, as before they emerged at the other side many pineapples had become casualties to the Grenadier bayonet. Predictably many names were taken.

It was customary for the troops to be visited by the 'brass' when in town and a Guard of Honour was found by the 6th Battalion. Sid was selected for this parade but was thrown off during the first rehearsal because once again his forage cap was not up to the required standard. He was proud of his old cap which had seen almost as much service as he had. Not too disappointed at missing the extra drill, he felt sure he would get over it.

No one was sure when their new ship would arrive and a routine ensued. Every week the Battalion packed up and marched out of its billets down to the docks. After some time it would become clear that there was no ship and the troops would return to their temporary home at the school. No one seemed to know why there was confusion about their departure date. But the guardsmen were happy to remain in Durban for as long they could, as a great time was being had by all. After a month of the routine in the Eastern Cape Town, the Battalion once again marched down to the docks, many men had made dates on the assumption that they would soon return. When they arrived on the quayside the troops suddenly realised that all was not well. Instead of the usual empty dock there stood a large and very old looking ship. The H.T. Ascanius looked as though it had seen better days. Forming up on the quay were hundreds of soldiers from the New Zealand Division. They had obviously disembarked from the sad looking ship and they had nothing good to say about her. Some of the Kiwis said they would not get back on board even if ordered to do so. The Grenadiers unfortunately had no option. Before anyone had any time to say farewell to the city they had come to like so much, they were boarding the Ascanius.

To their surprise, the White Lady once again appeared on the quayside to give them a farewell performance. Her operatic tones rang around the docks, as the Guardsmen waved goodbye to the many civilians who had come to say farewell. Her voice was joined once again by a powerful male baritone coming from the deck of the troopship. The voices combined with others to form an impromptu chorus.

The female singer was obviously enjoying the experience, but she would have been mortified if she could have seen the mystery baritone. The voice belonged to none other than Guardsman Delderfield who was seated on one of the open-air latrines. The other men in the vicinity were doubled over with laughter as the Guardsman sang as loud as he could. This was the last time that the Grenadiers would meet their White Lady. Most of them were not aware that her name was Perla Seidle Gibson, she was a native of Durban and a well-known opera singer. Perla had sung to thousands of departing allied troops and was regarded as something of a saint. Her own husband was serving in North Africa, and her officer son was later killed at Cassino. Shortly after his death she overcame her own grief to give an emotional performance to departing South African troops. She was a brave lady who would be long remembered by the Grenadiers.

As the remainder of the Battalion embarked, there was another distraction, this time from the gang-plank. The Battalion Sanitary NCO, otherwise known as the 'Number One on the Plunger', had managed to drop his rifle whilst struggling with his baggage. He had watched helplessly as the Lee Enfield dropped into the black waters below. The unfortunate man was descended upon by a succession of angry NCOs and Warrant Officers, none of whom were able to recover the rifle.

Later that day, the dejected Sanitary NCO was approached by another Corporal who told him that his rifle had been located. 'It's in Davey Jone's locker, mate', he said, sniggering and turning on his heel. The confused sanitary man, who was not the 'brightest lamp in the box', then set out in search of a Corporal Jones D, so that he could reclaim his personal weapon.

The Sixth Battalion left Durban on 15th August. The ship's anti-aircraft defences were found by 12 guardsmen equipped with Bren Guns. Before they left the harbour, a number of the troops decided to dispense with the old sun helmets that they had been issued, these were unpopular and impractical, so they were dumped over the side. They were left in the ship's wake, bobbing up and down like scores of tiny boats. The old ship was filthy. It must have been used as a collier at some point because there was a thick layer of coal dust everywhere. The guardsmen were put to work cleaning up the mess, in order to make their transport habitable. Unlike the Strathmore, there was no ventilation on the old steamer, and life below decks was incredibly uncomfortable. They steamed north through the Indian Ocean with the heat becoming ever more uncomfortable. There was trepidation as they passed through the straits of Madagascar. Word had filtered down that Japanese submarines had been recently sighted there.

By 21st August, a good number of men had reported sick. Most were fairly minor but there was the occasional serious illness. There were many cases of vomiting and diarrhoea and most of the men put this down to the filthy condition of the ship. There was also a shortage of decent drinking water. The ship was now a day overdue and the boilers were apparently overheating.

The Ascaneius continued its voyage across the Indian Ocean, dropping anchor off Aden in order to refuel, before travelling into the Gulf of Suez and the Red Sea. The temperature below decks was now 100 degrees fahrenheit and was unbearable. To make matters worse, word was received that torpedoes had been fired at a ship between Aden and the Red Sea.

Their own ship escaped any submarine activity but, approaching Suez, two enemy aircraft were spotted by the men posted on anti-aircraft duty. The planes were too close for comfort and the Bren gunners prepared to defend the ship. As the aircraft passed overhead the gunners made themselves ready to be attacked. But the enemy aircraft must have been at the limit of their range, and they soared off into the distance. The incident served to remind everyone that they were now within the reach of the Luftwaffe, and the air sentries remained very alert.

The troopship finally docked at Port Tewfiq near Suez, it was a great relief to all aboard. Apart from the obvious dangers that they had faced, it had been a miserable voyage from Durban. It was 7th September 1942, and their journey from Liverpool had taken almost four months. They may have reached the Middle East, but their journey was not yet over. The Grenadiers were hurriedly disembarked because another visit from the Luftwaffe was anticipated. The Germans had seen the troopship and would now be aware of the presence of British reinforcements. Transport was provided and the Battalion was driven to a tented transit camp. The tired dusty troops settled into their tents for the night, but were disturbed by a huge air raid on Port Tewfiq. The bombs could clearly be heard and it sounded as though the port was getting a real pounding. Sid was glad that they were not still on the Ascanius. He had already become accustomed to the smell of the desert. It was all very familiar, and the sound of the distant explosions also brought back memories.

It was not long before the Battalion was moved again, this time to a huge tented camp at El Qassassin to the east of Cairo. This move was by train from the nearby railhead. Boarding took much longer than expected as there were crowds of Egyptians selling their wares. The 'gazoos' sold lemonade and all manner of goods to the young guardsmen. Those who had previously served in Egypt were wiser. The train eventually departed, and the troops soon found themselves in the desert wilderness with nothing but sand to view.

The Suez Canal came into sight as did the great lakes, but the passengers were pleased to arrive at their eventual destination. Qassassin was part of the 8th Army complex to the west of the town of Ismalia. It was full of troops from various regiments and corps, all destined to join the fight against Rommel. The camp consisted of large tents which could hold a Platoon of men. These were pegged down over four feet deep pits, which were designed to provide some protection from air attacks.

As always there was a good deal of administration to be done. The troops were allotted tents, and mosquito nets were drawn. In the following week the less experienced men were introduced to the desert environment, route marches and schemes, digging trenches and so on. The Battalion were issued with the new Mark 4 Lee Enfield rifle, and there was much debate about the merits of both new and old weapons. The SMLE had been in service since 1903 and was proven in war. But the new Mark 4 was quicker to mass-produce and had a few perceived improvements. Outwardly there was little difference, although the new spike bayonet was most unpopular.

About once a week the troops were allowed to visit Cairo. It was a long dusty ride in the back of a truck, about 60 miles, but most thought it was worth the trip. At 18.00 hrs they would start the return journey and the weary troops would be asleep by the time they returned. The battalion's vehicles had been sent to a workshop to be repainted and fitted for the desert. Once this had been done, they were ready to move forward.

On one occasion, the camp routine was broken when a Platoon, under Lieutenant Strang Steele and Sergeant Bolan, was sent to a nearby South African camp. The Platoon had been sent to 'put down' a mutiny, and no one knew what to expect. When they arrived, they saw a group of about twenty African soldiers drawn up in two ranks. They had apparently refused to obey orders. The Grenadiers were drawn up facing the aggrieved Africans, bayonets were fixed, and they were stood at ease. The group was then addressed in their native tongue by a South African Captain. His words were translated to the Grenadiers as he spoke. 'These soldiers are from the famous British Guards and they do not question orders. Half an hour ago they were asleep, and now they are here facing you without question or complaint!'

The Platoon was then called to attention. Their arms were sloped, and they marched up and down in front of the watching mutineers, eventually halting, turning once again to face the unhappy assembly, before being stood at ease. The Captain then informed the Africans that they would now do their drill as the Guardsmen had done. They were called to attention and turned to their right. All but about five of the group obeyed the order. Those who persisted were quickly placed in close arrest, and manhandled into the back of the Grenadier trucks. The remainder were informed that their disobedience would be punished, but that those in arrest would be sent for courts martial.

The five mutineers were handed over to the Military Police. Their fate was never discovered by the Grenadiers. The South African captain was most grateful to the guardsmen, for showing such a fine example and for defusing the situation. The mutineers may have presumed that the guardsmen's weapons were loaded and that they would have been used if ordered. They would have been correct.

Most of the men had assumed that the Sixth Battalion would soon be joining the 8th Army in its fight against the Afrika Korps. They were shocked, and somewhat disappointed, to discover that they would in fact be travelling to Syria where 201 Guards Brigade was forming. At the end of September, the Battalion departed for Syria. They were split between the road party, and those who travelled in the relative comfort of the train. Sid as usual accompanied his officer on the road party. The vehicles crossed the Suez Canal, into the hot barren landscape of the Sinai Desert and its frequent sandstorms, which were familiar to Sid.

There were specially built stopping places for the vehicles. Trucks were forbidden to stop on the road as the heat caused them to sink if their heavy weight remained for too long. If a vehicle broke down, and it was not possible to tow it, then it had to be pushed off the road and left for recovery at a later date. The landscape was ever-changing as the convoy passed into Palestine, through orange groves and cultivated areas, past Tiberius and the Sea of Galilee, then down hill until they were below sea level.

It was at this point during a short stop that a conscientious Platoon Sergeant, realising the historical and religious significance of their location, decided to make sure that the men shared this knowledge. Pulling up the canvass at the rear of the truck he announced that, they were close to Lake Tiberius, there was a weary disinterested acknowledgement from the dark interior. 'Miracles were performed here you know', he said. 'Well we could bloody well do with one now', came the reply. The Platoon Sergeant decided that this would not be the time for some religious education and he returned to the front of the truck, vowing to leave the guardsmen in their ignorance in future.

Eventually the troops passed into Syria, through the little village of Qatana. Not a soul was to be seen, and they continued into a bleak and desolate plain. After about four miles, they passed through the camps occupied by the Headquarters of 201 Guards Brigade, and the Coldstream and Scots Guards. A little further on they reached their destination. In a flat dusty plain they came across a collection of rickety looking huts, tents and vehicles. It was 3rd October. This was to be home until further notice. Sid's initial impression was not favourable. They were obviously miles from anywhere, and the snow-capped mountains did not suggest an easy route to civilisation.

The Companies and Platoons were allocated their accommodation, mostly in the huts which were constructed from old and very poor quality wood. The buildings were lined with asbestos, and were roasting hot during the day. There were windows but no glass. Hessian hung from the frames instead. A good deal of clearing up had to be done before the huts were habitable, and the troops set about their task with resignation. The CQMS issued palliasses which had to be stuffed with straw and placed on low trestles covered with boards. These uncomfortable beds would have to do for months to come.

As always, the Battalion routine soon settled people down. Guards were mounted, parades and inspections were held, and desert training started in earnest. Everyone was aware that the other Battalions in the Brigade had been in the desert much longer, and the Grenadiers were anxious not to be found wanting. They need not have worried. Both the Coldstream and Scots Guards were reforming with replacements sent from England. Both Battalions had fought valiantly, but had been decimated at Tobruk, and they needed time to rest and retrain.

The desert training was much tougher than any they had experienced before. There were schemes which required the troops to survive in the desert for extended periods of time. The environment tested men, vehicles and the re-supply system. Many of the men suffered badly with blisters. More time was spent on weapon training and shooting. There were also special courses run on unfamiliar subjects such as mine warfare. Mines were being extensively used by both sides, so it was very important to know how to lay and to lift them. Sid, like everyone else, found it hard going, but was impressed at how quickly the younger men adapted to their environment. The Battalion was becoming stronger by the day, and the seniors were confident that they could match any other Battalion in the army.

It was during this period that Captain Gwyer and Sid had a 'fall-out'. There had been a number of trivial incidents that came to a head with Gwyer telling him that he was 'idle'. Sid was understandably indignant and had no regrets when he was told he was to return to a Platoon. He had been servant to Gwyer since long before the war. He had matured and grown a little tired of the job. No doubt his officer had detected his lack of enthusiasm and had also become frustrated. It was a sad way for the relationship to end. But Sid felt relieved at not having to worry about looking after someone else's administration. The down side was that he was promptly handed a Bren gun to look after. This was a bit of a burden on the route marches. However, he often saw Captain Gwyer marching away with his limp, and remained secretly proud of his officer's determination.

It became very apparent that 201 Brigade would not be ready for some time, so thought was given to recreation for the men. Leave was organised by Company, and trucks were organised to Damascus. Sid, Wally and the others greatly enjoyed the break from the desert. They took every opportunity they could to travel to the city, where Arabs, westerners and uniformed soldiers intermingled. Wally became a regular and was allegedly on first name terms with some of the French Military Police. Longer leave periods were arranged in Beirut. Those who were prepared to make the train journey from Damascus, over the snow-capped mountains, were rewarded with views of the Mediterranean, and the Lebanese city on its shore. Beirut held many attractions for the troops, but few were able to visit more than once. They always returned to the routine of tough desert training.

Now that Sid was back in a Platoon as a 'Duty Man', it didn't take long for his potential to be recognised. There was talk of him being placed on a drill course, in order to be promoted to Lance Corporal. The course never materialised, probably due to the intense training that was being undertaken and he took it in his stride. He soon mastered the Bren gun. As an experienced man he found that he was able to frequently help the younger guardsmen.

Rumours were rife about how the war was progressing and there were stories about new specialist units being formed. Everyone had heard about the Commandos and many Grenadiers had volunteered. A great number of them had joined Number 8 Commando. Another newly formed unit was the Long Range Desert Group. The LRDG had been formed at the end of 1940, and a 'Guards' patrol had been recruited from guardsmen who were then serving in Egypt. Volunteers had been asked for from 201 Brigade. Sid heard that Guardsman Bishop, a man he knew well, had been seconded to this shadowy group. He imagined that Bishop would soon be driving around behind enemy lines, dressed as an Arab and creating havoc. The idea was a rather appealing one.

It soon became commonplace to advertise for volunteers from the Battalion, to join various units and organisations. One day, Sid was told that a couple of NCOs from the SAS were interviewing candidates. No one had any idea who the SAS were, so there was speculation that the South African Signals must be short of men. In fact, in 1941 the Special Air Service had been raised by David Sterling. Largely from the remnants of Number 8 Commando, it was a unit comprised mainly of Guardsmen. The SAS, often working alongside the LRDG, had already caused a good deal of damage behind enemy lines.

When the real identity of this mysterious unit was revealed, Sid, along with a number of other Grenadiers, became very interested. His enthusiasm was further fuelled when he set eyes on the NCOs who were acting as recruiters. Sergeant Major Riley of the Coldstream Guards was accompanied by Sergeant Kershaw, a Grenadier. They looked very fit, bronzed by the desert sun and hardened by what Sid imagined were daring raids behind enemy lines. Riley explained the role of the unit. It was music to the ears of young men like Sid, who were seeking adventure. The NCOs told the assembled Grenadiers how they had hit the Germans hard by using unconventional tactics behind their own lines, and how they had struck fear into the Nazi heart. Riley went on to explain that all candidates would be required to undergo parachute training, and a tough selection course. They didn't want time wasters, and this would be no picnic for those who volunteered.

Parachuting at this time was regarded as a very dangerous occupation and many would-be candidates were deterred by the thought of jumping from an aeroplane on to the baked desert floor. Those who volunteered were unaware that David Sterling himself had spent a considerable time in hospital, recovering from an attempt to teach himself how to parachute, which had resulted in a temporary paralysis of his legs. Once the briefing was over, a handful of men put their names down.

Sid thought very hard about volunteering. There was no sign as yet that the Sixth Battalion would be leaving Syria. The lure of adventure finally made up his mind, he had to volunteer. He wondered if he had done the right thing, but couldn't help the feeling of anticipation that had come over him. This was a real chance to get back at the Germans, and it would be an escape from the somewhat repetitive Battalion routine in the bleak Syrian desert.

Chapter 11

The Special Air Service

It wasn't long before the volunteers were called for. They were instructed to pack up their equipment, and once their documentation was complete, they were loaded onto a truck bound for the Canal Zone in Egypt. Sid knew several of his fellow passengers. There was Dougie Wright, a fierce but well respected ex Kings Company man. Guardsmen Bill Thomas, Dickie Holmes, Sergeant 'Jumper' Workman, all of whom he had seen around. Sitting at the end of the seat was Jim Kosbab. Sid imagined that some people would be glad to see the back of Kosbab, but he was glad that this tough and proven soldier was joining them. The group speculated about what type of training they would be doing and on their likely chances of being accepted into the SAS. Kossie expressed his delight at having escaped the 'bullshit', and his enthusiasm for getting back into the war before it was over. The dusty journey was not as bad as they remembered from their outward trip. After several days of travelling they arrived at Kabrit on the shores of the Bitter Lakes in Egypt.

The SAS had established their training base at Kabrit and usually returned there after operations. It had not been easy for the first volunteers, and they had undertaken some difficult raids. 53 men had taken part in a night parachute drop into enemy territory in late 1941. Of these, more than thirty were killed or captured. This was a devastating result, for a unit with an initial strength of only sixty or so veterans from number 8 Commando. The survivors returned having learned some tough lessons. But, undeterred, they forged a working relationship with the LRDG. Over the course of the following year many spectacular small-scale raids

Jumper Workman, 'somewhere' in Italy

were mounted. Some of the men that now inhabited the camp at Kabrit were veterans of such raids and they certainly looked the part. The new arrivals were struck by how fit everyone looked. They were obviously a very tough bunch who deserved respect.

The prospective SAS soldiers were put into a squad of about thirty other men. They were from all sorts of regiments, but Sid noticed that the biggest single group of men seemed to be from the Guards. However, there were a good number of Gunners and a few men from other infantry regiments. Any volunteer who was a Non Commissioned Officer had to revert to the ranks, but none of the former NCOs seemed to be concerned.

He got to know another trainee from the South Wales Borderers, by the name of Noriega. His new friend had seen a fair bit of action, and wore the ribbon of the Military Medal on his chest. He was small in stature, but Sid soon discovered he was fit and very capable. The group were struck by the lack of the usual army red tape. There were few parades but, best of all, the rations were far superior to those that had been available in their own units. Sid felt that so far it looked as though they had made the right choice, and he got as much of the good food as he could.

No time was wasted in starting to train the volunteers, and their first full day started with PT. This was very different to the PT in the Battalion. All the instructors seemed to be Warrant Officers and experts in their trade. The trainees were also conscious that they were being constantly watched, and assessed for any weaknesses.

As always, Sid was able to cope with the PT, even though the standard of fitness was higher in this group than in others he had experienced. There was a great

The infamous Jim Kosbab M.M.

deal of map reading to be done. Although he already held his First class certificate, he found that he was learning new skills all the time. He soon became competent at negotiating the desert terrain at night, something for which he had never before been given the responsibility. There was plenty of weapon training too, and not just the weapons that he had been taught previously. There were German and Italian machine pistols and rifles to be mastered. He was soon able to strip and assemble the weapons of his enemies as quickly as those of his own army. Time was spent on the range firing the lethal hardware and some of the new additions that had come from across the Atlantic. Sid had seen the Thompson Sub-machine Gun but the M1 Carbine was a new one for him. The Carbine was a .30 inch semi automatic rifle favoured by the US army, but its simplicity, light weight and high rate of fire became popular with the SAS.

PT was held every day except Monday. This was because the trainees were permitted to visit Cairo on a Sunday, and it was thought that a day may be needed for them to recover from the experience. The group soon discovered why the rations were so good. The level of physical activity was far greater than in their battalions. A huge amount of calories were burned off, running, route marching and map reading.

A few men fell by the wayside. Others decided that parachuting was not for them when the training started in earnest. Various catwalks and platforms had been built at the camp. These seemed ridiculously high, but the troops were expected to run along them, jumping from one platform to another. There was to be no hesitation and confidence was quickly built. Those who froze at the thought soon returned to their units. Others were less fortunate, and sustained serious injury in falling from the platforms. More basic 'parachute' training was conducted by jumping from the back of moving trucks to practise landing. A small railway track had been constructed, and a rail truck was used to good effect. Men could be seen jumping from the fast moving vehicle and landing hard in a cloud of dust. Inevitably the injury rate was very high.

An obstacle course was also constructed and the trainees were tested on it. But this was no ordinary obstacle course. There were all manner of difficult obstacles to negotiate, rope bridges, catwalks, trenches, low wire entanglements, and walls supported by scaffolding poles. Smoke grenades often obscured their view, and filled their already burning lungs with acrid smoke, as live ammunition was fired over the heads of the crawling troops. When they reached the end of the obstacle course they were often required to prove their marksmanship on the range. It was exhausting work, but Sid loved it. His confidence was improving, and he felt sure that he could make it into the SAS.

Those men who survived the early weeks were sent on the Parachute Course. There was great trepidation in the group, even after the hardships that they had survived. Parachuting was a new art and the accident rate was high. Sid was only too aware that there would be no second chance if he got it wrong. He had recently attended the funeral of a Warrant Officer that he had met briefly since his arrival. The unfortunate man had been killed when his parachute had failed to open. Sid tried not to think about the terror that the poor man must have experienced as he fell earthward.

Grenadier Guards SAS men 1943. Left to Right; Dougie Wright (later M.M.), SSM Feebury (later D.C.M), Bill Thomas (died Sardinia), Jim Kosbab M.M. and Sid Dowland (later B.E.M)

The Parachute School was nearby and he duly reported with a few others for his course. There was plenty of jumping about and rolling, as well as parachute packing, before anyone went anywhere near an aircraft. It was soon discovered that the aircraft was exited by means of a circular hole in the fuselage. Sid had imagined that they would jump out of a door, so this was something of a surprise. Timing was crucial. Any error of judgement often resulted in the unfortunate parachutist smashing his face against the fuselage, causing a broken nose and lost teeth. The instructors explained gleefully that this was known as 'Ringing the Bell'. There were no reserve parachutes to rely on, and any malfunction of the main canopy would result in death.

The great day came and Sid joined a 'stick' aboard the aircraft. When his turn came around he gritted his teeth, and jumped through the hole in the floor without ringing the bell. His heart pounded. But he breathed a sigh of relief when he looked skyward and saw that his canopy was open. The aircraft was now fast shrinking as he floated toward the desert floor. He was amazed at how quickly the ground rushed up to meet him, and his planned controlled roll turned into a crumpled mess. The parachute collapsed and he was surrounded by dust, but he was uninjured. He was elated, it was a fantastic experience, and his initial thought was to do it again as quickly as possible. His wish was granted, as the course required them to complete two jumps a day, before lunch. The trainees were not allowed to be qualified as parachutists until they had completed five jumps. Then the group progressed to exiting Wellington Bombers through the door. Sid completed the course

Parachutists

and returned to the SAS camp feeling ten feet tall. He was one of the first of the group to complete the course, and it felt great. He was now given a set of wings to sow onto his uniform and the rank of parachutist. This new title seemed a little strange after several years of being a guardsman, but he was now being paid two shillings a day more, so it was bearable.

Although plenty of men had dropped out from the course, the Guards remained the dominant group. All of the Grenadiers were still at Kabrit, Dougie Wright, Kosbab, Thomas and others. But there were yet more Grenadiers who had joined the SAS earlier. There were Sergeant Kershaw, George Cass, and Squadron Sergeant Major Feebury, yet another impressive Grenadier who had been one of the originals who had joined from No 8 Commando. The group were now a part of 1st SAS and had been issued with new berets. These were sand coloured and bore the new badge of the regiment, the flaming sword of Excalibur, bearing the motto 'Who Dares Wins!' The badge was mounted on a backing of dark blue and light blue cloth. It was said that this was in honour of the first men recruited by David Stirling. 'Jock' Lewes and Tom Langton had rowed for Oxford and Cambridge respectively, and their old university colours were now being worn by SAS men all over the Middle East. Predictably both officers were guardsmen.

Each man was issued with a menacing looking Commando dagger and a .38 Webley pistol. Most of the guardsmen chose not to wear the new daggers. The old hands had advised them against this. In their trade the risk of capture was high. Any man found with the murderous looking blade on his person, could expect rough treatment. There were plenty of men who enjoyed their new status and the lack of close supervision. Some of them took full advantage of it. They could be seen swaggering around with the pistols strapped to their hips. They often used the desert road signs for target practice.

Kossie was as outspoken as always and was quick to tell such men what he thought of their attitude. His confrontational approach brought predictable results and he became unpopular in some quarters. Those who knew him well were prepared to put up with the odd indiscretion. Each man was expected to be well turned out, and to maintain the standards of a guardsman, without the rigorous supervision that would be present in the battalions.

Around Christmas 1942, 1st SAS was visited by their commander, David Stirling. This was the first and last time that Sid would see this legendary figure. Stirling was captured in January 1943. After making a great nuisance of himself, he was eventually incarcerated in the infamous Colditz Castle, where he spent the remainder of the war. Sid was very impressed with the presence of this Scots Guardsman and those who surrounded him. Some were virtual legends already, having taken part in many daring raids.

1st SAS consisted of A, B and C Squadrons, and Sid's group made up the newly formed D Squadron. C Squadron was now made up of Free French Paratroopers. There was also a large detachment of Greeks in the regiment. There were usually eight men to a patrol, and four or five patrols to a Squadron. The patrol was usually made up of an officer, a sergeant, two corporals and four parachutists. However, this number was increased or decreased according to requirements. The NCOs were selected from those men who had held rank in their own units. There was little science involved in selecting men for each patrol.

One day, a large group of men was drawn up, and Sid was approached by Lieutenant Duggan, a fellow volunteer who he knew well. Duggan, a tank regiment man, told Sid to stand to one side as he wanted him to be in his patrol. Sid did as he was told, and watched as the others were 'picked' for the remaining patrols. The process was a little like choosing playground football teams, with a little trading thrown in. Dougie Wright had spotted Sid, who he thought was not allocated to a patrol, and shouted, 'Looks like you'll be winning the war on your own, Sid'. Kosbab said, 'He'll be OK, cos he's a good map reader, so he'll always know where we are'.

Before long the Patrols were organised and everyone had been allocated. SSM Feebury was ever present with advice and experience. Sid was happy to have such a respected and capable Warrant Officer as their Squadron Sergeant Major. Those men who had held rank before, and who had survived the selection process, were promoted once again. Sid's talent was recognised and he was handed two chevrons, becoming a full Corporal overnight.

A period of naval training followed at Kabrit. There was a naval petty officer there to organise this phase of the training. The troops trained on inflatable dinghies, collapsible boats and even whalers, becoming quite proficient. They were soon issued with their vehicles, American made Willys Jeeps. These vehicles had been especially adapted for their desert environment. A special cylindrical condenser had been fitted to the front of the radiator, to assist with cooling the engine, and to conserve water, which would always be in short supply. A series of brackets was fitted all over the jeep. Into these were fitted a miraculous number of jerry cans containing water and petrol. 90 gallons of fuel was normally carried in this way, in addition to the extra fuel tanks already fitted, which gave the jeeps a range of several hundred kilometres. Every nook and cranny was stashed with stores and supplies. Many pounds of explosives, to be used for demolitions, and rations to last them for up to two months behind enemy lines, were crammed in. In addition to the troops' personal weapons, most of the jeeps were equipped with their own armaments. Pintle mounted machine guns were bolted to the bodywork in front of the passenger seat. These were often large Browning .50 calibre, but there were many other types, including the Bren, and twin mounted Vickers guns which had been salvaged somewhere from British aircraft. Any other essential equipment hung from the sides of the jeeps, in rucksacks and other containers.

After familiarisation with the vehicles, more training, and much preparation, D Squadron left Kabrit to join the operations against Rommel. A and B Squadrons were already operating deep in the desert. At long last the Afrika Korps was on the run. D Squadron was commanded by Major Lord George Jellicoe, a Coldstream Guardsman. Jellicoe was an experienced officer who had taken part in a number of daring raids already. He had narrowly escaped capture in occupied Crete, and was greatly respected by the men.

The long journey through the desert was plagued by engine problems and by punctures. Kosbab was driving Sid's jeep, and the air turned blue every time the vehicle ground to a steaming halt. The Squadron continued without them, but the little group was able to catch up. Sid's navigational skills didn't let him down, no mean feat, as their direction was found by no other means than the sun, compass, or by the stars. After a very long dusty journey, the now complete D Squadron crossed into Libya, and eventually arrived on the outskirts of Tripoli.

They soon discovered that the allied advance had been swift and that Tripoli was now in British hands. They wasted no time in entering the city. There was an air of jubilation. Smiling allied troops marched through the streets in great numbers. The Highland Division were present and bagpipes could be heard. The dusty SAS men, some wearing Arab head-dress, attracted some curious looks. The array of weaponry mounted on the jeeps was also most unusual. There was no time to share in the liberation celebrations, and D Squadron drove through the city and out the other side. It was there that they met a group of men from B Squadron who were returning from their recent operations. They were bearded and filthy in appearance, but they were none the less relaxed. The two groups gathered around the jeeps and discussed the situation. The D Squadron men were keen to hear what B Squadron had been up to.

After a brief exchange, Earl Jellicoe drove off in his jeep to seek clarification of the situation ahead, and to confirm what role D Squadron would play. After a fairly lengthy period of time, the Squadron Commander returned with the news that D Squadron was no longer required. Jellicoe had met someone he referred to as the 'Commander', and Sid assumed that he was talking about Montgomery himself. It had been decided that although there were pockets of enemy still in the area, the Germans were beaten, and there was no real job for the specialists of the SAS. There was some disappointment among the men that they would still not be getting a shot at the enemy. However, there was nothing for it but to return to Kabrit.

It was January 1943, and with no imminent operation planned, D Squadron set about their training once again. Unknown to the men, another reorganisation of 1 SAS Regiment was planned. D Squadron was moved again, this time to Palestine. When they arrived, they set up camp at Athlit, near Haifa on the coast. There was more naval training, and Sid learned that they were to become specialists in this type of warfare. There was demolitions training, much more intensive than any that he had previously experienced. He learned what quantity and type of explosive was required to cut through various types of materials.

They were also introduced to the limpet mine, a disk-like explosive device, which could be attached to the bottom of enemy shipping by means of magnets. Some of the men thought that it was ironic that having trained as parachutists, they were now spending endless days diving under the sea with explosives strapped to their chests.

They became expert swimmers and some of the men could stay below the surface, without the aid of oxygen tanks, for an incredible period of time. Tommo, a Scots guardsman, and fellow member of Sid's patrol, was particularly proficient in this field, leading some to think he was 'half fish'. Oxygen and flippers were not generally used and Sid found that he did not enjoy diving beneath ships. It was clearly an exceptionally dangerous practice.

A great deal of training was carried out with the Royal Navy, and the men of D Squadron soon learned the use of various nautical terms. The sailors often 'took the mickey', but were astounded when they saw how slick the SAS men were with their boat drills. On one occasion, Sid's little group were paddling into the harbour. He was positioned at the bow, and was dictating the time for the rowing. The unusual sight had drawn the attention of the Navy who were unaccustomed to seeing the army behaving in such an uncharacteristic way. As they reached the jetty, the officer in Sid's dinghy shouted for him to 'Make fast'. Sid replied with a Grenadier 'Sir', and promptly tied off with a clove hitch. The watching sailors were astounded, and exclamations of surprise were heard from above.

In April, D Squadron was renamed the Special Boat Squadron or SBS. The Squadron was divided into three Detachments, L, M and S, so named after their commanders, Langton, Mclean and Sutherland. Sid's Patrol was placed in 'L' Detachment. He and the others regarded themselves as the 'Best of the Best', and desperately wanted to have a go at the Germans. Not all of the training took place at sea. An exercise was organised near Beirut in the Lebanon. The plan was to 'raid' a number of allied headquarters locations. There was a great deal of night movement and long tiring marches carrying heavy rucksacks.

During one night move, Sid was leading the group when they came to a steep ravine, with a deep river at the bottom. It was necessary to climb down the steep sides and as Sid made the descent he suddenly heard a shout from above. Parachutist Murray had lost his footing and he tumbled down the ravine. Tommo shouted to Sid to grab the man. He reached out and grasped the flailing mass of arms and legs as he passed, but the momentum dragged Sid after him. Both men splashed into the river and went under. They were still wearing their rucksacks, which weighed about 50lbs, and struggled to reach the surface. It was a terrifying moment. But miraculously both men managed to scramble to the bank, where they were hauled out by the remaining patrol members. Sid lay on the bank coughing, and gulping in great lungs full of air. As the two had swallowed a good deal of the dirty water, the officer in charge insisted they go to the local Military Hospital where they both received various injections to prevent disease.

Some of the other patrols faired a little better. SSM Feebury managed to gain entry into a British Headquarters where he literally took papers from the desks. The sense of security that had previously existed in the headquarters, was shattered, and the exercise resulted in a tightening of security. Unfortunately, the sentries were unaware that an exercise was taking place, and one of the SAS men was badly injured during the raid. This was an accepted war time risk and the incident soon faded into memory.

Soon after the exercises in Beirut, the SBS moved to Algiers where they carried out more training, this time with submarines. Launching inflatable boats from a submarine was no easy business, and a great deal of time was spent mastering the technique. When a submarine was not available, an MTB or other type of vessel would be used. On one occasion, Sid and the others were trying to climb aboard their little boat which was being held by a group of sailors. They were not making life easy for the SBS men and Sid snapped at them, 'If you lot can't hold this bloody boat still, I'll get some WRENs to do it'.

The soldiers got on well with the submariners, they were a breed apart, and the SBS quickly recognised this. The junior ranks were accommodated in the mess decks. Sid's reaction was one of horror when he saw the living conditions. The sailors lived in incredibly cramped conditions that would have made even the Ascanius seem luxurious by comparison. There seemed to be a constant smell of diesel oil which made one feel sick after a while. The sailors moved around the boat in silence, a skill that the soldiers had not yet mastered. They were constantly berated by the submariners, and reminded that any unnecessary noise could result in the boat being attacked. It took a while to settle into a routine when aboard. There were many differences to their way of life. There seemed to be no day or night, which in itself was rather disorientating. At meal times, each man peeled his own potato which would be set aside, and returned to him cooked. Sid thought this was a little odd, but he didn't complain.

Their drills improved as they became more aware of the environment. They became quite adept at climbing aboard their little dinghies in the dark. The commander of the submarine would give the SBS commander a compass bearing to his objective from the sub, and the group would start the long paddle to the shore. This was a very hit and miss business. The only indication of their location was given by the submariners. It was difficult to plan for the changing tides or the wind, and they often ended up a good way from their intended destination. The 'pick-up' was equally difficult as they had no direct form of communication with the submarine. They were simply told that the sub would be standing off shore on a particular date for a number of hours. The SAS men would have to shoot a bearing to the supposed location, and then paddle out to sea in the hope that they would see the vessel.

There was a general feeling that all this training at sea would soon be put into effect as a live operation. Many practice runs were made from the sub. On one exercise the son of a prominent British politician was attached to Sid's patrol. The group were wary of this newcomer, who clearly had not trained with the SBS before. The dinghies were launched from the sub, as usual, and they paddled ashore without difficulty. When they reached the beach, the SAS men jumped from their boat and pulled it from the surf. To their amazement the young officer remained in the boat as they pulled it onto the beach. Only when there was no possibility of his feet getting wet did he jump clear! Sid and the others were not only surprised, they were disgusted. This was not the sort of officer they had become accustomed to. Sid thought that Noriega would kill the man on the spot, but somehow he restrained himself. Fortunately the officer's attachment was short lived. He later became very well known, but Sid's opinion of him remained low.

The SAS soldiers forged a great working relationship with the submariners. When they were in Algiers many enjoyable evenings were spent with the Navy men. To his great surprise, Sid discovered that one of the submariners was an ex-Kings Company man. They had not served together but they had many mutual acquaintances, and lots of stories were exchanged about the First Battalion.

It was around this time that Sid and the other Grenadiers learned that while they had been moving around North Africa, the war in Tunisia had been progressing. 201st Guards Brigade had been committed against a range of hills known locally as the horseshoe. The plan had been to open the way to the Mareth Line and to kick Rommel out of the region for good. The SAS men heard that things had gone badly for the 6th Battalion. But it was to be some time before they learned the full extent of their old Battalion's losses. On 16th March, the Grenadiers and Coldstream had been launched against an enemy position which they had been led to believe was weakly held. Poor intelligence had led to an attack against a heavily defended area through numerous minefields. In its first battle, the 6th Battalion lost around 280 men, 81 of them killed. Colonel Archer Clive had been wounded and twenty-four officers had become casualties. Among the dead was Captain Gwyer. The commanding officer was one of the last to return across the Wadi Zess from their hopeless position. He was subsequently awarded the DSO. The Grenadier SAS men were saddened, but did not yet know just how bad things were. In the meantime, their determination to hit the Germans was stronger than ever.

At the end of June there was a tension in the air. It was no surprise when they received a warning order for an operation. D Squadron moved from its temporary base, at Phillippville, to Algiers on 22nd June. They were warned to prepare for a 'submarine operation'. Some of the men had been taken ill around this time. It was presumed that it was some sort of local bug that had struck them down. Jumper Workman in particular, was very ill and had to be omitted from the operation. Sid thought that Jumper would be furious when he recovered. Kosbab was also omitted because of a medical problem. Despite his obvious frustrated appeals, the decision stood.

The party was assembled and Lord Jellicoe gave a briefing on the objective for this mission. It was to be called 'Operation Hawthorn'. They were to embark on 28th June. They would travel by submarine, and would disembark at several different points, on the West coast of enemy held Sardinia. Next, the patrols would move independently, on foot, to attack a series of German airfields where they were to cause as much damage as possible. Their extraction was to be on foot to the east coast, where they would attempt to rendezvous with a submarine for the home leg. Many of those present thought the move to the coast with the enemy in hot pursuit would be more than a little tricky. Jellicoe had been forbidden from taking part in the raid for security reasons, and overall command passed to Captain Verney.

There were to be six patrols commanded by Captains, Verney, Brinkworth, Imbert- Terry, Thompson, and Lieutenants Duggan and Cochrane. Thirty men were to take part, and two submarines were to be used with the patrols split between them. Each patrol was given a code name after a flower or a plant, 'Periwinkle', 'Mistletoe', 'Daffodil', 'Jasmine', 'Hyacinth' and Sid's own patrol which would be known as 'Bluebell'. This patrol would consist of SSM Feebury, Tommo and Noriega, in addition to Lieutenant Duggan. Most of the other Grenadiers were to be on the raid, including Dougie Wright, Bill Thomas and George Cass. One unexpected addition to the group was an American Italian interpreter. This was something of a surprise to most of the men, as he had done no preparatory training.

On the afternoon of the 28th, Sid's party boarded HM Submarine Severn, and the remainder of the raiding patrols installed themselves on a second vessel. That evening, under the cover of darkness, both submarines set sail for Sardinia. With so many SBS men aboard there was scarcely enough room to move, and the sailors were even more sensitive than normal to any noise.

The Patrols of Captain Thomson and Lieutenant Duggan were to be landed on the evening of 30th June or 1st July, if the conditions were favourable. After several hours at sea almost everyone was feeling ill. It was unbearably hot, and several of the men had fits of vomiting and diarrhoea. Everyone assumed that this was due to the unpleasant conditions aboard the cramped sub. One small bonus was that the sailor running the ships store came from Dorset, and he quickly recognised Sid's accent. The two exchanged stories from home and a little of the ship's rum ration found its way into his kit.

As they made slow progress below the waves, there was no improvement to the men's condition. Sid too was feeling quite ill. Dougie Wright was by now very sick, and it became clear that he would be incapable of taking part in the Op. The decision was made that he would have to remain on the sub, and would play no further part in Operation Hawthorn. The American attached to the group was already unpopular. The SAS men were naturally suspicious of this 'outsider', and when he was caught smoking, some of the men were furious. This was something that just was not done on the sub. Most of the group were smokers, and this breach of discipline was regarded as a serious development. About 24 hours into the voyage, Mr Duggan and SSM Feebury came down to the mess decks and announced that there were to be some changes to the plan. Their original objective had been changed. They would now be attacking an emergency aerodrome at Villasidro, and they would also land a day later. This meant that routes, bearings, and rendezvous, would all have to be changed and Sid checked these with the other patrol members until they were all satisfied on the alterations. He noticed that Tommo looked bad, but they were all feeling rough. Anyway it wouldn't be long until they got out into the air.

Chapter 12

Sardinia

HMS Severn surfaced off the coast of Sardinia on the evening of 1st July. There was virtual silence on the boat. The atmosphere was very tense, this was the most vulnerable time for a submarine. The crew were experienced, they had done this before and the risks were well understood. The SAS men had assembled with their equipment and were prepared for a swift exit. The longer the sub was on the surface the greater the risk of being spotted. They had said their farewells to the crew much earlier and as they squeezed themselves through the hatches, there were slaps on the back and many whispered expressions of good luck.

As he hauled himself through the final hatch, Sid smelled the salty sea air and he was surprised at how dark it was outside. His eyes had become accustomed to the red filtered light inside the sub and it took a short while for his sight to adjust. The submarine's wet decks glistened in the moonlight, and it was surprisingly warm. He was helped to his feet by an unknown sailor, and the dinghies were pointed out to him. He handed his rucksack to the sailor, and carefully slid into the small inflatable boat, dropping the last couple of feet and landing on his backside. Next, he received the rucksacks from the remainder of the patrol, and stowed them aboard the little boat. He helped to steady the next man as he dropped over the side and then took his usual place at the bow. Sid brought his carbine up alongside his body and stared into the night. There was no sign of land, or anything else for that

matter, just the reflection of the moon on the surface of black sea, and the occasional white topped wave.

They had practised this many times and the patrol was complete in a matter of moments. The sailors allowed the dinghy to break free of the sub, and the raiders started to paddle for the shore. There was a final wave from the men remaining on the deck before they disappeared down the hatches. When Sid next looked back, a few minutes later, the submarine had disappeared completely. To his left he could see Captain Thomson's patrol in their boat, steadily paddling for the shore. Mr Duggan had been given a compass bearing by the submarine commander. Sid, at the front, constantly checked his own compass to ensure that they were heading in approximately the right direction. The sub's Captain had told Duggan that they were about a mile from the shore and they stared intently into the darkness for any sign of land. It seemed as though the little craft were making good headway and the group expected to see the outline of Sardinia at any moment. But it didn't appear. They paddled for over an hour, but there was still no sign of land. The bearing was checked and double checked, as more precious time passed. Sid became anxious. If they were only a mile out they should be able to see land by now. When two hours passed with nothing but the sea in all directions there were some grave faces aboard the boat. But there was nothing to be done but continue paddling. There was concern that if things had gone drastically wrong, and the sub had surfaced in the wrong place, they could still be on the open seas at first light. They would be virtually defenceless if they were spotted.

After almost three hours there was no change in their situation. The paddling had tired them, and regular breaks were necessary. Duggan frequently stared through the binoculars in search of the Sardinian hills, without success. Suddenly a slap on Sid's shoulder was followed by an outstretched hand pointing forward. As he stared into the darkness he saw the faint silhouette of land at last. The paddling became more urgent, and the hills looked closer with every stroke of the oar. They could now hear the surf breaking on the beach, and the rocky hills rose above them. They were more alert now. Blackened faces scanned the coastline for any sign of activity, and weapons were pulled closer. Finally, after three and a half hours, they reached the shore. Sid jumped into the surf and was quickly joined by the others. The boat was dragged ashore at the double, and they took cover under a rocky outcrop.

They were joined by the other patrol. Once present, the two officers moved forward, off the beach, and began to climb the hillside in order to recce the area. Sid's patrol fanned out as sentries, the way they had rehearsed. He handed an entrenching tool to a member of the other patrol, as they were responsible for burying the boats. Sid noticed that he was sweating profusely, even though he was soaked to the waist and the night air was now cool. He put this down to tension but he noticed that Tommo seemed to be shivering uncontrollably. Sid held his carbine into his shoulder and stared into the night, but he could hear Tommo, who seemed to be mumbling to himself. Something was definitely wrong.

Just as he made up his mind to go and see what the problem was, SSM Feebury arrived, closely followed by Mr Duggan. The route ahead was apparently clear and they were to move as quickly as they could. Sid went back to the location of the boats in order to check that all was well. To his horror he found that the other patrol had already moved off, but they had only buried their own boat. He was quickly joined by the SSM who was furious at this setback. The two deflated the boat and scraped a hole in the sand. Their only means of escape now suitably camouflaged, they rejoined the others.

Mr Duggan was now with Tommo, and Sid watched a worried exchange between his commander and the SSM. Thomas was obviously sick. He must have contracted the same bug that had affected Dougie Wright and Jumper Workman. It was now 03.30 and much time had been lost since leaving the sub. First light was in about an hour, so it was essential that they get as far from the beach as possible, and locate a suitable hiding place in which to pass the daylight hours. The climb up the rocky hillside was very steep and hard going. Unusually, Sid was feeling the physical strain and was dripping sweat. From the very start of the climb Tommo was in deep trouble. He was trying hard not to be a burden, but was falling behind. He was placed in the middle of the patrol, pulled from the front and pushed from behind. But it was difficult to maintain this approach on the rocky slope. Feebury and Duggan pushed on, to try and find a lying up place. Tommo once again fell behind. Sid went back to help and to his horror found that Tommo had lost his carbine and a bag full of bombs. The sick man had no idea where the missing equipment had gone and was almost delirious.

When Duggan returned, a short search was made for the missing kit but it couldn't be located. At the top of the cliff they headed off once more on a bearing due east. It was almost dawn, but there was no sign of life, no buildings, animals or roads. Duggan pushed on. Eventually it became clear that Tommo could not continue. The decision was made to lie up and see if he recovered. A small dip was found behind some boulders and the sick man was rested between them. They covered him to keep the heat in and administered sips of water. The SSM said that Tommo was displaying the symptoms of malaria and he was given some quinine. Sid realised that he too may have the disease, as he had been feeling unwell. He dosed himself up with anti malarial tablets and quinine, but still felt very rough.

As the sun came up, they took turns as sentries and Mr Duggan studied the map intently. Later in the morning, Duggan left to recce the area. He was clearly frustrated by this unexpected turn of events and wanted to make up for lost time. Most of the group managed to get some sleep, and they ate some of their rations. SSM Feebury wore his characteristic Arab head-dress and Sid thought that he looked just like a tough Bedouin. In the afternoon, Duggan returned and reported that there was still no sign of life. This at least was good news. According to the map there was a river about five miles away. It was decided that they would allow Thomas to rest until it got dark, they would then move closer to the river. If Thomas was still sick they would have to leave him. No one wanted to leave a sick man behind in an uninhabited area but they all understood the logic. There was a job to be done and they had all accepted the risks when they volunteered.

At this point Duggan decided to share another piece of bad news with the patrol. Apparently the skipper of the submarine had got his bearing wrong, and the pre-arranged rendezvous for their pick up would have to be changed. There was nothing that could be done now. The pick up was arranged for a week's time, and there were more pressing matters at hand. Although Thomas was still ill, he seemed to have recovered a little and was now making sense, Sid still felt very bad, but thought he would be able to continue. The SSM spoke to Tommo and asked if he thought he could make it the five miles to the river. Tommo immediately replied that he thought he could. As darkness finally fell on the hillside, the patrol made their final preparations. Bearings were checked, and rucksacks were heaved onto shoulders before they finally set off in the moonlight.

A very short distance had been covered when Sid's attention was drawn to a brief commotion ahead. Tommo had collapsed and fallen over a bush. There was no longer any doubt that to continue with him was not an option. Mr Duggan must have given this scenario some thought during the day. Sid had also been struggling and was clearly showing similar signs of malaria. Duggan announced that Sid was to remain behind with Thomas, and do what he could for the gravely sick man. He was also told to treat himself, in case he became much worse. If the two recovered in time, they were to join the rest of the patrol at the rendezvous. If they got worse, they should give themselves up in order to get medical attention. But this was to be a last resort. They should not surrender until after the raid had been launched.

Sid had no intention of giving up, but Tommo's condition was clearly serious. Further instructions were given to ensure that maps, Lewes bombs, escape money and other items were destroyed or buried before they were captured. Duggan went over the routes and bearings with Sid again, and told him to make sure that Thomas understood when he recovered. Enough time had been lost. After handshakes the two groups parted for the final time. Noriega waved, and followed on after Feebury.

Sid watched as they disappeared into the darkness and felt very alone. He sat down next to Tommo, who was now sleeping, and made an appraisal of his situation. He was stranded, alone with a gravely sick man, behind enemy lines. To seek help would mean compromising the operation, and to remain where they were would not help Tommo. His own condition was worsening and the two had a limited water supply. It would be a week before any pick up was possible. By then the enemy would be looking for them on the coast. All things considered, the situation couldn't have been much worse. It was perhaps as well that he was unaware that the second submarine had developed mechanical problems. It had returned to Algiers without dropping the remaining patrols.

The two rested all the following day and once again Tommo seemed a little better. Sid tried to get him to take some quinine but unsuccessfully. Because of his constant fever, Tommo was drinking water far too quickly. Sid was concerned that their small supply would not last. He encouraged the sick man to drink a little less, but to no avail. By now both were weak, but they understood that they had to reach water that night, or their supply would run out.

After dark they set off once again toward the river marked on their map near Capo Pecora. Their movement was painfully slow. It was necessary to rest frequently. After several hours they had covered only two or three kilometres. But they eventually reached some high ground, overlooking a Wadi and a railway track. By now their water supply was exhausted, but Sid could see the moon reflecting off a river on the far side of the rail tracks. Both men were dead beat and suffering high fever. Tommo was in no state to go on, so Sid took their water bottles and started the long descent down the hillside. He was now seriously ill himself. He underestimated the distance to the river, taking much longer to reach the water than he expected.

There was no sign of life and the only sound was from the gurgling of the water as it flowed past. He filled the bottles and started the climb back up the hillside. The return journey was very hard going and Sid found himself stumbling over rocks in the darkness. He was forced to rest frequently as his fever made him feel dizzy. It had taken much longer than he had expected. By the time he had returned to the area where he had left Tommo, the sun was coming up.

The ground suddenly looked very different and his friend was nowhere to be seen. Sid walked left and right in patterns. Several times he was sure that he had found their hiding place, only to have his hopes dashed. Hours passed, and as the sun rose he became weaker. He started to feel dizzy again and in desperation he called out to Tommo. There was no reply. By mid morning he had become delirious himself and he collapsed on the hillside. The rest of the day was spent drifting in and out of consciousness. He was able to drink some water, but was too weak to move. He remained in that position all night. In the early hours of 5th July he felt strong enough to continue the search for his lost pal. After much searching he eventually found his friend, only 200 yards away, the sun was now coming up once again.

The Scots Guardsman was in a desperate state. He had been 24 hours without water and initially did not recognise Sid. Tommo had removed his shirt and boots, and had apparently lain in this position for at least a day, under the hot Mediterranean sun. He was sunburnt and his lips were cracked and dry. Sid dragged him into the shade and immediately got him to drink some water. He applied ointment to his cracked lips and spent the rest of the day doing what he could to make Tommo more comfortable. He brewed tea, soup and stewed some dried apricots, to try and build up his friend's strength. Tommo dropped off to sleep and seemed fairly peaceful for most of the day. At around 6 p.m. he suddenly started to pant heavily. Sid tried to wake him, but to no avail. Eventually he stopped breathing altogether. Sid desperately tried to revive the man, but it was obvious that he was dead. Nothing more could be done. Guardsman Leonard Thomas was just 20 years old.

Sid had never felt so alone in his life. He sat next to his dead friend and the grief descended upon him. It would have been very easy to just give up and surrender at that moment. But his training and natural determination took over. His mind started to assemble a course of action which, for the time being, distracted him from the sense of loss he was experiencing. He couldn't leave Tommo the way he was. So he wrapped the dead man in his sleeping bag, and scraped a shallow grave. He buried his friend under the cover of a small bush. He marked the spot with a wooden cross, which he fashioned from dead wood.

He also buried Tommo's equipment as he had been instructed by Lieutenant Duggan. He retained as much water as he could and boosted his own meagre ration supply from Tommo's rucksack. He thought that he may still be of some use if he reached the RV, so he kept some of the Lewes bombs and his own weapons. The remaining daylight hours were spent studying the map and checking weapons. He ate some of the rations, as he knew there was a tough night's marching ahead of him.

Once it was dark, Sid hoisted his rucksack onto his back, checked his compass bearing once again, and set off into the summer night. He felt much better than he had been the previous day, but was still weak. He was conscious that he should make up as much ground as he could. The raid was due to take place on the fourth night after they had disembarked. He realised that he would be too late to take part in the action. He decided to make for the RV. Mr Cochrane's party would be in place there, to meet the raiding patrols on the eastern side of the island, before extraction.

The going was very hard. There seemed to be little or no habitation in this part of the island, so he moved relatively quickly. It was necessary to stop and drink water regularly. He used this opportunity to check the map, and to listen for any sign of life. There was none, save for the sound of the crickets and the occasional bird. For the next three nights he continued his trek, moving mainly at night, and resting during the day. He was confident that he knew his approximate location. According to the map, there was a village which should come into view before too long.

On the evening of 8th July the village of Montevecchio duly appeared where Sid expected. None the less, he was relieved that his navigation had been correct. His movement had been slow and he needed to press on. But the village was situated directly in his path. To go around it would take many hours of climbing the surrounding hills. He felt that in his current condition this might take all night. He moved himself to a position over looking the little village. Dogs could be heard barking. But there was very little sign of any human activity, apart from the dim lights emanating from the small windows in the houses. He settled down to watch the village. He had made up his mind to risk moving through the narrow streets. It looked quiet enough and he would save a lot of time. Once the lights went out and the population had settled down for the night, he would make his move.

In the early hours, everything seemed to be silent. All the lights seemed to have been extinguished. It was now or never. Sid moved as stealthily as possible down the rugged hillside toward the village. He stopped frequently to listen, and to stare into the night. His biggest fear was that his presence would be detected by one of the many dogs, and that this would wake the whole village. He was soon moving through the tiny cobbled streets. Some of the houses had shutters over the windows and they all seemed to be in darkness. The walls were painted, or whitewashed, in pale colours and he felt that he was badly silhouetted on this particularly light night. In the event of being spotted he had decided to play the part of a German patrol. He thought that if he was confident enough he could convince the villagers to mind their own business. As he passed by the tiny dwellings, he could smell human habitation and he hoped they were all sleeping soundly.

He was almost at the far edge of the village when a dog suddenly started to yap. The animal's bark echoed through the streets. Sid thought it might be heard in Rome. He had to get out of town fast and he broke into a jog. He soon found that, in his current state, he couldn't continue this for long. He dodged into an olive grove, once out of the village, and continued his hasty retreat. Behind him he imagined that villagers were spilling into the streets to see what the noise was. He once again climbed the hillside and started to feel a little more secure. He was soaking

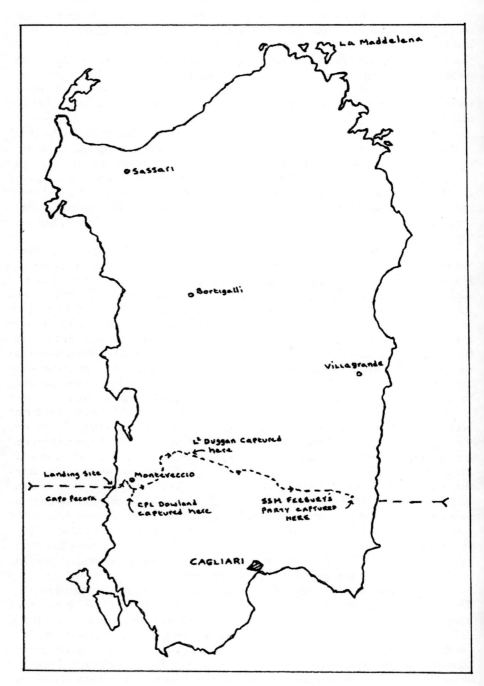

Operation Hawthorn, July 1943

with sweat and gasping for air. He sat down with his back to a large rock facing down the hillside toward the village.

When he managed to bring his breathing under control he listened once again for signs of pursuit. This time there was very definite human activity coming from below. As he watched, there were lights coming on in the houses and smaller ones, perhaps torches in the streets. There were more dogs barking now too. There were voices, men's voices, and it sounded as though someone was giving instructions in Italian. Sid felt sure that he hadn't been seen. Surely a dog barking didn't usually bring this sort of response. Something was wrong and he decided it would be un-wise to hang around in this area. By dawn he needed to be as far away as possible.

He once again continued his lone march into the countryside. Just before first light he was close to exhaustion. Ahead there was a wood, and he thought this would provide some cover during the day. He settled into the little copse and made himself as comfortable as possible. As the sun came up, it became apparent that the wood was not as thick as he had thought. It was too late now, it was broad daylight, and the surrounding countryside looked very open. He would have to sit it out un-til dark. He checked the map. He was unsure of how far he had travelled since the incident in the village. But he hoped that he had put sufficient distance between himself and whoever had been moving about in the dark. During the morning he drifted off into a light sleep, but constantly woke with a start, disorientated and confused.

During the late afternoon he heard voices. They were close but he couldn't see them. They were clearly getting closer. To his horror he suddenly spotted two sil-houettes no further than twenty yards away. They were male, civilians and were headed straight for his position. Sid flipped open his holster and slowly drew his .38 revolver, should he shoot or hide? Suddenly it was too late. They had seen him and were clearly startled. He decided that he couldn't shoot two civilians, and any-way the noise would bring everyone else down on his position. He would have to bluff it.

'Buon Jiurno', he called, in what he thought was a confident German voice.

There was no reply from the startled Italians. They nodded, and hurried on their way. Sid cursed his luck, did they buy it? He wasn't confident and considered risking a daylight move from his current position. A quick glance through the trees confirmed that there was precious little cover. He decided to stick it out for a few more hours until the light was gone. As a precaution he buried his maps, money and other items. He once again settled down and drifted into a disturbed sleep.

In the evening he awoke to find that the sun was going down. He was relieved. Soon it would be dark, and he could get away from this compromised hiding place. As he once again checked his equipment, he thought that he heard movement. He pressed himself into the undergrowth. Yes, there were voices and something was burning.

He raised his head slightly and could see that the wood was on fire. Damn it! Was someone after him or was this an accident. He would have to sit it out. The fire rapidly took hold and moved toward him. The smoke was choking and before long he had to move his position away from the flames.

Sid understood now that someone was trying to burn him out. He hoped that it was the two civilians, and not a platoon of Germans. As the heat increased he accepted the inevitable, and decided to make a dash from the wood. He grabbed his carbine and hauled himself onto one knee. His rucksack was hoisted over one shoulder and he prepared to run. As he looked up, he suddenly found himself staring at an Italian Corporal who was pointing a rifle at his chest. There was a shout, and the man was joined by another soldier. Sid realised that the game was up. More men arrived, and he walked out of the wood with his hands in the air.

The soldiers were edgy and reluctant to get too close to him. There were at least four of them and an officer. They were scruffy and ill shaven but the officer seemed to know what he was doing. The SAS man was quickly disarmed and his equipment taken away from him. He was searched but only for weapons. Sid noted that they had failed to find his escape map or compass. The troops were soon joined by the Caribinieri. He was positioned between the soldiers, none of whom attempted conversation during their march to the local police station. He couldn't help thinking that it was a little strange that the Italians didn't appear too surprised to find him alone in the wood. He was experiencing mixed emotions. There was a sense of failure at being caught. But at the same time he was almost relieved to know that it was all over. These emotions soon passed, and by the time they arrived at the police station he was already thinking about escape.

Chapter 13

In the Bag

In the village a large crowd of civilians had assembled. Sid was surprised that so many people had gathered so quickly. Heads bobbed up and down to get a better look at the prisoner. Children jumped in the air to catch a glimpse of him. At the tiny police station he was again searched. One of the policemen found his escape hacksaw blade. He wasn't bothered. They still hadn't located his silk escape map or his two small compasses. The whole thing was conducted in full view of the villagers. They crowded at the doors and windows, where they chattered excitedly.

His equipment was laid out on a desk, and the soldiers took turns at handling his Webley revolver. The weapons were removed, as was anything else that the Italians thought might be a threat. But most of his kit was returned to him, although he noted that the guards kept his soap. He thought they were welcome to it, as several looked as though they were in need of a bath. He was treated fairly well by his captors, they were by no means friendly, but no one had in any way abused him. He noticed that the guards became nervous if they were left alone with him, and they all kept their distance. As soon as he was left alone, he concealed his escape map in the lining of his bush shirt, and hid his second small compass. He also had a tiny trouser button compass which he made secure.

After about an hour another army officer arrived from the local garrison. He took Sid's number, rank and name, and made an attempt to question him further. But Sid refused to talk. The officer was quite officious. Like the others he knew he was dealing with some sort of highly trained commando, and he lacked the confidence to press his interrogation. The officer and a group of soldiers then marched him to the local garrison headquarters, which was about 8 kilometres away. When he arrived, he fully expected to be met by a Gestapo interrogator, or at least by a German officer. Neither of these materialised and he underwent a series of amateur interrogations. Even the local priest was called to try and glean some fragment of information from him, but without success.

Sid decided that there would be no harm in telling them about Tommo, in order that his friend could have a decent burial. He showed an officer the location of the grave on the map. A few hours later, the soldiers returned with Tommo's carbine and revolver. They had located the grave without difficulty and they assured him that Tommo would be buried in a proper cemetery. The officer further commented that Tommo probably died from malaria. Sid was surprised that they had been able to tell this, until the officer revealed that Sergeant Mckerracher, and Bill Thomas from Captain Thomson's patrol, had died in the local hospital. There could be no doubt as one of the soldiers had a photograph of his Grenadier pal. This was devastating news. He had now lost three friends. It sounded as though the op was turning into a disaster for L Detachment.

Sid was visited by the same doctor that had treated his friends in the hospital. The middle aged Italian confirmed that in his opinion the two had contracted malaria in Africa. The local priest and the Italian Company Commander told him that all three of his friends would be buried in the local cemetery. Sid was well treated by the Italian soldiers and as there were no cells available he was held in the company office. A twenty-four hour guard was mounted on him.

Before very long he was on good terms with the soldiers, who took great delight in teaching him Italian. The Company Commander had introduced himself as Captain Carlo Beneventi of 1st Company, Regiment Costello. He was a decent sort, and he informed Sid that he was shortly to be moved and that he would be interrogated once again. Beneventi told him that he was concerned that his superiors would have Sid shot as a spy if he refused to talk. He was at pains to point out that this was nothing to do with him, and was out of his control.

He was permitted to take exercise in a small walled courtyard which was overlooked by a series of tenement buildings. The guard provided some water. He decided that he should get himself cleaned up, as he was filthy from his ordeal in the hills. He stripped off and started to scrub some of the dirt away. When he looked up there were female faces in nearly all of the tenement windows. He had caused quite a stir and the guards quickly came and took him back inside. Sid never discovered if it was the women or their husbands who had complained.

The local priest visited from time to time, but Sid never trusted him and was careful what he said. During one of these visits, the priest told him that the allies had landed in Sicily. In fact the first landings had taken place the day after his capture on 10th July. This was the first good news that he had heard in over a week. If Sicily fell, his chances of liberation would be greatly improved. Perhaps this had been the reason for the raid on Sardinia, to prevent the Luftwaffe and the Regia Aeronautica from interfering with the landings. It all made sense now. Jellicoe

must have known of the invasion plans, which was why he had been forbidden from taking part in the raid.

The next day he was put on a bus for Bortigali, he was escorted by two Caribinieri who sat either side of him. The bus was full of civilians who were curious about him. The priest too had found his way onto the bus. One of the Caribinieri took it upon himself to tell the passengers all about the prisoner. Sid was able to understand some of the briefing. The policeman was clearly relating the story of how Tommo had died, and how the Englishman had buried him and marked the grave with a cross. This seemed to go down well with the deeply religious catholic peasant folk.

Several hours later the bus arrived in Bortigali and he was handed over to the army once again. This seemed like a much more professional operation. His interrogator this time was a colonel, who was very relaxed and confident. This was a little more daunting and he remembered Beneventi's warning. The Colonel spoke through an interpreter, and immediately put him off guard by referring to the submarine. Sid didn't fall into the trap of confirming his means of insertion and the Colonel laughed. He already knew a staggering amount of information about the operation, which he said Captain Thomson had told them. Sid didn't believe it, but he was alarmed to hear that Thomson too was in the bag. That only left Gill and Corporal Shackleton from 'Daffodil'.

The interrogation continued for a few more days. Sid kept as quiet as he could. He was confident that he hadn't given anything away, but remained curious at the level of information the Italians seemed to have. His malaria flared up from time to time and made life very unpleasant. During his last session with the Colonel he was told that Mr Duggan had been picked up too and that he was very ill. He guessed that Duggan too must have contracted malaria, and he wondered what had happened to Noriega and Feebury.

When the Italians had exhausted their supply of questions they decided to move their captive once again, this time to Sassari in the north west of the island. His new home was a large police station complete with cells. These were filthy, and infested with fleas and other insects. But once his cell door was locked and the guard had walked away, he heard hushed English voices. Sid quickly pushed his face to the small barred window in the door. Across the corridor he could see another identical, rusty cell door and in the window a familiar face. It was Corporal Gill from Captain Thomson's party. The two had a brief whispered conversation. He discovered that Gill shared a cell with Cpl Shackleton, the last member of Daffodil patrol. Gill went on to say that Sergeant Cass and Murray were in the next cell, and that Sergeant Scully and Wilson were in hospital.

It was not possible to have any lengthy conversations because the guards made frequent patrols of the corridor. He sat on the floor of his cell. He was pleased to see a familiar face, and felt better knowing that he was not alone. He was still uncertain about his future. Would the Italians really shoot them? Hitler had certainly issued an order stating that Commandos were to be shot, so it was quite possible. He wondered about the success of the mission. Clearly Daffodil patrol had all been captured, as had most of Bluebell, but the presence of Cass and Murray meant that Mr Cochrane's party too had been unsuccessful. The two men in hospital were from Captain Brinkworth's 'Jasmine patrol'. Gill had seen the four other members, including the American who had been attached. Sid guessed that the officers were being held somewhere else. and he hoped that the two remaining patrols had fared better.

During the following days he was questioned again. But this time his interrogators wore civilian clothes, and he imagined that they must be Fascist officials of some sort. They were rather pompous, and clearly saw themselves as 'Spy Catchers'. Sid was relieved that they really didn't know as much as they thought. He was informed that he was to be treated as a spy, and could be shot if he failed to cooperate. One of the men informed him that the American had given himself up, because he was fed up with being messed about by the English. He had told his captors everything. This was an alarming development, and Sid wondered if it could it be true?

When the Italians had finished with him, he was permitted to mix with the other captives and they each filled in the gaps. The American had been a damn nuisance from the start and had not got on with Captain Brinkworth. He had apparently gone missing and the remainder of the patrol had spent two hours looking for him, without success. The American had later claimed that he was captured on 7th July, but one of the other prisoners had seen a document which recorded his date of capture as the 3rd. This would explain the activity in the countryside and the reason why the three patrols had all been caught before carrying out their raids. It also meant that the Italians were aware of their presence even before Tommo had died. The captives were furious. But the American had already been moved on. Sid also learned that some of the prisoners had been mistreated. Captain Thomson had been held in chains and kicked by civilians when he was captured. Most of the party seemed to have been affected by malaria to one degree or another.

After a few days in the police station, Sid and the other prisoners saw their officers being brought in. By straining his head at the bars he was able to see Captains Verney, Imbert-Terry, Brinkworth and Lieutenant Duggan. He was pleased to see that they were all alive, but the presence of Verney and Imbert-Terry meant that all of the patrols had been captured. The little party only stayed for about an hour before being moved on, but Sergeant Cass was able to speak to them briefly. Duggan had been very ill but seemed to be coping and the others still appeared to be fit and determined. Cass was unable to discuss the mission with them, and it was assumed that none had reached their objectives.

The following day, Sergeant Scully joined the prisoners in their flea-infested cells. Scully had been desperately ill and had been confined to the local hospital. His condition had improved slightly and the Italians, fearing he might escape, decided he should be locked up again. It was obvious to the others that Scully was still very sick. They protested to the guards that he should be sent back to the hospital. The guards showed little interest and their requests to speak to someone more senior were ignored.

A couple of days later the prisoners were suddenly moved once again. They were all pleased to be leaving the filthy, infested cells behind, and made the most of the fresh air during the journey. Their new home was an old prison at Sassari. As they drove through the gates, Sid was struck by how depressing the stone walls looked. From the time they arrived they were treated exactly like convicts. Their guards seemed completely oblivious to the Prisoner of War status to which they were entitled.

The SAS men were initially crammed in six to a cell in a ridiculously small space. Their protests were eventually noted and three of the party were moved to a separate cell. Sid and the others explored their new accommodation. It was soon discovered that Captain Thomson and Mr Cochrane had scratched their names on the wall, indicating that they had been held there for ten days.

By now Sergeant Scully had developed severe dysentery. The poor man was desperately ill, and there were just two small pots in the cell to be used as a lavatory. Sid and Corporal Shackleton hounded the guards, in order to get some sort of medical attention for the sick NCO, but the only response from the guards was 'dopo' and 'domani'. No amount of badgering could even persuade them to allow Scully out of the cell to the toilet. Scully was by now bleeding, and suffering badly day and night.

They soon learned that there were more of their raiding party being held in the old Sardinian prison. Jacques, Kilby, Johnston and Schofield were all there too. When they first arrived Sid had noticed that there were four Americans being moved from their cells. They were supposed to be Commando types, but he doubted this as they all looked overweight and fleshy. He also learned that the American they had recently come to loathe, had been held in a cell with Jacques and Schofield. They had been allowed to mix with the four Americans and had freely walked into each other's cells. Sid thought this very strange, as the SBS men had been forbidden from speaking to each other and they had been kept separately. It was all very suspicious, particularly as the Americans had been moved as soon as the other British prisoners arrived. The captives discussed the matter endlessly. They hoped to have the opportunity to question their so-called interpreter.

The group were often required to work in the prison, chopping wood and similar jobs. Many of the guards were simple peasants and were quite affable. Sid often found himself discussing football with a young guard as he worked. England had defeated Italy 3-2, at Highbury in 1934. He took great pleasure in explaining how Eric Brook and Ted Drake had scored three goals in the first twelve minutes of the match. There were many hardships and shortages for the Italians at this time and the Englishmen told stories of the plentiful supplies in England. These stories were of course untrue, but the facts couldn't be allowed to get in the way of a good tale. Some of the young guards took it all in and could be seen to salivate when Sid told of the mountains of chocolate and vats of milk, which were overflowing England's green shores.

Not all of the guards were pleasant young country boys and one day Gill, a tough man and a holder of the Military Medal, found himself being badgered by an obnoxious Italian. Gill had had enough, he threw down the blunt axe and shouted at the guard to 'chop it your f****** self'. The Italian went crazy. This wasn't supposed to happen, prisoners did as they were told without question. He gestured wildly with his rifle and took two steps toward the prisoner. But something in the eyes of the Englishman told him he was too close already. The Guard summoned the 'Brigadier Chief', a pleasant middle aged man who was unable to share the concern of the younger guard. There was a brief exchange between the two, and Sid surmised that the guard had been told to shut up and get on with it. A tense situation was defused and the SAS men thought they had won a small victory.

The group were kept in the stinking conditions for a further five days. Scully was still denied medical attention and they did whatever they could to make him as comfortable as possible. On the fifth night they were suddenly frog marched from their cells and Sid wondered if this was it. Were they to be shot? Or were the Gestapo waiting for them. Each prisoner was eventually led into an office where he was met by an interpreter. He was told that they were all to be transferred back to the military headquarters the next day. From there they would be moved to a prison camp. To his surprise, Sid's personal possessions were returned to him, and he was marched back to his cell. The silk escape map was still hidden in the seam of his shirt, and the two small compasses were safely concealed.

At three o'clock the following morning, the prisoners were woken by a commotion. They were told to gather their things and were moved outside. Sergeant Scully was to remain behind and the interpreter assured them that the NCO was to be returned to hospital until he was well enough to travel. Sid said his goodbyes and Scully wished them all well. It was tough to leave their friend this way but they doubted if he would have survived a long journey.

The British soldiers were loaded onto a truck and were chained together in pairs to prevent any escape. Sid found himself shackled to Murray, whom he had not seen for a while, and the two chatted on the journey back to Bortigali. When the little truck arrived at their destination the troops were again unloaded and their shackles were removed. They were addressed by an Italian Colonel who told them that they were no longer suspected of being spies, and that they would be treated as Prisoners of War. Their pay books were to be returned, and they were to be moved to a Prisoner of War Camp.

They were guarded by large numbers of Caribinieri, and there were few chances of escape, particularly as many of the men were still very sick. Sid's malaria continued to flare up from time to time, but he was able to keep the illness under control. The party were moved on once again, this time to an old prison camp at Villagrande. Their new cells were every bit as grim as their old ones, but there were more familiar faces here. The rest of the raiders were already in the camp, Sergeant Scott, Corporals Richards and Hannah, Parachutists Mcmillan, Hand, Rogers, and Noriega, and Lance Corporal Brown. Even SSM Feebury was in the bag.

Before long the group were able to swap stories and Sid discovered that after Duggan, Noriega and Feebury had left him, they had reached their objective. The three had camouflaged themselves at the perimeter of the airfield and had planned to carry out the raid after dark. Unfortunately, at dusk the aircraft took off and did not return until dawn. This had continued for three nights and Mr Duggan had become very ill. Eventually all three had been captured, but not before laying their explosives on a railway line which was subsequently destroyed, causing a train to be derailed. Noriega was very weak having succumbed to malaria also. When the captives were allowed to exercise, SSM Feebury picked up Noriega and carried him outside, in order that the sick soldier would get some sunlight and fresh air.

Even though the operation had been plagued by bad luck, it had not been a total failure. After the problem with their submarine, 'Mistletoe' and 'Periwinkle' patrols had returned to North Africa. There they quickly hatched a plan to parachute into Sardinia, from a Halifax, on the evening of 8th July. The drop went well and the raiders reached their objective without difficulty. A daring raid resulted in three Junkers transport planes and one Messerschmitt fighter being destroyed. The party escaped from the airfield and evaded capture for several days. But, after a number of narrow escapes, Captain Imbert-Terry's and Captain Verney's patrols were also captured.

The SAS men were held in the primitive camp at Villagrande for a further two weeks. On the whole they were treated fairly well but the accommodation was filthy.

The food was barely adequate, however the prisoners understood that there were severe shortages on the island. They doubted if the civilians were eating very much more. Most of the men suffered with dysentery or malaria. Kilby, the group medical orderly, worked tirelessly to treat the prisoners in whatever way he could.

He prepared a medical report on each man. His reports detailed any illness or injuries suffered by the men, and were designed to be passed to a qualified medical officer when one became available. Kilby quickly learned enough Italian to be able to dispense with an interpreter. He gained the respect of the guards, who sometimes came to him with their own medical problems. He was regarded as something of a hero by his comrades, and Sid felt proud that they had such a man in their ranks.

Eventually the group was moved yet again, but this time they were on the move for over a week. At first they were marched toward the coast, passing through many small villages on the way, where they caused great excitement. Some of the villagers tossed them fruit which was gratefully received. Next they were put on a train which was painfully slow in its progress. During one of the many halts, the train was approached by several civilians some of whom passed apples through the windows. It didn't take long for the prisoners to spot a gorgeous blonde girl. They gestured for her to give them a cigarette. The blonde, who was clearly enjoying the attention, duly passed her cigarette packet to Sid, indicating that he should take one. Unfortunately the group had not received much charity of late. Sid took the packet, handed round the cigarettes, and returned the now empty packet to the girl. She was outraged that her goodwill had been abused in such a way and stomped off, leaving the Englishmen shouting their thanks.

The Caribinieri that had escorted the prisoners were decent types. Naturally they had become well known to the prisoners, who treated them as harmless boys. The SBS men laughed and joked with their captors and even playfully snatched their rifles and inspected the barrels. They were very aware that escape from the island was virtually impossible and they had decided to wait until a decent opportunity presented itself. The party stopped off at various locations secure enough to hold them, until they finally arrived on the island of La Maddelena, on the northern tip of Sardinia. It seemed sure that they were going to be transferred to the Italian mainland from this little island. Shortly after arriving they saw that their officers were also being held there, and some of the party managed to exchange a few words with them. Significantly, Captain Brinkworth pointed out that the American had been a traitor, and said that they should have nothing to do with him if he reappeared. Mr Duggan wanted to know what had happened to Tommo, so Sid wrote a brief report on a scrap of paper which was smuggled to the officer.

That night as the group settled down to sleep, there was a tremendous commotion. Guards ran around shouting, and vehicle engines roared into life as lights came on all over the compound. Some time later, they learned that some of their officers had escaped. The troops were delighted at the reaction of their Italian gaolers, who were clearly in a state of panic. The NCOs speculated about who may have escaped and what their plans might be. It was clear that there was very little chance of getting off the island. They couldn't have been gone very long before the guards had discovered their disappearance.

About three hours later Captain Verney and Captain Imbert-Terry were brought back to the compound. They had been discovered in the harbour, where they had stolen a small rowing boat. The Italians were initially fooled by the Englishmen, who passed themselves off as German naval officers when challenged. But they were soon identified and recaptured. Their plan had been to reach Corsica, where they thought they might get more help from the French population. The two men were manhandled and brought before an Italian officer who was red with rage. The Italian slapped Imbert-Terry's face hard and shouted at the two Englishmen. The NCOs were outraged at the mistreatment of their officers and they made a note to remember the Italian's name for future reference. The escape attempt had been courageous, but the chances of the two officers reaching Corsica alive were very slim. It was perhaps as well that they had been unsuccessful this time around. Unfortunately, the escapees were left totally at the mercy of the still angry Caribinieri, and they were left lying face down for the next twelve hours. They were frequently kicked, and hit with rifles. Other policemen amused themselves by pouring water over the helpless officers. Imbert-Terry was by now suffering with dysentery which made for an extremely unpleasant evening.

The following morning the whole group were frog-marched down to the docks, although their officers were kept well away from them. Security was much tighter and Sid surmised that the guards had all received some form of admonishment. They had been joined by two American airmen, who seemed pleasant enough, and were accepted into the group. The two were appalled at the stories of the treacherous interpreter, and vowed to spread the word among other American POWs. Waiting at the quayside was an Italian destroyer with smoke rising from the funnels. The group were marched directly toward the gangplank, so Sid assumed that this would be their transport to the mainland. He was proved correct.

Once aboard the warship, they were led below decks and locked inside various storerooms and other accommodation. It was quite hot below, and Sid wondered how long they would be locked away. He needn't have worried as the Italian sailors were a friendly lot, and the prisoners were frequently brought on deck The sea air was very refreshing, after the weeks they had spent confined in filthy cells, and they made the most of it. The destroyer was moving at full speed and the prisoners assumed that there must be a considerable threat from allied aircraft. The sailors were very keen to speak to the Englishmen, it seemed as though they had taken on almost celebrity status.

There was no chance of escape from the fast moving vessel, so the SAS men made the most of the situation. They gratefully accepted the iced water and even some wine that was served to them. The ship sailed on through the night, leaving the little island of La Maddelena behind them. Ironically, Mussolini himself would soon be a captive on the tiny islet, although no one could yet imagine this. They crossed the Tyrrhenian Sea and eventually docked at a small port about fifteen kilometres from Naples. Many of the ships crew shook hands, and wished the soldiers well as they were led down the gangplank.

Chapter 14

Italy

The Italian soldiers who waited on the quayside were less friendly, and much more suspicious of the allied prisoners. The little party was closely guarded and loaded onto a waiting truck, which conveyed them to the nearby railway station. Sid noticed that the area had been heavily bombed, and he presumed that the railway had been the intended target. Twisted tracks curved upwards and there were many destroyed buildings. A single railway track seemed to have survived the bombing and he assumed that this would lead them to the POW camp. Despite the bombing of their town, the local civilians were friendly toward the prisoners. He also noticed that a number of anti American posters had been defaced.

They soon boarded a train with their guards, who promptly pulled down the blinds when they saw the SAS men talking about the bomb damage. The next part of the train journey was fairly lengthy. It took them north to Rome, then east through the mountains, almost to the Adriatic coast. The wooden benches were by now very familiar, but still most uncomfortable. The officers were taken from the train at a place called Chieti. It was clear to the rest of the party that they were destined for different camps. Sid wondered if they would see their officers again.

About eighty kilometres further north, the remaining men were disembarked at Porto San Giorgio, where they spent the night. Those members of the group who were not sick were constantly looking for opportunities to escape. They felt sure that if the allies captured Sicily, they would soon be advancing up the Italian mainland, and would be within reach. Unfortunately, their guards seemed equally conscious of their intent, and they were continuously and closely watched.

The following day the party were transported to POW Camp 59 at Servigliano. As soon as they arrived, the prisoners became aware of a very different atmosphere in the camp. Until now they had been guarded by policemen, sailors and a mixed bag of generally disinterested Italian soldiers. Things here were very different. Their gaolers were harsher and more focussed on detail, a fact that was reinforced with a very thorough search. Lance Corporal Brown objected to being manhandled by the Italian soldiers, and told them so in no uncertain terms. The officer in charge barked some instructions and pointed at Brown. He was immediately taken away by two guards to the solitary confinement block. He remained there for a whole week. This was a harsh lesson quickly learned by the remainder. There would be discipline in this camp and they would have to be more cautious of the Italians.

Camp 59 housed several thousand allied POWs, including many Americans who had been captured during the first US actions in North Africa. The wooden huts which provided their accommodation were basic, but adequate. The prisoners kept the huts as clean as possible, but it soon became apparent that the old timber buildings were infested with mice. The tiny grey rodents were everywhere. They scampered under beds, behind walls, and in roof spaces. The new arrivals were split between several buildings, which housed a number of British and Commonwealth troops.

The British and American prisoners were kept in separate accommodation. Sid soon learned that there were different rules for the treatment of the two nationalities. The American prisoners were issued bed sheets, unlike their British allies who slept in just blankets. This was apparently in retaliation for the treatment of Italian POWs by the British. In America, prisoners were not required to work during the day, whereas in Great Britain they were. Needless to say the Italians reciprocated by forcing the British to carry out building work and repairs. Unfortunately for the fascists, they soon learned that the British were masters at looking busy, whilst actually achieving very little. The SAS men laughed, and said that this was a skill mastered by every British soldier soon after enlistment. Great care was taken to sabotage as much of the work as possible, and many a newly built wall was seen to collapse when leant upon by the guards. The Italian officers raged at the prisoners, their frustration made obvious by their red faces. They were doubtless made even angrier by the unconcerned reaction from their captives, and the many scarcely concealed smirks.

Within a few days Sid had become acquainted with a Coldstream Guards Sergeant by the name of Hird. Curiously, Hird was the only British soldier accommodated with the Americans. He had been captured in North Africa, on an operation with the Guards Patrol of the LRDG, and was incarcerated with a large group of Americans. When the prisoners were transported to Italy, Hird explained that he was a British serviceman and not an American, but the Italians had refused to acknowledge the fact. No doubt it would mean a large amount of paperwork for his captors, so Hird was informed that he was now American. There were certain advantages, not least of which was the issue of bed sheets.

Sid often visited Hird in the American lines where he was known as 'Slimy Limey'. He became accustomed to the very forward and loud manner of the 'Yanks'. To his amazement he was shown a 'War Map' which was painted on one of the walls within the Yank hut. The map was coloured, to show areas occupied by the Allies and by the Axis forces. It was incredibly detailed. During his visits he noted that the map changed constantly, to show the allied advances. He was very surprised that the Italians permitted the practice, until he noticed that the guards frequently came into the hut to study any changes to the war map. It seemed that the prisoners were better informed than the Italian guards. But Sid had no idea what the source of their information was and he assumed that someone must have access to a wireless.

The camp routine was incredibly mundane. There were frequent roll calls to check the numbers of prisoners, and the men were locked into their huts at night. The guards were meticulous during the roll calls. Some of the old hands said that the Italians were more conscientious than the Germans when it came to accounting. During the day there was very little to occupy the troops and various activities were organised. As always, Sid was keen to take part in any sport that was going and he volunteered to play in a cricket match. The Americans looked on disapprovingly as the Englishmen ran up and down between their improvised stumps.

When Sid's turn came to bat, he slugged a huge six. It soared through the air and crashed straight through the window of the Italian Headquarters building, where the ball came to rest in the commandant's office. The Americans were suddenly full of enthusiasm, and they cheered and laughed loudly. The infuriated Italian Adjutant emerged from the building, holding the cricket ball, and the guilty batsman watched as a sentry pointed towards him. The Italian nation was not famous for its love of cricket, and Sid wondered if he was to be sent to the slammer. The ball was eventually returned and there were no reprisals, but he breathed a great sigh of relief. The Americans were most impressed, and they frequently asked if he could do it again.

There was plenty of paranoia in the camp, some of the Americans were of Italian descent and they spoke the language fluently. The tale of the treacherous interpreter had spread through the huts and there was mistrust of any man who seemed too cosy with the guards. Anyone accused of being a 'stool pigeon' could expect rough justice, especially from the Americans.

As Sid expected, the food in the camp was very basic. A quantity of rice was issued regularly and this would be cooked by the prisoners themselves. There was no cutlery, so knives and forks were improvised from old tins, strips of metal and even button sticks. Three small bread rolls per man were issued per week, and these were considered as luxuries. Some of the men ate these immediately, but Sid decided he would save as much food as possible in case the opportunity to escape presented itself. Unfortunately he had not counted on the mice, who found their way into his rucksack to attack the bread. He tried various methods of discouraging the persistent rodents but no matter where he placed his food they reached it.

Occasionally Red Cross Parcels got through to the prisoners and these were issued one between every three men. The rather basic British versions were much smaller than the grander American and Canadian parcels, but they were none the less well received. The American version contained powdered milk, but the British one had tins of the more popular condensed milk. The Italians were keen to prevent food hoarding and they punctured all of the milk tins before issuing them. The captives soon learned to counter this tactic by stuffing the holes with paper and using the milk as an adhesive to reseal the tins.

A French Legionnaire in Sid's hut expressed his disgust at this English milk. Sid countered by asking 'where the bloody French Red Cross parcels were'. The two never hit it off. It was clear that the Frenchman was no fan of the English, a fact that Sid had difficulty understanding, since so many of his countrymen had been keen to board English ships at Dunkirk. He later heard a rumour that the Frenchman had been one of the thousands who had fought against the allies, in the early days of the North African campaign.

The guards carried out regular searches to prevent stockpiling. But it was soon discovered that by leaving a bar of soap from the Red Cross parcel on one's bed, these searches could be avoided. The parcels contained all sorts of other goodies, such as tins of 'bully beef', which were soon wolfed down by the captives. Most of the SAS men took a more considered approach and soon accumulated a cache of escape rations in their rucksacks.

The thought of escape was never far from the minds of the former SBS raiders and there were more than a few concealed compasses and maps in the camp. Many of the officers told the men that Italy would soon be liberated and that it was pointless to try and escape. None of Sid's pals shared this view and they discussed escape plans frequently. No one could have predicted the events that were to take place in mid September.

The Allied invasion of Sicily had been a bloody affair, but Patton and Montgomery had succeeded in pushing the Germans off the Island. The British Fifth Division was now pushing its way north on mainland Italy. On 9th September the Allies captured Salerno. The desperate fighting there had been preceded by the fall of Mussolini, and Italy's surrender, on 3rd September. The Germans moved quickly to disarm the Italians and to secure their defences. Despite these allied successes, the British and Americans were destined to face another two years of tough fighting in the Italian hills.

The prisoners knew only that the Italians were being driven back, so it was a great surprise when the Commandant of Campo 59 announced the news of Italy's capitulation. There was a great deal of confusion. The Commandant told them that the Germans would probably take over the camp. The men speculated about what the Nazis would do with them. Some thought there would be no change, others thought that they might be transported to Germany. Some even suggested that the Germans wouldn't bother to come, as they would be busy fighting the allied advance.

The senior officer in the camp, a British Captain, issued an order forbidding the men to try and escape. No doubt he feared that there would be a massacre if they tried to break out in a disorganised fashion. To the amazement of the prisoners their guards were reinstated, they couldn't understand it. The commandant had told them that they should leave before the Germans arrived. Why were the guards suddenly back in place? Everyone seemed confused, even the Italians. The SAS men got together to discuss the situation and they agreed unanimously that they would break out as soon as they could. Some of the group tried unsuccessfully to escape straight away and were soon returned to the compound.

On 14th September, a rumour circulated that the Germans had taken over a nearby camp, and that the Italians were going to set them free before the Germans arrived. That evening, SSM Feebury passed the word around the camp and the SAS men got together. It wasn't long before the whole group was knocking a large hole in the perimeter wall. Sid was joined by Sergeant Hird and a couple of his yank pals from the hut. In the darkness he could see other large groups of men attempting to escape. Each of the SAS men carried his own stockpiled escape rations and there were plenty of escape maps and compasses concealed in their clothing.

Once through the wall, the group proceeded to cut its way through the perimeter fence. They were in the open now and they hoped that the rumours of Italian nonchalance would prove to be founded. The answer was provided when a bullet cracked over their heads and thudded into the ground not far in front of them. It was followed by another and another. Each man in turn squeezed through the fence and sprinted for the undergrowth in front of them. Several more shots were fired and Sid became conscious that the guards seemed to be trying to scare them rather than to kill them. The camp loudspeaker suddenly barked into life and a flustered Italian voice instructed the guards to cease fire. It seemed as though the sentries were as usual, poorly informed about events and were simply obeying their existing orders.

Chapter 15

On the Run

The escapers were soon out of sight in the undergrowth, and Sid felt more secure. It was pretty clear that the Italians were not going to pursue them, so there was time to take in the scene. The lights of the camp perimeter were now distant. The sound of the loudspeaker had given way to the high pitched tone of the crickets. The smell of the olive groves filled his nostrils. To him, they smelled like freedom itself.

Although there was no sign of imminent pursuit, everyone understood the need to get as far away as possible by first light. Sooner or later the Germans would be scouring the hills for them. Those close to the camp were the most likely to be picked up. After two months in captivity, Sid had no desire to be back behind bars. Evading capture was not going to be easy, once the shooting had stopped. Scores of other men had decided to seize the opportunity to escape. In the darkness, he could see other groups all around and he was anxious to get away from them. He wasn't sure who was leading this group, but assumed that SSM Feebury was at the front. Most of the D Squadron men had escaped from the camp together, except those who were too sick. There were about thirteen of them in the party, including the yanks. Kilby, the medic, selfless as always, volunteered to remain behind with the sick men. This almost certainly meant that he would be transferred into German custody.

They had broken out at about 23.00 hours, and for several hours they pressed on into the darkness. Sid had no real idea where they were, but he thought they were heading roughly south east. For a long period they climbed up the rocky hillside until they reached a fairly remote area. There was no sign of life or civilisation in any direction, and the whole group halted among the rocks. They moved together into a large circle and the situation was discussed. It was generally agreed that it would be madness to continue as one group, so decided to break into smaller teams of three or four men. The SBS men broke up into groups they had worked with before. But Sid was obliged to remain with Sergeant Hird and the three yanks, because he had the escape map and a compass. Hird was clearly a good man, having come from the LRDG, but he was less confident about the Americans.

There was a great deal of discussion about what route to take from here. Some said that they would head for the coast, and that they would hitch a ride in a fishing boat to southern Italy. Others said that they would head south along the coastal plains by the most direct route, in order to make good time. Sid had thought about this for a long period of time. He had studied his escape map, and had already decided to take the most difficult route, over the Gran Sasso Mountain range. Gran Sasso itself was the loftiest peak in the Apenines. The mountain groups in that area towered up to 10,000 feet. This would take much longer than the more direct route along the coast, but he reasoned that fewer escapees would be on this course, and he was less likely to encounter large concentrations of Germans. Hird saw the logic in the plan and quickly agreed. In the absence of a better plan, the Americans too went along with the idea. They were no doubt conscious of the fact that both of the 'Limeys' had been used to operating behind enemy lines and seemed very competent.

By dawn, the large group had dispersed in different directions, and Sid found himself acting as unofficial group leader. He decided that they should press on, even in daylight. The surrounding countryside seemed sparsely occupied and he was still anxious to get as far away as possible. There was no sign of life in the hills apart from the occasional farmhouse. Some fields had been sewn with crops, and it seemed to be relatively safe to continue. The sun rose gradually higher in the sky, until around mid-day the little group were exhausted. It was decided that they should rest until the evening, when they would continue their march. None of the escapers had eaten since the previous afternoon, and Sid was feeling rather hungry. It was only now that it dawned on him that none of the others had brought any escape rations. He grudgingly allowed them to share some of his rations but couldn't help thinking what an idle bunch they were. He wondered if he would be better off on his own, but the memory of the long nights he had spent alone in the Sardinian hills was still fresh.

The following day they set off once again, constantly on the look out for Germans and where possible avoiding all habitation. Unfortunately, other groups of prisoners were using a similar route and the same tactics. Inevitably, many of these men met up in the hills and valleys. They swapped information on sightings of Germans. Sid was keen to avoid these groups as he felt that they would increase the chances of the Germans locating them. It had not occurred to him that many thousands of allied POWs had been turned loose by the Italians, and that most of them were heading south. The Germans had moved quickly and were sweeping the hillsides for the fugitives. Scores of men had been recaptured and put on trains for Germany. The process was to continue for months to come.

During the late afternoon he spotted another group of POWs on the other side of a river. He decided to cross over and see if these men had seen any Germans. But half way across he slipped on a rock and fell heavily on his knee. As he staggered to his feet wincing with pain he saw that he was bleeding badly. Once he reached the cover of the far bank he examined the wound, and found that it was much worse than he had at first thought. He applied a makeshift dressing and when Sergeant Hird had conferred with the other group he attempted to carry on. It quickly became apparent that they would have to lay up for a while, at least until he could arrest the bleeding.

Hird had proved himself to be a resourceful man and he quickly located a small mountain chapel which appeared to be deserted. The group occupied the tiny church where they spent the night. The next day, they were discovered there by an ageing Italian monk, who soon proved to be sympathetic and trustworthy. The monk brought them some small scraps of food and tended to Sid's injured knee. The old man poured alcohol directly into the open wound and Sid almost leapt through the ceiling. A clean dressing was applied and with rest the bleeding finally stopped. The monk told them that the Germans were all over the countryside. They had rounded up many allied escapers, but they had not yet shown any interest in the immediate area. The little group decided to stay put for a few days, in order to allow Sid to recover, and for the Germans to move on.

The little chapel was incredibly peaceful and there was a stream nearby, so life was tolerable. The monk was able to supply them with some bread, and occasionally a few potatoes, which were quickly devoured. The little group were grateful to the old man, as he was taking a great risk. The Germans would almost certainly have him shot if he was caught. It was clear that most of the hill people had no time for the fascists, but which of them to trust was another matter. As always Sid was impatient and anxious to move on, so after a few days rest, they thanked the monk and continued their march into the hills.

For several days his knee was stiff and painful, but eventually the pain started to subside. He changed the dressing whenever he could, and checked for signs of infection but fortunately there were none. Their march was long and arduous. It was often necessary to skirt round villages where they thought they might be betrayed, even though they felt drawn toward the little hamlets. The small supply of food that Sid had stored was soon used up between them. They foraged for fruit and vegetables whenever they could, but even these were in short supply.

One afternoon they found themselves looking at an isolated farmhouse in a steep sided valley. One of the Americans suggested that as it was a lone house it would be worth the risk to approach the occupants and to see if they could get some food from them. There were nods of approval from some of the others, but Sid disagreed. He felt that something was wrong about this house. The Americans told him that he was being over cautious. One of them volunteered to go to the house alone to see if anyone was at home. Sid had noticed that smoke was coming from the chimney of the little farmhouse. He said that he thought this was strange, as the occupants should be working in the fields at this time of day. They agreed to move a little closer before throwing caution to the wind. Fifteen minutes later, the four fugitives peered over a dry stone wall at the windows of the house, which was now only about a hundred yards away. The sound of a gramophone could clearly be heard coming from inside. This was strangely inviting.

The Americans had just about made up their minds to walk down to the house, when the door suddenly opened and a figure stepped outside. To their amazement they saw that it was a man dressed in field grey, with a rifle slung over his shoulder, he was wearing the characteristic coal scuttle helmet of the Wehrmacht. The door opened again and another figure appeared, shouting at the first man. There were other voices coming from inside. It soon became clear that the farmhouse was being used as a billet for German troops. They were probably quartered there whilst they hunted down the escaped POWs. The little band of escapers rapidly turned about and headed back into the hills, using the stone wall as cover. It had been a narrow escape and a valuable lesson to them all.

About a week later, the group once again ran into another large party of fellow escapers. This time they were Yugoslavs and there were almost fifty of them. Sid was amazed that they could even consider moving around in such a large group. The Yugoslavs said that there were Germans everywhere. It was difficult to find a safe route through, as all the bridges and check points were well guarded. When they found that there was an SAS man and a LRDG man in the group they were very impressed, and wanted to follow on with Sid in the lead. He was horrified. It was totally impractical and he attempted to dissuade the group leaders from this course of action.

Once they discovered that the intended route was over the Gran Sasso mountains they became less enthusiastic. To his relief they dropped the idea of following him. One of the Americans was of Yugoslav descent and he was able speak the language fluently. He was in conversation for a very long time. When he came back to the group he announced that he would be departing with the Yugoslavs. It seemed that they had managed to convince the American that Sid's route was madness and that he would be better with them. A second American decided to take his chances with the large group of Slavs, and the two parties went their separate ways, wishing each other well.

Sid was convinced that his route selection was correct and was not at all bothered at the loss of the two yanks. Hird was a good man and the remaining American was the best of the three in Sid's opinion. He was a country 'hic' from Iowa, but was reliable enough and easy going too. They had covered many miles since their escape from the camp, but it was difficult for Sid to fix their exact location. The map scale was very small and only the major navigational features were shown. Through necessity they had avoided villages and roads where possible, so much of the navigation was guess work. He worried that they were not making enough progress, food was in short supply and the winter was fast approaching. He was happy that their direction was correct, but they would need to move quicker.

The three set off once again and were forced by the terrain to follow the line of a road through the mountains. After many hours, they suddenly heard the sound of vehicle engines approaching. They quickly got off the road and into some small bushes. Sid strained to see through the foliage. He soon realised that the vehicles were German, worse still, they were loaded with heavily armed troops. To his horror, the vehicles stopped about a hundred yards short of their position, and he heard commands being shouted. The metallic clang of the tailboards confirmed that the German troops were dismounting. It was too late to run for it, they would be seen for sure and would most likely be shot before they got very far. They would have to sit tight and hope that the Germans didn't see them.

He watched as the soldiers formed up on either side of the road and started to march towards their hiding place. He estimated that there must be about a Platoon of them, probably infantry, and well armed too. It would only be a couple of minutes until they were right on top of the alarmingly thin bushes in which the ex-POWs were concealed. Sid glanced to his left and was horrified to see a pair of legs and British boots sticking out in the open. By stretching, he was able to kick Sergeant Hird's legs, which were quickly withdrawn into the bush, just as the lead German drew level. He could clearly hear the sound of their jackboots on the road, and pressed himself into the ground, praying that none of the soldiers would look into the bush. The first man passed by without even looking at their hiding place. There was an agonising five minutes as each enemy soldier walked past them. As the trio hugged the ground they could clearly hear German voices just a few feet away. His prayers were answered, and the enemy Platoon passed them by without further incident.

The following day they approached an old farmer at work in his fields. The man was friendly and only too pleased to help them. Sid felt uncomfortable asking this civilian for help but they were tired and very hungry. The old man made them welcome and shared the little food that he and his daughters had. The meal was based on pasta with virtually no meat, but the three eagerly wolfed it down, and were grateful for the kindness of the farmer. The Italians informed them that the Germans were all over the local area and that they had visited the farm only the day before. The farmer thought that they were unlikely to return for some time as they were clearly sweeping the area in a systematic fashion.

After spending a day at the farm, it was decided that they should stay and rest up, until they were sure that the Germans had moved on. The old man was very happy for them to stay, and his daughters giggled merrily at the thought of having three young men around. There were very few men in the villages, most were serving somewhere with the army, or had taken to the hills to avoid the Germans. Many were fearful that the Germans would shoot any young man they found on suspicion of being a Partisan.

For the next week the three escapers remained at the little farm. They slept in a hay loft and were fed by the farmer's daughters. In return they helped in whatever way they could, chopping wood or working in the fields, but always with one eye on the horizon for Germans. There was no sign of life in the surrounding countryside and they started to feel fairly secure, Sid noticed that the young girls seemed to have lost their initial coyness and were becoming very friendly. The old man didn't seem to mind. In fact he encouraged the girls to spend time with the foreigners. Sid also noticed that Sergeant Hird was becoming very friendly with one of the girls in particular, and he thought trouble was brewing.

At the end of the week he suggested that the group should think about moving on, winter was fast approaching, and the Germans should have left the area by now. Hird disagreed and felt that they should stay a little longer. Sid compromised and dropped the subject for a couple of days. When he once again suggested moving, the American agreed with him, and they looked to Hird for his opinion. To Sid's utter amazement the Coldstreamer announced that he would not be coming with them. He had fallen for one of the farm girls and had decided to remain at the farm indefinitely. Sid tried to talk sense into the older man. But Hird told them that he had more chance of staying out of captivity at the farm, than they would have wandering the hills, and trying to cross the German front line. The American too tried to persuade the NCO to leave with them, but to no avail. That afternoon, Sid and the Yank shook hands with Sergeant Hird and wished him well. There were hugs and kisses from the farmer and his daughters as the two set off once again across the fields and into the mountains.

The going was hard, and the two couldn't decide which was worse, climbing the steep hillside or sliding down the other side, only to be confronted with yet another formidable slope. That night the pals discussed Sergeant Hird, and pondered what he might be up to, now that they were miles away in the hills. They laughed and hoped that he would be safe at the farm.

Two days later they picked up another stray, this time it was a Londoner, from the Tank Regiment. He had escaped from a camp some distance from theirs and had also had his share of narrow escapes. He confirmed that all the bridges he had seen were heavily guarded by the Germans. All three were now tired and hungry. Once again, they decided that as the civilians they had encountered were friendly, they should risk entering a village.

That afternoon they walked into a tiny hamlet. They had watched the old buildings for some time before deciding that it was safe to enter. The villagers were friendly enough but were clearly frightened. The escapers had not encountered this level of fear, in the civilians they had met so far, and they wondered why they were so scared. Their questions were answered when an old man, who they took to be the village elder, returned with a young Englishman. He too was an escaped POW and had been there for several days. He told them that the Germans had moved into the village the previous day. They had discovered his hiding place and had dragged him out into the street. The Nazis had fired a burst from a sub machine gun around his feet. The man was still shaken, apparently the Germans were in a rush and decided that they couldn't take him with them. He had thought that he was about to be shot, but the Germans left the village. The soldier was told that the patrol would return and if he left the village, they would track him down and shoot him.

He was clearly terrified and took the threat seriously. Sid told the man that he should join them, and that they should immediately get as far away as possible. The soldier replied that he was going to stay put, rather than risk being shot. The other escapers told him that he was mad and that the Nazis would send him straight to Germany. They pleaded with him to change his mind, but the German threat had clearly terrified the man and he would not be persuaded.

Sid and his companions had no intention of hanging around to be recaptured, and they quickly set off once again into the hills. Later on at another village, they discovered the reason for the newly found fear amongst the Italian peasants. Mussolini had been rescued from captivity in a daring raid by German forces. The dictator had been held by Anti Fascists in an Apennine ski lodge, which as it turned out was not far from their current position. Otto Skorzeny's commandos had whisked him away to safety and he had started to broadcast on the wireless. He promised the return of his fascist government, and the hill folk were terrified at the prospect. Anyone found guilty of aiding an escaped allied prisoner could expect severe punishment. The Germans and their fascist allies had carried out many summary executions in the mountain villages. There were still plenty of civilians who were willing to assist them, in spite of the dictator's broadcasts. The same people offered them food, when they were hungry themselves, and many allied soldiers benefited from courage and generosity of the hill folk.

Groups of escaped prisoners and individual escapees were everywhere. It was impossible to avoid them, and they sometimes joined together for the night. The parties often changed, as men decided that their chances would be improved by swapping groups. The American in Sid's party decided to leave them. He was replaced by a young South African, and was later joined by a Canadian Flying Officer.

Sid was sorry to see the Yank go. He liked him, and they had spent a long time together. The Yank had proved useful, as his boots were much sought after by the hill farmers. On one occasion they had arranged a swap with a local civilian, a bag of potatoes for the American's boots. The potatoes were a godsend, but the Italian never got his boots, as the group made tracks before he realised that he had been conned. Sid privately thought that the real reason for the Yank's departure was that he didn't get on with the Londoner, but there was nothing he could do.

The Germans were now being sighted more often and in greater numbers. He felt sure that they were getting closer to the front line and wondered how they would manage to reach the allied lines without being shot by either side. Although the civilians were scared, the fugitives had come to realise that most of them would help if they could, provided that there were no fascists in the villages. They scrounged sandwiches, fruit and whatever else was on offer. On one occasion they rested in a village with a New Zealander they had run into. He had been a sheep farmer before the war, and he wasted no time in stealing a sheep and slaughtering it. They had a wonderful feast, but had to hide the evidence, as the shepherd soon missed the sheep and was suspicious of the allied soldiers.

They often asked the peasants if they had seen any Germans and this local intelligence proved to be very valuable. When a woodcutter was spotted alone beside his little hut, the three soldiers struck up a conversation with him. They were invited inside the tiny building for a drink with the Italian. He apparently didn't want them to be spotted outside. The three men managed to communicate well with the woodcutter, who told them that there were lots of Nazis about. As they chatted, the civilian suddenly stood bolt upright, the look on his face immediately told them that all was not well.

'Tedeschi!' he said. Sid leaned round the door frame to see a burly German soldier slowly walking up the hill towards the little hut.

There was only one door and this faced directly towards the German. There was no way they could leave the building without being seen. There was only one room and hardly any furniture. The only possible hiding place was under the single bed in the corner. The woodcutter gestured for them to hide and all three of the fugitives somehow squeezed themselves under the tiny bed. Sid couldn't help thinking how ridiculous the scene must look. He felt that they were bound to be seen immediately. The German reached the doorway and the three men clearly heard his boots on the wooden floor. From his exposed position, Sid could see the lower half of the enemy soldier. He had a Schmeisser sub machine gun tucked under his arm and his steel helmet hung from his belt. From their hiding place they clearly heard every word of the conversation between the woodcutter and the soldier. It sounded fairly pleasant as the German attempted to communicate in the Italian's native tongue.

The civilian had positioned himself at the doorway directly in front of the bed in order to limit the German's view. The two chatted for what seemed like an age, before the soldier cheerfully said goodbye, and walked back down the hillside. Sid had no idea if the man had been alone or part of a patrol, but he couldn't believe that they hadn't been spotted. They were greatly in debt to the woodcutter. He had risked everything for them, without even being asked. Much later they left the little hut, having heartily thanked their Italian saviour.

The little party got on well and Sid became fond of the young Londoner. He was a cheerful type. The two laughed as the tank man related the story of the Englishmen and the South African hiding under a woodcutter's bed. That night, for the first time, they heard the sound of artillery fire. They realised that they were very close to the front. From their daytime hiding places, they were able to watch German armoured vehicles and tanks, moving to and from the sound of the guns. Both men wondered how they would be able to avoid them. The weather had become much colder now and it frequently rained. They were poorly equipped to be high in the hills in the winter. They used whatever cover they could to shelter from the wind and the rain but they were often soaked to the skin. The mountain tops were covered in thick snow and they wondered how long it would be until all the hills were turned white.

They moved only at night now and were much more cautious. The thought of being recaptured when they were so close to the allied lines was unbearable. There may have been less chance of being seen in the darkness, but it was murder trying to find their way down the rocky slopes. In this part of the country, the roads clung to the sides of the steep rocky hills. The only way to proceed was to clamber down the slopes, before crossing the roads, and continuing the descent into the valley bottom. It proved almost impossible to climb down slowly. The loose rocks and gravel usually carried them down at an ever-increasing speed, until they were flailing like madmen, and struggling to stay upright.

That night, Sid led as they clambered down a hill. Predictably, the momentum took him, and as usual he was sliding earthward at a very rapid rate. He struggled to see the road as it approached. He knew it was there somewhere, but it was too dark. Suddenly he was on the road, and attempting to keep his balance as he tumbled forward. He hit something hard and was knocked completely off his feet. He was winded, but as he hit the tarmac he realised he had hit another human being who had also been knocked off his feet. The sound of a rifle striking the road, and the clatter of a steel helmet on the tarmac told him it was a German. Sid's companions who had tumbled onto the road just behind him shouted, 'Jerry! leg it!'

The Londoner was already sprinting down the road as fast as he could, followed by the South African. Sid was up and running as fast as his ragged desert boots would allow. He ditched his little rucksack as he heard a shout from behind, 'Halt!' There was no chance whatsoever of any of the fugitives halting. It was very dark, and Sid hoped that the German would not be able to hit a moving target. The Londoner and the South African suddenly disappeared off the road, and Sid followed. They once again tumbled down the hillside, quicker this time. The trio fell repeatedly, cutting their knees on the sharp stones. The expected gunshot never came, and they were able to disappear into the countryside.

Just before first light they located a small barn and concealed themselves inside. The trio discussed their narrow escape and wondered why the German had not shot at them. They concluded that the poor man must have been completely stunned when he was struck by Sid's tumbling frame. Tired as they were, they couldn't help giggling at the thought of the German who must have thought he was being attacked. They wondered if the man had needed to change his trousers when he reached his billet. Sid complained that he had lost his rucksack containing his old cardigan, and the cribbage set that he had carved at camp 59. The others told him he was lucky he hadn't lost his head. They laughed until they cried, but were brought back to reality by the sound of artillery fire once again. There were a lot more Jerries between them and safety. The tired pals soon dropped off to sleep. When they woke it was dark once again.

That night they moved along a valley bottom, crossing and re-crossing the same river several times. It was impossible to use the bridges because of the level of enemy activity. The moon was behind cloud and it was exceptionally dark. Voices were suddenly heard and the three men froze. They were definitely German. An engine had started up, there were more voices, and the trio realised that they were in the middle of some sort of German concentration. There were silhouettes of large vehicles now visible, and the smell of cigarette smoke hung in the air. It was a still night and noise was carrying a good distance. But the Germans were close, probably no more than a hundred metres.

After sitting tight for what seemed an eternity, they decided to press on slowly. The river was crossed again. There seemed to be no end to the German activity around them. Sid trod carefully but expected to be challenged by a sentry at any moment. The challenge never came, and after several hours of picking their way through the enemy formation, the noises ceased, and there were no more silhouettes to be seen. First light was only an hour or so away, so the fugitives made there way up the hillside until they found a secure hiding place in which to spend the following day.

When daylight came, they found that they were overlooking a small hamlet and they watched as German troops passed through the village for most of the day. The Germans all seemed to be heading away from the front. Several truck loads of troops stopped in the village, to loot whatever they could lay there hands on. The civilian population seemed to be missing and Sid assumed that they had been evacuated. As they watched the Germans load their booty onto the trucks, there was a sudden rush of air and a high pitched whine, as an allied shell dropped just short of the village. The loud crump and plume of black smoke was enough to encourage the Germans to exit the village. They drove off with great haste, as more shells landed. The bombardment continued for some time and at one point the explosions fell close to their own hiding place. The pals huddled in the rocks for protection until the shelling stopped.

When the noise from the artillery had subsided, and the valley returned to its normal tranquil state, movement could be heard behind them. At first Sid thought that the sounds were probably made by an animal, but as he listened, he realised that the noises were made by a human being walking over the rocks. He cautiously peered over the top of the boulders that formed his hiding place, praying that he would not see a German patrol. About fifty yards away, to his relief, he saw an old man. The three soldiers guessed that he was a shepherd and they debated whether it was safe to approach him. Sid thought that the old man may be able to tell them how far away the allied troops were. He had also become increasingly concerned about the presence of German minefields. He felt sure that the Germans would have laid mines across the path of any likely allied advance.

The civilian was startled when the three bedraggled young men rose up from their hiding place, but they were able to calm him fairly quickly. Once the old man had recovered, and he realised that they were escaped POWs, he became quite friendly. He spoke virtually no English, but Sid's Italian was good enough to decipher the shepherd's ramblings. He told them that the Germans were rapidly withdrawing in this area, and that he knew of no big German positions in front of them. Furthermore, there were no minefields to his knowledge, and the best news of all, he had been told that Canadian soldiers were only a few miles away. This news was fantastic, but they had to be cautious. The shepherd could be mistaken, or the Germans could be planning a counter attack. There were still many things that could go wrong.

The old man wished them luck and they all shook hands before parting. The three pals were excited and tempted to set off in a southerly direction immediately. But they managed to restrain themselves until it got dark. Sid's biggest concern now, was how to cross the allied front line without being shot. He was fairly sure that most of the enemy were now behind them. But it would be no easy task to convince the front line troops that they were on their side, before they opened fire.

After several hours of cautious marching, they encountered a very open flat plain. They were concerned that this would be an ideal place to lay a minefield. But they decided to push on, albeit carefully. At first they moved very slowly, stopping to check the ground ahead for any sign of disturbance. However, their confidence grew when no deadly mines were spotted. An hour later they were across the plain and once again into a rocky valley. Sid estimated that they had travelled at least five miles. If the shepherd was correct the Allies must be close. They advanced more cautiously now, it was a light night, and they didn't want to be mistaken for Germans.

As they picked their way through the rocks, an object on the hillside suddenly caught Sid's attention. It was familiar to him, and out of place amongst the rocks, although it took a few seconds for him to recognise it. There at the side of a rock, a few metres above them, was a Bren gun magazine! There was no mistake, its curved shape was obvious, and it was reflecting the moonlight. Sid grabbed his companions' arms and they halted. This was a dangerous moment. The Bren gun indicated that this was most likely a sentry position. They were probably being watched right now. If the sentry thought they were Germans he would open fire. They had to identify themselves and quickly. Sid called out, 'Is that the Canadians up there'? No reply. 'We're escaped POW's, British'. No reply. 'Are you Canadians? We're British POW's'.

There was a rustle from the rocks above and voice called softly, 'C'mon up'.

The escapers raised their hands to show that they were unarmed, and clambered up the hillside. They expected to be told to stop, so that the sentry could get a better look at them, but he called them straight into his position. They were expecting a grilling, but the sentry seemed completely satisfied about their identity. A second man led them back into the Canadian position, to an NCO, who was sleeping in a small scrape under a large tree. Sid imagined that this must be the Platoon Sergeant. He thought that the man would now take their details and confirm their identities. A tired and disinterested face appeared from under a blanket. He briefly welcomed them back to their own side, then instructed the young Canadian soldier to take them back to his Company HQ. There was little or no movement to be seen during the short journey back. The next group of Canadians were equally disinterested, in turn sending them further back to the Battalion HQ.

The pals became aware that these troops were all exhausted. They must have seen some tough fighting in recent weeks, so it was hardly surprising that they were not really interested in a couple of stray Englishmen. Sid didn't care, they had made it. He was elated. The weeks of hard slog up and down the mountainsides had been worth it.

Eventually they were guided to the Canadian Battalion HQ. Their guide left them, shaking hands and wishing them well. The HQ was made up of a collection of camouflage nets under which a small group of vehicles and tents were arranged. The ex-POWs were ushered into a tent. A small lantern burned and they could see various maps laid out on a table. They were approached by a tall man who was wearing khaki battledress and the rank of Lieutenant Colonel. This must be the Commanding Officer. Sid stood rigidly to attention, saluted and reported, 'Corporal Dowland 1st SAS Regiment, parent Regiment Grenadier Guards, Sir'. His startled companions were obliged to follow suit, stating their details to the Canadian Colonel. The Officer greeted them warmly, congratulating them on their escape and shaking their hands. He enquired about the route they had taken and was particularly interested in the location of the local enemy troop concentration that the three had stumbled through. After about fifteen minutes they were handed over to an NCO who issued them with some blankets, a steaming mug of tea and a place to sleep. Sid curled up under the blankets and fell into a happy, satisfied, and very deep sleep.

He was woken several hours later by a deafening crash. For a moment he was startled and disorientated until he remembered where they were. Even then he wondered if he had dreamt of reaching safety. There was another crash and he realised that this was German artillery. It was close, but fortunately not falling on his own position. The Canadian NCO reassured them that this was quite normal. If the Germans knew their location, the 88mm shells would be falling on them already. Sid, awake now, replied by telling the Canadian that they had been shelled twice in 24 hours, once by the allies and now by the Germans, the Canadian chuckled.

It was almost daylight now. The new arrivals were led down to a small field kitchen where a group of tough looking soldiers in steel helmets queued for their breakfast. Mess tins were handed out to the Englishmen and they joined the queue. Sid was aware that the Canadians were looking them up and down incredulously. He became aware of their appearance for the first time. None of them had shaved for quite some time. Their clothes were little more than dirty rags which hung from their skinny frames. A stocky man standing in front of them glanced down at Sid's feet and said, 'Hey Bud, if them boots were mine, I'd have them framed'.

Sid looked down and surveyed his sorry looking desert boots. The soles were hanging from the boots and remained in touch with the uppers only by means of some rusty wire which he had wound around the two rapidly separating parts. One of the heels had completely gone and his sock was visible through a hole at the front of the right boot. They were only designed for about eighty kilometres of marching and he had come much further than that. The state of his footwear did not detract from the pleasure of his first meal back in allied territory. The three pals savoured every bite. Later the Canadians produced a map and Sid traced his route. The POW camp had been roughly on a line with Ancona, half way up the Italian coast and they had crossed over the lines not far from Foggia. He estimated that they had covered several hundred miles in the preceding weeks. He had selected by far the toughest route, but it had paid off.

The trio soon left the sound of artillery fire behind them, as they were loaded onto a three-ton truck which was headed toward the rear. They peered out of the canvass at the back of the lorry and were able to see columns of allied troops marching on either side of the road. American made jeeps were heading up and down the muddy tracks carrying all sorts of stores. Many of the vehicles heading towards the rear were laden with stretcher cases and heavily bandaged casualties. It was raining heavily now and the roads had turned to thick mud. Sid was glad that they would not be spending any more nights in the mountains. He wondered where the others were, had they all made it back or were they still in the hills. The site of the heavily laden infantry at the sides of the track reminded him of the 6th Battalion and he wondered where they were now. He didn't yet know that the 3rd and 6th Battalions of his regiment were both fighting in Italy.

Chapter 16

Freedom

They were transferred from one means of transport to another and eventually were put on an American train. The carriages were full of ex-POWs of many nationalities and the troops swapped stories of capture, near miss and escape. Some of the men had been recaptured by the Germans and had escaped from the trains they were put on. There were even some men who claimed to have escaped three times. They had all been surviving on very little food for weeks, if not months. The boxes of rations that were placed in the carriages were soon shared out and devoured. Whenever the train stopped the troops all piled out to make a 'brew'. It was a luxury that had been missed in captivity and the hot mugs of tea were generously passed around. As the old train puffed through the Italian countryside, the detritus of war was only too obvious. There were knocked out tanks and ruined houses all over the place. Parts of the railway track had been destroyed and replaced. There were burned out rail trucks in places, bearing testament to the ferocity of the allied air attacks.

The POWs were eventually disembarked at the southern port of Taranto where they were herded to a temporary camp. On the way, they passed columns of Italian prisoners and laughed at how the tables had turned. Some of the group couldn't help themselves and shouted insults at the Italians, accompanied by appropriate hand gestures. The next few days were filled by military administration, forms were filled in by the score and there were interviews and medical inspections. The Quartermaster was not generous when approached for new items of clothing. But Sid did manage to get a new pair of boots, even the QM saw that there were no more miles left in them.

All the troops were anxious to know what was to become of them, some wanted to return to their units, but most wanted to get back to England. Sid thought that he would be returning to the SAS. After all they had spent a great deal of time training him, and he felt sure that he would get back to them soon. His hopes were further raised when he bumped into another SAS man that he had known briefly in Kabrit. The soldier looked fit and well, and was dressed in what appeared to be a new uniform. Sid asked 'where he had got the gear from', and the man explained that 2nd SAS were based down the road, not far from Bari. He had scrounged the uniform from them. Sid then asked why he had not stayed at the SAS camp. The man replied that initially he had done exactly that. But he had been discovered by the authorities who threatened to post him as a deserter, unless he returned to Taranto. He went on to explain that it was compulsory for POWs to return to the UK. Sid further discovered that the casualties in the Guards regiments had been very high. All Guardsmen were being sent back to England so that they could be reassigned.

He bumped into a few familiar faces from camp 59 and discovered that he was the third man to reach the allied lines. The first had also been an SAS man, who had hitched a lift along the coast on a fishing boat. The camp monotony was broken when Sid was called to the administration office. He was met there by an officer wearing the SAS badge and parachute wings, who explained that he was to be taken to the camp of 2nd SAS for debriefing. The officer ushered him into a jeep and the two chatted all the way to Bari. The lieutenant was interested in the details of the raid and what had gone wrong. He also wanted to know how the Italians had treated them. Before leaving, Sid was warned that he was to return to the holding camp the following day, or he would be posted as a deserter. It was great to be back with men from the SAS. They knew how dangerous the mission on Sardinia had been. He was able to relate to them much better than the mixed bag of men that he currently shared his accommodation with.

At Bari he wrote a detailed report about the raid and his escape. He mentioned the treacherous American soldier, the deaths of Tommo and the other SAS men, and how Kilby had selflessly remained behind to look after the sick. The report was typed by a Coldstreamer, who said that it was an amazing story, like something out of a novel. Sid assured him that it was all true. He had not seen any of his fellow raiders but he felt sure that if they were not safely 'home' yet, they soon would be. He asked the SAS officer if he could rejoin 1st SAS or be attached to 2nd. But the officer replied that there was nothing he could do, as all POWs were being repatriated. The issue was further complicated because Sid still suffered with malaria, which had not been properly treated when he was a prisoner. To his utter disgust he was soon sent back to Taranto.

The ranks of the freed prisoners continued to swell, as more men were liberated or escapers got through. Eventually, they were put on a ship which sailed to Bizerte on the coast of Tunisia. Bizerte had been the last axis stronghold in Tunisia, and had been liberated by the American 1st Infantry Division. As the ship docked in the old French Naval port, the troops were able to see ancient Byzantine buildings mixed with more modern structures. There was rubble in the streets, and bomb damaged buildings could be seen in large numbers.

Once they had disembarked from the ship, Sid and the other passengers were loaded onto transport, and taken to a huge staging camp on the outskirts of the town. There were thousands of troops, and hundreds of vehicles, all trying to negotiate the narrow streets. It was a very slow journey. The transit camp was far from luxurious. There were hundreds of bell tents, erected in rows to accommodate the many troops who, for one reason or another, were passing through the port. No one was supposed to be there for long, so the facilities were basic. However, there was a NAAFI nearby where they could get a mug of tea and a 'wad', to kill time.

He endured the monotony of the staging camp for a week, before a troopship bound for England eventually arrived. There were lots of ex-POWs aboard, each with a similar story to his own. Many wounded troops were being sent home for medical attention. The voyage back to England was much shorter than his outward journey. The allies now controlled most of the Mediterranean, and although there was still an air threat, and the possibility of a stray U-boat, it was not necessary to take the long trip around the Cape and across the Atlantic. The voyage was uneventful and it seemed to the passengers to take forever for the shores of England to come into view. They had learned that they were to dock at Liverpool and those who could, lined the decks for a glimpse of England. It was wet and foggy, but this was home. They were all very glad to be back. It was late December 1943.

When the process of disembarkation began, Sid made his way onto the quayside. He was suddenly accosted by two familiar faces. Johnston and Schofield had been members of 'Hyacinth' patrol on the Sardinian raid. They too had escaped from camp 59 and were being repatriated together, as they had originally both come from the Royal Signals. They shook hands warmly, and exchanged stories about their adventures. They were all keen to learn the fate of the other SAS personalities who had escaped with them. The two signallers had been on the run with Sergeant Cass, and Sid was desperate to hear how their fellow Grenadier was. He was devastated to learn that George Cass had been shot dead by an Italian fascist. The Signallers filled in the details. Apparently the group had been apprehended by the Italian, who held them at gun-point. George, daring as ever, had thrown his coat at the fascist and had attempted to overpower the man. But he had been shot in the process. The remainder of the group had managed to escape, but they owed their freedom to George. Sid remembered his friend's face and his defiant attitude. Cass was always the one to confront the prison guards, or to take the mickey out of them, often to his own detriment. But this time he had paid the ultimate price.

He later learned the fate of some of the others. Sergeant Scully had apparently turned up in Tripoli, although no one knew how he came to get there. SSM Feebury had made it back, but had left Hannah with Shackleton, in Moschia. Hannah was desperately ill with pneumonia and could not have continued. Noriega had also been sick in camp 59. He had never really recovered from his sickness on Sardinia. No one had heard from him since. There had been rumours of an SAS medic treating sick soldiers on the run in the hills. It could only have been Kilby. The three pals hoped that their heroic friend had made it to safety behind them. Captains Verney and Imbert-Terry had, unsurprisingly, also avoided the Germans to reach freedom.

Having reported to the authorities in Liverpool, as instructed, Sid was duly processed and sent on leave for six weeks. He drew his rail warrant and ration book before heading off to the railway station. It was great to be back home, but things were different now. It seemed that there were Americans everywhere, and people seemed to be very used to the war. When he had left England a year earlier, the threat of imminent invasion was only just receding. Now there was a more optimistic mood in the air. North Africa was in allied hands and Italy would surely soon follow. As the train steamed ever southward, his thoughts were full of the events of the preceding twelve months, places, names and above all faces. He wondered where they all were, Dougie Wright, Kosbab and the others. He thought of the friends that he had left behind, especially poor Tommo, and the many pals from the 6th Battalion. Had they survived that fateful first battle? What he couldn't know was that the Sixth had been the first Grenadier Battalion to land in Italy. They had been fighting hard ever since. In November 1943, as Sid was crossing over the lines, his old Battalion were coming down from the heights around Monte Camino. They were able to muster only 263 men for duty and the Battalion was never again sent into action.

Poole was much as he remembered from his last visit home. There were still plenty of sandbags about, and the blackout was still in force. As he turned into the street he had grown up in, he noticed that there were changes. One of the houses quite close to his own had been bombed. Only the ruins of the house remained. There were neat piles of bricks, indicating that the explosion that had wrought so much devastation had not been recent. He subsequently learned that the whole family had died in the house. As he stood in front of his mother's house, he tried not to think about how close the German bomb had been to his own family.

He knocked on the front door, and after a short delay his mother's face peered around the gap. She looked confused for a few seconds, then recognition suddenly spread over her features. The door was wrenched open and she flung her arms around her son. She was quickly joined by his sister, who was still living at home. There were squeals of delight. When the initial commotion subsided he was dragged into the house where he was greeted by George. It was great to be home, but it took some time for his mother to recover from the shock. It had been over a year since she had last seen him. The War Office had informed the family that he was listed as missing. There was a suspicion that he was a prisoner, but this had never been confirmed. His mother didn't even know for sure that he was alive, until she opened her front door that December evening.

He had six weeks to catch up on the family events of the last year. He was saddened to hear that his brother was a prisoner of war of the Japanese. Walter had been captured when Singapore fell in February 1942. Confirmation of his fate had come much later. Sid was able to appreciate what his brother might be going through, but he decided not to share this information with the rest of the family.

All repatriated POWs were sent on leave with double rations, in order to build them up before returning them to duty. His mother was delighted to hear that there would be some extra food on the table. Rationing was still strictly enforced and many items were in short supply. Each adult was allocated only one and a quarter pounds of meat, and one egg, a week. Sugar, cheese and butter were also still in short supply. It was great to sleep in a proper bed, to be close to his loved ones, and be able to relax properly, for the first time in ages.

Getting to know his family again was very enjoyable. He visited all his local relatives who were delighted to see him home safe and sound. Inevitably there were local pubs to be visited, where plenty of old acquaintances were renewed. He expected to see plenty of men in uniform, but the number of gum-chewing Americans in his home town surprised him. They seemed to be absolutely everywhere. People were generally surprised to see him back. When they learned that he was a repatriated prisoner they assumed that he had been sick and had been returned through the Red Cross. They often enquired, 'Sick were you?' 'No, I bloody-well escaped!' he would reply through gritted teeth.

He was proud of his considerable achievement and resented anyone who might suggest, even inadvertently, that he had somehow got home via an easier route.

He was also a little irritated that no one had heard of the SAS. After a while he dropped all reference to his new regiment. Christmas at home was a great occasion, as were the New Year celebrations. 1944 arrived with great optimism and everyone prayed that this year would see the defeat of Hitler's forces.

In early February he once again said goodbye to his family. He boarded a train, this time bound for an obscure army camp in Croydon. He had been instructed to report there in order that he could be correctly administered. He wasn't entirely sure what that meant. But he still harboured the hope that he would eventually return to the SAS. The 'Second Front' was surely coming soon and there was bound to be a role for the SAS. The camp was fairly relaxed, at least by the standards of the Guards, and Sid found life there rather uninteresting. He was subjected to a series of very thorough medical examinations. The doctors repeatedly asked about his malaria and seemed content when he told them that he had not had any recurrences since Italy. He was kitted out with new battle-dress uniform and other essential items.

He thought that things were returning to normal, until he attended an interview with a young bespectacled Captain. The rather serious young officer filled out some official forms, then launched into a series of rather odd questions. He placed a pair of pliers on the desk and asked, 'What are these?' 'Err, pliers Sir'. 'And how do you use them?' Sid hesitatingly replied with the rather obvious answer. He was then shown a diagram of a piece of machinery and was asked to indicate which way the various cogs turned. He managed this to the satisfaction of the officer and thought that he was now probably being certified as 'sane'.

The officer then asked what his original Regiment had been. When the Grenadier Guards were mentioned he looked up, and put down his pen. 'There is no point in going any further. All Guardsmen are to return to their Regiments, it's a War Office order'. There was no point in trying to appeal. The officer went on to say that casualties in North Africa and Italy had been heavy in the Guards Regiments. All available men were required at Regimental duty. Within a couple of days Sid was on a train to Windsor, back to the Training Battalion he had left in 1941.

Chapter 17

Windsor

The railway station at Windsor was all too familiar to him as he stepped down from the train. There were plenty of other men alighting in Windsor. Most of them seemed to be Grenadiers, although there were also Americans and Canadians. He walked the route to Victoria Barracks that he had taken many times before, and was soon standing at the guard room presenting himself to a young Lance Sergeant. The guard commander eyed his unfamiliar SAS cap badge and parachute wings suspiciously, but didn't ask what they represented. Sid was relieved. He had grown tired of explaining the role of his adopted regiment. The sound of foot drill could be heard from within the barracks, and the high pitched screams of the Squad Instructors reminded him of the Guards Depot. He wasn't looking forward to soldiering in England.

As always he was sent for the Commanding Officer's Memoranda and he 'fell in' when the bugle sounded at the Orderly Room. It was here that he discovered 'Snapper' Robinson was still the Sergeant Major. There were other familiar faces that didn't look like they had been far from Windsor since 1941. Sid joined the long file of men who were to be seen by the Commanding Officer. There were several in close arrest, complete with their escorts standing in front and behind them.

He was approached by a Warrant Officer, who looked at Sid's parachute wings on his battledress, and SAS badge in his beret. 'Are you joining the Battalion?' Sid sprang to attention and confirmed that he was indeed rejoining. 'Well, you can get rid of that badge and replace it with a Grenade. Understand?' He gave the only reply that was appropriate in the circumstances, 'Sir.'

Next, a young officer who had been loitering nearby approached him, and he once again sprang to attention. 'And what is that cap badge?' He asked. 'Special Air Service, Sir'. The officer looked confused and then asked what he was doing back in Windsor. Sid replied that he was an ex-POW and had escaped from occupied Italy. The young Subaltern looked impressed. 'Where were you captured?' 'Sardinia, Sir'.

'What on earth were you doing there?' 'Sabotage, Sir.'

There was a distinct reaction in the queue of waiting men, as heads turned to discover the identity of the 'Saboteur'. The inquisitive young officer was called away, and the interrogation ended. But the obnoxious Warrant Officer had witnessed the whole conversation, and now looked rather sheepish. Sid noted that the man didn't bother him again. His appearance in front of the Commanding Officer was very brief. He was once again required to answer a series of questions about his activities, over the last year or so, before being marched out.

Within a week the Sergeant Major had discovered that Corporal Dowland had never attended a drill course. This situation simply would not do. All Grenadier Non Commissioned Officers had to follow this path before being promoted. Sid was immediately told that he was to attend a course the following week. His morale suffered a further blow when he received a letter from the War Office. It informed him that, due to the fact that he had not been 'war substantive' at the time of his capture in Sardinia, he would have to revert to the rank of Lance Corporal. He simply couldn't believe what he was reading. What a way to reward initiative and hard work! After all he had been through, the army had seen fit to reduce him in rank, and cut his pay! As if all this was not bad enough, he was constantly being badgered by Officers and Warrant Officers who, in his opinion, 'had never seen an angry man, much less an enemy soldier'.

This was a very unhappy time for him. He found that adjusting to the Windsor regime was harder than he had anticipated. People like Sid were not popular. Life outside the Grenadier Guards simply did not exist for some of the seniors. They were suspicious of anyone who had served anywhere else. It was as though no one else was doing any work and that by serving elsewhere they could in some way lower standards on their return. No one had any idea what the SAS did, and Sid grew tired of trying to educate them. He couldn't help thinking that there were too many people in the Training Battalion hanging on to a cushy number. Some of the Officers and NCOs had seen no active service at all, but this didn't prevent them from generously giving their views on warfare. There were, of course, plenty of men who had seen more than their share, men who had served in France, North Africa and Italy, some of whom had been wounded. He was by no means the only ex-POW in the camp either.

In early February, news filtered through that in January the Fifth Battalion had landed at Anzio with the allied forces. They now joined the 3rd and 6th Battalions in Italy. The fighting had been fierce, and the advance slow and costly. Sid couldn't help thinking about the officers in Camp 59, who had told them to sit tight until the allies arrived. He had made it all the way home, and the allies were still far from winning the war in Italy. He thought that it was a safe bet that some of them were now safely installed in a fresh camp, somewhere in Germany.

His drill course began on a wet Monday morning. It was all too familiar. He had spent hours on this parade square years earlier. He was now being drilled by instructors who in some cases hadn't been out of England since. He had hoped that he might have been appointed Lance Sergeant in a couple of months, but instead he had been demoted, and was now sweating up and down the square. This was not what he had expected at all. Here he was, marching up and down at a rapid pace, on the same drill square, with squads of young guardsmen being newly drilled

Although his morale was close to rock bottom, he managed to stick it out and passed the drill course with flying colours. Next came a weapons course, followed by a similar phase in tactics. He found these far more interesting and his previous experience was put to good use. It was while he was on the tactics course that he encountered none other than Major Sir Thomas Butler, his old Company Commander from Number Four Company in the 6th Battalion. Butler asked what on earth Sid was doing back in Windsor. When he heard his reply he was most interested, and arranged for the two to meet after the current tactics lesson.

The reason for Butler's interest was that he too had been a POW, captured along with a hundred or so other Grenadiers at Mareth. He had escaped together with Captain Bonham-Carter. The two discussed their adventures, and discovered that they had selected similar routes across the Gran Sasso. Sid admired this officer, who was clearly a great leader of men. Butler had since been awarded the DSO for his actions during that fateful battle. There were several officers who, like him, had returned from Italy or North Africa. They were very different to some of the others who had not seen service outside England, and had no idea what war was like. Later that night, he thought about his time in the Italian hills, and chuckled to himself when he realised that his old Company Commander must have been fairly close to his own position, most of the time they were on the run.

This period of depression didn't last too long. Someone was working behind the scenes, and after a very short period of time, he was promoted to Lance Sergeant. He felt that an injustice had been righted and cheered up a bit. His promotion changed things considerably. He was now a 'Mess Member' and was expected to train the Guardsmen and recruits who were passing through the Training Battalion. On the Battalion drill parades he was now drilling a squad, which was much more interesting than simply square bashing.

Massed arms drill was sometimes carried out and the Sergeant Major would position his rotund frame on the veranda of the married quarters. This vantage point overlooked the parade square and he was able to spot any man who was being idle, he would shout across the square, 'Company Sergeant Major, that man second from the right in the rear rank is idle, lock him up.' There would be a pause and the sound of hobnailed boots on tarmac as the guilty man was identified. This would be followed by the tell-tale calling of the time, 'Left, right, left right,' as the idle man headed for the guardroom.

Officers were not spared the agony of the square either, and the Sergeant Major was often seen, drilling them mercilessly, as the Adjutant looked on. The Battalion drill parades were not taken too seriously by most of the men who had war experience, they had seen far more frightening things than 'old snapper' on the veranda above. The Adjutant was the Marquis of Hamilton who had 'buck-teeth' and appeared rather 'knock-kneed' in his riding breeches. Drill Sergeant Jones was 'pigeon-toed' and marched in a peculiar inverted manner. These two characters, when combined with the Sergeant Major's rather round appearance, gave the parade a humorous feel. Some of the veterans regarded the Saturday parade as a pantomime, and struggled to conceal their mirth as the three main characters played their parts.

Once his courses were complete, and he was able to relax a little, Sid was able to turn his attention to something that had played on his mind for a very long time. When he left for the Middle East he had been unable to say goodbye to Pat. He had thought of her frequently during his spell overseas. He now wanted to renew their relationship and he made contact at the first opportunity. Pat had no idea what he had been up to while he was away, but she had been informed by Sid's mother that he was listed as missing. Before long the two were happily courting as though he had never been away. The boys were pleased to see him too, they had grown considerably and they seemed to enjoy his company. The happy couple visited all their old haunts but Sid was disappointed at the way the old town had changed.

During his last tour there were plenty of troops around, but they were mainly guardsmen and Household Cavalry troops, with a few local chaps thrown in. The situation now was very different. The surrounding area was home to thousands of soldiers, many of whom were living under canvass awaiting the 'Second Front'. They were permitted to visit Windsor during their time off. The town was now

jam-packed with soldiers from the United States, Canada, Poland and a whole host of other Commonwealth nations. There were almost a hundred pubs in the Windsor area but some of these were more popular than others. They became overcrowded. That inevitably led to friction between the various units and nationalities.

Many of the British troops greatly resented the Americans, and were quick to remind them that Great Britain had stood alone against the Nazis whilst the Yanks had looked the other way. The Americans, not given to turning the other cheek, often responded by reminding the Limeys that they would be talking German right now, if the U.S. had not come to their rescue. The Military Police of both nations were often required to intervene. Sid and Pat soon learned that Peascod Street was a place to be avoided when the troops were in town.

In time, Sid was posted to Number Seven Company at the Etonian Country club. This was commanded by Major Stanley, whose CSM was Bill Nash, a man greatly respected in the Sergeants' Mess. The training here was more to his liking. There was plenty of field training and PT. The platoons regularly ran up and down the Long Walk. The carriageway linked the Castle to the huge mounted statue of King George III. A rifle range had been constructed in the park and this was very well used. Every two weeks or so the various platoons carried out a ten mile forced march. This was supposed to be completed in under two hours. There was a great deal of competition between the various instructors to see whose Squad could finish quickest. Many of the instructors in the Company had no war experience and Sid soon found himself in great demand. He was often required to join other platoons at the request of their Platoon Sergeants. He spent a great deal of time working under Sergeant Alan Dobson whom he also admired as a good soldier. Because of his experience, he was sometimes given a platoon to run without supervision, a task he greatly enjoyed.

The spring turned into summer and at last the long awaited news came. On 6th June 1944, the Allies landed in Normandy. Everyone eagerly followed the reports of progress in France. The early days were very tense. As the weeks passed there was more confidence that the foothold in northern Europe would be held. The Guards Armoured Division left their holding area near Brighton and crossed to France later in the month. The First and Second Battalions saw their first action at Cagny on 18th July. Thereafter, a steady flow of men went to and from Windsor, as replacements went forward and wounded soldiers arrived from hospital.

During that summer the enemy introduced a new and terrifying weapon to their arsenal, the V1 rocket or 'Buzz bomb'. The fearful buzz of their engines was often heard in the skies over and around London. The borough of Croydon was particularly hard hit. Nearby, Caterham too was struck including the Guards Depot. On 18th June one of these weapons crashed onto the Guards chapel at Wellington Barracks during the Sunday service. It killed 121 soldiers and civilians, and injured many more. The regimental headquarters of the Grenadier Guards in Birdcage Walk was also extensively damaged. When word reached Windsor there was a great deal of anger. Many Grenadiers were among the dead. In the following days the troops were much more wary. When the tell-tale engines were heard above, the Duty Drummer blew the call, 'There's a bomber overhead'! and shelter would be sought. Everyone listened carefully, in case the characteristic buzzing noise suddenly stopped. Silence was the signal that the devastating missile was about to plunge earthward. Mercifully, Victoria Barracks was spared. However, a number of the feared weapons fell on the surrounding area. The closest was only three miles away, when the local destructor chimney in Dedworth was destroyed.

Guardsmen were coming and going all the time, and often moved on fairly rapidly, dependant on where they were required next. Some went to the Guards Armoured Training Wing at Pirbright. Others disappeared as replacements for the Battalions fighting in Italy. There were sometimes gaps in the programme, and the officers often devised schemes to fill them. As there were a number of escaped POWs in Windsor, there was some enthusiasm in the officers' mess for an escape and evasion exercise.

One evening the Training Company was assembled for a briefing on this test of initiative and resourcefulness. The troops were to be loaded into the back of a number of enclosed 3-ton trucks. They were to be driven to a series of unknown drop off points, from where they were to get back to Windsor using their own initiative. The NCOs were to be dropped off at separate points and had to try and capture as many of the troops as possible on the way back. Sid kept his mouth shut, but he thought this was a pointless exercise. It would be simple to get back to Windsor, and the number of NCOs hunting them down was so small as to be ridiculous. He had just completed a week as Sergeant in Waiting, and was quite tired. Furthermore, he was next for guard, and did not fancy spending the evening stumbling around the Berkshire countryside. He made up his mind that he would take this one easy, particularly as there was no training value that he could see.

The trucks, full of troops, left Victoria Barracks once it was dark. Sid tried hard to keep his bearings, which was not easy to do when the canvass at the back of the truck was lashed down. The troops in the back of his vehicle had a variety of experience. Some were very green and fairly enthusiastic about the exercise, but others were more experienced and less keen. One of these men was 'Wacky' Jones. Sid was well acquainted with Wacky. They had served together in the 1st Battalion and had both come out of Dunkirk. Wacky had stayed with the Corps of Drums in the same Battalion. He had returned to France with them in June, where he had been wounded early on. He had recovered from his wounds and was now waiting to be posted. Jones left Sid in no doubt that he questioned the value of the exercise, but diplomacy required no comment from an NCO. Somehow he couldn't see Wacky crawling through the fields in an effort to impress the company officers.

When his turn came, Sid jumped down from the back of the truck into the darkness and watched as the 3-tonner disappeared into the night. He thought that he had managed to keep a reasonable idea about the direction they had been following, and given the time they had been on the truck, he guessed that they couldn't be too far from Reading. The thought had no sooner entered his head when a bus appeared around the bend. As it got nearer he was able to make out the letters at the front announcing its destination, Reading! He didn't even think about his actions, two minutes later he was comfortably seated at the back of the bus. It didn't take long before the old vehicle entered Wokingham. Sid recognised the town immediately. He had stayed several times with an old friend whose parents had been evacuated from Dover. This was too good to be true. Never one to miss an opportunity, he left the bus at the next stop, and half an hour later he was standing on the doorstep of his pal's house.

The lady of the house recognised him immediately and welcomed him inside. When he explained the reason for his presence, he was invited to sleep over, an offer that was too good to refuse. The next morning he awoke refreshed, and was served a delicious fry up before catching the first Windsor bound bus. He waited until the designated time before returning to barracks, where he joined the remainder of the troops. As he had suspected, hardly any of the guardsmen had been caught. He guessed that a few of them had devised plans similar to his own, as had the other NCOs. Later that afternoon, there was a de-brief and the guardsmen were asked to explain how they had evaded capture. The officer in charge pointed at Wacky Jones and asked how had he got on. The wiley Drummer immediately replied that all had gone well until they got near Windsor, when suddenly Sergeant Dowland had leapt out from behind a bush and nabbed them. Wacky grinned at Sid as he was congratulated by the officer. Neither of them had seen each other at all in the last 24 hours, but Wacky rightly assumed that Sid would not contradict him. The two laughed about the episode much later when they were out of earshot.

The Sergeant Major was apparently trying hard to get Wacky sent back to a service Battalion, a fact that Wacky frequently made public when the opportunity arose. Several of the men who had served in France, thought that some of those who hadn't been at all, should go before those like Wacky, who had been twice already. Sid thought that his chances of getting back into action would be good now that there were six Battalions fighting overseas. He approached the Sergeant Major about this possibility. He was told bluntly that there were no vacancies and he was to stay put. He thought that he would continue to pursue the matter. However, a sudden recurrence of malaria confined him to hospital, and that was the end of the matter for the foreseeable future.

Malaria kept him from training for a few weeks and he was visited in hospital by a Grenadier officer who clearly had his welfare at heart. The young officer provided the entertainment when he paused in the doorway and asked, 'Is malaria infectious?' Some of the other patients were veterans of the campaign in North Africa, and they were forced to conceal their amusement at the officer's naivety. Once the disease relented, Sid was discharged from hospital. He resumed his duties, training the constant flow of manpower through Windsor. He was frequently surprised at the diversity of background among the troops. There were even a couple of Platoons of ex RAF men who had transferred in bulk to the Grenadiers. They were good quality men and some had served in France in 1940. They too resented being treated like raw recruits, when they had been closer to the Germans than some of the instructors. There were many outstanding athletes serving in the regiment at this time. The Training Battalion boasted a particularly fine boxing team, not surprising when their heavyweight was Jack Gardner.

Life in the Training Battalion became fairly straight forward as the training cycle was repeated. The platoons usually went to Minehead in Somerset, to carry out realistic training which included live firing. But most of them also visited the local field firing area at Medmenham near Henley, on the river Thames. Each platoon usually left Windsor on foot, during the early evening, to make the sixteen mile journey to the range. Ammunition was carried in their equipment and the journey usually included a night crossing of the Thames by collapsible boat. On arrival at the range, final preparation was carried out before the inevitable dawn, 'Advance to Contact'.

When the exercise was complete, they once again returned to barracks on foot. The Corps of Drums usually met the platoon about three miles from camp, at the 'Nags Head' pub. They provided musical accompaniment for the remainder of the journey. The Commanding Officer usually met the troops at the gate where he took their salute. There was more live firing conducted locally at St Leonard's Hill, where a number of unoccupied buildings were used for house-clearing exercises. There were route marches to the ranges at Pirbright. The troops normally spent the night there, in cold Nissen huts, before returning to Windsor on foot the following day.

The possibility of a quick posting was never far away. Inevitably Sid's sporting talents were recognised once again. He played regularly in the company football and cricket teams, before being snapped up by the local civilian football team, Windsor and Eton FC. It was a real bonus to be playing civilian football, especially when they were prepared to pay him for something he loved doing. Windsor and Eton FC flourished during the war years with a surfeit of quality players from the Grenadiers and Household Cavalry. Pat was never far away and their relationship flourished. He often thought that she alone had kept him sane, during his difficult adjustment back to regimental duty.

The summer passed into winter and the progress of the war was followed by everyone at home. In September, the ill-fated Operation Market Garden had been launched in Holland, and the Guards Division had suffered many casualties. The war in Italy continued to rage. The 6th Battalion reinforced the 5th and ceased to be. The 5th Battalion too, having suffered terrible loss, in turn joined the 3rd Battalion who remained in Italy.

Sid occasionally bumped into men he had known in the 6th Battalion, and was able to catch up on the news of old friends. So many of them would not make it home. Jim Kosbab had apparently rejoined the 6th Battalion after his exclusion from the Sardinia raid. He was massively disillusioned to see his friends go into action without him, and then to learn that the raid had been a disaster, with no one returning. Kosbab was to prove his courage many times over during the Italian campaign. Unfortunately, his volatile character had not changed. He fell foul of the authorities and found himself in hot water once again. Sid also heard that Dougie Wright was still in the SAS and no doubt making a nuisance of himself somewhere in the Mediterranean.

1945 arrived, and although the war seemed to be going the way of the allies, there was no end in sight, particularly in the Far East, where the Japanese were contesting every inch of ground. At very short notice, he was once again dispatched from Windsor, this time to Hawick in the Scottish borders. There was a Grenadier Holding Company there. The troops were able to refine their infantry skills in a harsher and more testing environment, whilst waiting to be assigned to a Battalion. The town of Hawick stands on the confluence of the Rivers Slitridge and Teviot in the county of Roxburgh. Stobs Barracks was located just to the south of the town, on a bleak hillside astride the main Carlisle to Edinburgh railway line. It came complete with its own large sidings. The camp was little more than a collection of old huts on the moor, which had seen regiments come and go since before the First World War.

The current occupants were the Irish Guards Composite Battalion. They had responsibility for administering the holding companies, among other tasks, and Sid was to be attached to them for the foreseeable future. He soon noted that within the camp, there was a small collection of tents inside a closely guarded stockade. This was apparently a POW camp which housed some of the more fanatical Nazi prisoners. They were allegedly kept in isolation from the German prisoners at the nearby Wilton camp. There had been several escape attempts. The new arrivals were warned to stay clear of the captives.

No sooner had he arrived with the small detachment of Grenadiers, than the hut door was thrown open by a red faced Irish Guards Drill Sergeant, 'Who's Sergeant Dowland?' he roared. Sid stood to attention and identified himself, wondering what he could have done. 'You're playing football at 14.00 hrs, don't be late!' He was relieved but a little concerned that he was already known to the 'powers that be'. He turned up on time. The game was won and not surprisingly he earned a regular first team place.

This was all very well, but the weather in Hawick was appalling, and he often found himself playing in driving sleet or snow. The training here was tough too. The terrain was very demanding, and many of the young Guardsmen found it very hard to cope with the demands of the weather and the hills. The local town, although small, was pleasant and the population friendly. It was soon discovered that the town name was correctly pronounced as 'Hoick', although no one was able to explain the origin of this strange pronunciation. There was little to do by way of recreation, but to visit the local pubs where the game of quoits was played. On the rare occasions when the weather permitted, they could swim in the nearby Barne's Lough.

Once again winter gave way to spring, and summer eventually arrived. Sid had become accustomed to the training regime at Hawick. The 'Micks' had a very different way of doing things, but once he got used to it, things were fine. He returned to Windsor whenever he could. But a short leave pass simply wasn't enough after the long train journey from Scotland. Consequently he didn't see Pat and the boys as often as he would have liked, although he did manage several 'long weekends'.

Everyone now realised that the war in Europe was coming to an end. It was just a question of time until the Germans were defeated. Victory in Europe finally came on 8th May. There were great celebrations everywhere. Sid and the other instructors wished they could have been back in Windsor for the festivities, but it was not to be. There was plenty of fun to be had in Scotland, and the local publicans really pushed the boat out for the troops. It was difficult to believe that the Germans had finally been defeated. Five years had passed since those desperate hours on the beach at Dunkirk. There had been a great deal of hardship for everyone, and he couldn't help thinking about some of the men who wouldn't be coming home.

The following day there were lots of hangovers in Stobs camp and the conversation turned to the future. Although the war in Europe was over, there was no end in sight in the Far East. Most people thought that a Guards Brigade would be sent out to fight. They had been represented in every other theatre and it was reasonable to assume that at least some of the Battalions would be fighting the Japs within a few months. The training regime was eventually changed to reflect the next likely deployment to the jungles of the Far East, although this was rather difficult to achieve in the Scottish Borders. More Grenadiers arrived in Hawick until there were a substantial number of men detached there from Windsor

Completely out of the blue, Sid was told that he was to be posted to a Service Battalion. He assumed that he would be going to Germany to join the 1st, but was surprised to learn that he was to join the 3rd Battalion. He knew that they had ended the war in northern Italy, and assumed that they were coming home. Their destination was not yet known to him, and he assumed that they would be billeted somewhere in the home counties. When he learned the actual location that was to be home for the Battalion he was astounded, 3rd Battalion Grenadier Guards were destined for Hawick! There were now a significant number of Grenadiers at Stobs camp. They were all to be posted as reinforcements to join the 3rd when they arrived. The Battalion was to be reformed when it returned to England. Many of the longer service men were to be demobbed, and replaced by the newly drafted men. The immediate task for the Grenadiers at Stobs was to prepare for the arrival of the returning 3rd Battalion

The Grenadier veterans of Italy arrived back in England in late July and early August. Most were sent to Hawick by train, and many disembarked at Stobs Sidings. Unusually for the time, they were flown back in converted bombers. This meant that they arrived in packets over a period of days. The troops were only to spend one night at Stobs camp before going on leave. But Sid and the others busied themselves by placing the men in their temporary accommodation. He recognised many of the 3rd Battalion men from his service in North Africa. They were an impressive sight. The survivors of the campaign in Italy were deeply bronzed and fit in appearance. Each man wore the silver mailed fist insignia of the 6th Armoured Division on his arm. Some of the men were clearly not happy at being sent to Scotland but most were just pleased to be home and morale was high. No time was lost in sending the troops on leave, as most hadn't seen home for two years or more, and they were desperate to get away.

The following day most of the Battalion departed for a well earned leave, but not before the rumour mongers had circulated the story that, on their return, they were to be sent to Alabama to train with the US Rangers, in preparation for the invasion of Japan. One of the men also told Sid that he had seen Lance Corporal Harry Nicholls VC, recently repatriated from Germany. The man went on to say that he had seen the Commanding Officer, Lieutenant Colonel P T Clifton DSO, salute Nicholls as a VC winner, on his return to the Battalion. Nicholls had been a POW since being captured in 1940. Since the award of the medal in that same year, a second VC had been won in Italy, this time by Major Sidney who had been serving with the 5th Battalion.

When the Battalion returned from leave, some of the companies were to move into Hawick to another camp, a collection of Nissen huts which had been rapidly constructed. The setting was far from luxurious, but being closer to the centre of Hawick was a bonus. Sid, as part of the rear party, spent the following weeks preparing the site for occupation. It looked as though Hawick would be a very temporary home, everyone expected to be heading to the U.S.A or to the Far East very soon. There were lots of newly drafted men waiting in Hawick for the return of the 3rd Battalion. Most of the guardsmen with longer service were in the process of returning to civilian life, and their young replacements fully expected to participate in the forthcoming invasion of Japan. There was a fair degree of apprehension too. This would be D-Day all over again and no one underestimated how costly the operation would be to the allies. The Japanese had nineteen Divisions allocated to the defence of their homeland, not to mention aircraft and the dreaded Kamikaze bombers. The planned invasion was closer than most realised. 'Operation Olympic', the first Sixth Army landing on Kyushu was planned for 1st November 1945.

The Guards were, thankfully, not destined to fight in Japan. On 6th August, the first Atomic Bomb was dropped on Hiroshima, to devastating effect. It was followed three days later by a second, this time targeted on the city of Nagasaki. The war was effectively over before the 3rd Battalion had completed its leave, and no one was sorry. The Japanese surrender was formally completed aboard the USS Missouri in Tokyo Bay on 2nd September. There were great celebrations once again. The war was finally over, and people would be able to return to their peacetime routine once more. This was also a time for reflection. Victory had come at an awful price. The Grenadier Guards had lost 356 officers, and 4,707 men killed, wounded or captured.

When the troops returned to Hawick, the reformation of the Third Battalion began. There were a great number of men who had seen long service in Italy and who were to be discharged at the earliest opportunity. Large drafts of replacement guardsmen and Non Commissioned Officers had arrived from Windsor. The men at Hawick were broadly divided into two groups, 'old' and 'new'. A parade was held in a large Park in the town, and Princess Elizabeth inspected the Battalion which was effectively split into two parts.

This was a sad farewell to those who had fought so well in Italy, but it was also a new beginning for the fresh faced young Grenadiers who had arrived from Windsor. There were many who were relieved that their Colonel did not inspect them from the rear. No Battalion barber could be found and the men had cut or rather butchered each other's hair. There were some awful sights which the princess was thankfully spared. The whole Battalion marched passed their Colonel at the Hawick Town Hall, where she took the salute.

The 3rd Battalion fully expected to be in Scotland for some time. So when it was discovered that the 1st Guards Brigade was destined for foreign shores once again, the troops were incredulous. The Battalion was to be sent to Palestine to assist in the emergency there. The situation in Palestine had been deteriorating for some time and the British Government was struggling to maintain an even hand when administering two deeply opposed factions. The Jews were determined to establish their own state, and the Arabs were equally determined not to give up any more land. The Jews had formed their own self defence organisations, which became increasingly anti British.

In 1944, British personnel were being attacked by the 'Irgun Zvia Leumi' (IZL) a Jewish terrorist organisation which was becoming more and more extreme. The end of the war in Europe saw many thousands of displaced Jews with little option but to seek a new beginning in Palestine. The British, ever keen to show an even hand, sought to appease the Jews by permitting resettlement in Palestine, and to appeal to the Arabs by limiting the numbers. American President Truman requested that the British allow 100,000 displaced Jews to settle in Palestine. The request was quickly refused, fanning the anti British sentiment even more. International Jewish organisations began to send ship loads of refugees to Palestine, without British agreement. These refugees were regarded as illegal immigrants by the British. The Royal Navy intercepted many ships, in turn leading to violent confrontation and increased resentment toward the British. It was against this back drop of international anti British feeling, increasing instability, escalating terrorist attacks and a massive immigration problem, that the 3rd Battalion Grenadier Guards received the news of their new role.

There was scarcely any time for training. The driving Scottish rain and heavy mist could hardly have been worse preparation for the hot sun of the Middle East. Sid was glad to be back in a service Battalion. Recently promoted to Sergeant, he was keen to mould his new Platoon into an effective unit. Most of them were young men, fresh from Windsor, although there were a few old hands who had fought in Italy. He had been posted to Number One Company where he found that the CSM was none other than Bill Nash who had also come from Windsor. Major Hanbury, his Company Commander, was also well known to him, although he noted that his knew OC was now a holder of the MC. The Company second in command, Captain Rolls, also held the MC, as did Lieutenant MacCallum, one of the Platoon Commanders. There were plenty of people he knew in the Sergeants' mess and he made new friends every day. He enjoyed the feel of this Battalion. There was new enthusiasm, coupled with hard earned experience and confidence.

No one knew when they would be off to Palestine, but a group of Sergeants' mess members decided not to waste an opportunity to make a few bob. There was a 'Flapper Track' nearby where dogs were raced regularly for money. One of the CQMS had a reputation as a bit of an expert when it came to dog racing. A small syndicate was organised to purchase a dog, in order that it could be raced at the track, thereby earning the group a handsome profit. A dog was duly acquired and it showed great promise from an early stage. The CQMS and helpers met regularly on the football pitch to train the great canine hope. They watched with enthusiasm as it raced up and down the muddy playing fields. Each run was timed meticulously by the knowledgeable Colour Sergeant, until he was convinced that they were 'on a winner'.

According to his stop-watch this dog would compete with the best of them. Their prize mutt was entered in the next race, and a large crowd of eager Grenadiers arrived at the track hoping to make a handsome profit on this secret weapon. When the race eventually started the dog did not disappoint. It shot off at a tremendous rate, clearly buoyed by the occasion, it left the other animals for dead. The Grenadiers whooped with delight until their great hope reached the fist bend, where it failed to notice the track bending off to the left. It continued on the same bearing, until it left the track completely, disappearing behind a crowd of laughing Scots. It had apparently not occurred to anyone that training the dog in straight lines on a football pitch might not be the best preparation for a race on a circular track. There were many recriminations over the sorry episode but as always events overtook the troops.

Chapter 18

Palestine

The move to Palestine took place in early October. The Battalion travelled to Southampton by train, where they embarked upon the Liner Champollion. The voyage took a little over a week, and was largely uneventful. Sid thought that the ship was luxurious when compared to some of the others he had sailed on. On 22nd October their transport sailed into the port of Haifa. Some of the officers pointed out Mount Carmel. The town of Haifa sprawled over its northern slopes, but few of the guardsmen understood the significance of the mount. According to the bible, this was the sight of Elijah's confrontation with the prophets of Baal. It was here that god had hurled down fire to burn up Elijah's water-soaked sacrifice, in order to demonstrate his superiority over the pagan gods. The men did however notice the dry landscape that they were about to land upon. It was vastly different to the cold Scottish hills they had left behind. It was all very familiar to Sid, he had trained here with the SAS and he knew the region well.

Once the troops disembarked there was the familiar move to their temporary accommodation. The transit camp occupied by the 3rd Battalion was predictably filthy. A great deal of work was required to clean it up over the next few days. The Guardsmen were relieved when they were told to change into their KD uniforms, as the heat was making life rather uncomfortable. There were no signs of the terrorists they had been told to expect, and they soon received a visit from the High Commissioner who was none other than Lord Gort. The Battalion seniors were keen to show their distinguished guest that the Battalion was maintaining the highest Grenadier standards, and various inspections were carried out before his arrival. After a week or so, the vehicles arrived from Egypt, and Sid learned that they were to move to an area just north of the town of Acre about 15 miles away.

The bulk of the Battalion moved off to set up their new home, leaving Number Four Company in Haifa. Even as the road move was taking place, there were a series of disturbances throughout Palestine. A number of railway tracks were blown up by the IZL or the 'Irgun' as they were known by the army. Sid and the other troops learned of these occurrences when they arrived at their new home, 'camp 260', near the small town of Nahariyya. A curfew had been imposed. It was necessary for the Battalion to man a series of road blocks which were designed to prevent illegal transport, and to deter the terrorists. Sid's Platoon took their turn manning the road blocks. The young guardsmen quite enjoyed the task initially. However, the novelty rapidly wore off. Their nights were spent on deserted roads and the time dragged.

The Battalion constructed its tented camp fairly rapidly and a routine was soon established. Parades took place as normal, and troops daily mounted the road blocks and guards. Their accommodation was situated close to the sea, and the guardsmen were allowed to swim when off duty, although they were constantly reminded of the terrorist threat. As always, Sid was selected to play football for the Battalion. The team took on the Royal Artillery who thrashed them 8-1. He was furious, it was a crushing defeat. Some of the other sergeants were quick to pull his leg about the manner of the defeat.

In mid November the camp was unexpectedly struck by a dreadful storm. Tents blew away and personal possessions were scattered throughout. Everyone was soaked. It proved impossible to put the tents back up until the storm subsided the following morning. It was a thoroughly miserable experience for all concerned. The Brigade had not yet commenced full operations, as there had been little time to train. So once everyone was established, various schemes were undertaken to prepare the troops for their internal security duties. 'Cordon and search' operations were studied and the various techniques taught to the guardsmen, before being practised. The camp was set up to represent a village, with one of the companies detailed to act as the civilian population. The remaining troops established a cordon, to ensure no one could escape, before sending in teams of men to search for arms and explosives.

Learning these new tactics was quite interesting for the men and they were kept fairly busy. They were able to visit the local villages when off duty, but the larger towns were out of bounds most of the time. A number of local Arabs were permitted to work in the camp on various duties, and this helped the Guardsmen to concentrate on the more important job at hand. At reveille daily, some of the locally employed Arabs would tour the lines. Calls of 'eggs and bread' spurred the tired young men into action. Unrecognisable fried eggs, and misshapen Arab bread, were squashed into sandwiches and exchanged for cash. This was a popular perk and the Quartermaster suspected that the vendors were making a tidy profit from the ravenous guardsmen.

One of Sid's pals, who ran the accommodation store, had befriended a local Christian Arab, and the pair had been invited to spend the weekend at his home. The man lived to the north which had been largely untouched by the violence. They were able to gain a leave pass without too much difficulty. A pleasant time was spent with the man's family who seemed to be delighted to have the two British soldiers stay at their home. The two friends were able to repeat this enjoyable excursion several times during their stay in Palestine and they were always made welcome. There was plenty of sport, with swimming remaining very popular. In December, weekly leave parties were sent to Beirut.

All things considered, the first two months in Palestine had been fairly enjoyable. Standards of course had to be maintained and an Adjutants drill parade was organised. The dusty camp environment was unsuitable for such an activity, so the whole Battalion was transported five miles to an airfield where the parade took place. Sergeant Major Baker put the Battalion through its paces as if their desert surroundings didn't exist. If his eagle eye didn't spot idleness, then you could be sure that Drill Sergeants Hughes and Mitchell, DCM, would. Sid knew the Sergeant Major from his time in the first Battalion, where he had seen him as a young sergeant in the King's Company. The Guardsmen, as always, dreaded these events, and there was usually great relief if they were detailed for some other essential duty on the days when the parades were held.

Training was stepped up and it was necessary for the men to learn how to deal with the civil disturbances that were becoming more frequent. The Arabs and the Jews regularly rioted against each other, and against the British. Each faction had its own grievances which invariably culminated in violence. All of this was new to the guardsmen, so riot control techniques had to be devised. In mid December, a Battalion scheme was held to practise these drills. Number Four Company was detailed as the civilian 'enemy', and they dressed themselves in all manner of ridiculous outfits. As the exercising troops closed in on the protesting enemy, a full-scale riot broke out which was enthusiastically pursued by both sides. It took a great deal of effort to prise the two sides apart. At the conclusion of the scheme, the following morning, there were a large number of black eyes and minor injuries visible in the camp area. Some vital lessons had, none the less, been learned which the troops would put into action in the coming months.

Christmas 1945 soon arrived and was celebrated in the normal fashion. There were concerts and sporting competitions, and the traditional guardsman's Christmas lunch which was served by the Battalion seniors. A large bonfire was lit and most people managed to sink a few beers. The festivities were short lived, as on Boxing Day the emergency Platoon was sent to Nahariyya to search for illegal immigrants. A ship had foundered near the town, and it was estimated that around 200 people had landed illegally. Most of the 'illegals' had been spirited away by local Jewish sympathisers, so little was found, but this proved to be a taste of things to come.

Ships full of refugees were now regularly landing on the shores of Palestine and the Royal Navy was working flat out to intercept them. The Army and Royal Marines were repeatedly called upon to assist the Navy with boarding parties. Pitched

battles were often fought when the troops attempted to board the ships. Desperate men were encountered, armed with hoses, axes and even pistols. A number of men on both sides were killed, but these fatalities did little to discourage the flow of Jewish refugees.

In early 1946, it became obvious that the security situation was deteriorating. There was an increase in the number of attacks by the 'Irgun' and by members of the 'Stern Gang', an extreme splinter group. Airfields, police stations and armouries had all been singled out for attention by the terrorists. A number of attacks were carried out to the south of Haifa, and the Battalion was stood to in response. This was short lived and the normal routine was adopted once again.

Sid was able to take some leave, along with other members of the Battalion, and parties were sent to Cairo, Beirut and Luxor. These trips were carefully planned, as the 'Irgun' had started to kidnap off duty soldiers. He was required to participate in the annual Sergeants' Mess rifle shoot, along with everyone else who was available. He shot fairly well. A large wooden spoon was traditionally presented to the worst shot in the mess, and this dubious honour was won by Drum Major Booth. Great ceremony and much drinking followed the presentation, and the Drum Major was endlessly ribbed for the rest of the day. It was in stark contrast to the winner, Sergeant Barnes, who was congratulated and rapidly forgotten.

In mid January, electricity was finally installed in the camp area. It was a major improvement to the quality of life of those who lived there. Much improvisation was needed for the men to make life comfortable. Sid was able to utilise some of the wood working skills he had learned from his father. In his tent there was a small table which proved to be incredibly useful for a variety of tasks. Unfortunately, no chairs were available to the occupants. He rapidly set about locating some old crates and a few nails, from which he managed to fashion a basic but sturdy chair which delighted the other Sergeants in his tent. He manufactured a few other bits and pieces that proved useful, but the chair remained the pride of the tent, and was closely guarded by its occupants. The home made furniture was soon noticed by

The 'Pioneers' Palestine

other mess members who commented on how well made it was. Before long it had reached the attention of the Sergeant Major.

Sid soon found himself standing to attention in front of the RSM. The great man enquired as to where Sid had learned his carpentry skills. Then he pointed to a small shed constructed from scrap wood and old crates. The 'building' had been made for the RSM to sleep in. 'Could you make one of those?' he asked. Sid replied that he could make something similar, given the right tools. 'Well, Sergeant Perk, the Pioneer Sergeant, is leaving soon, how do you fancy a shot at the job?' Sid was surprised, but thought that he could handle the job and rather fancied a change anyway.

In a fairly short space of time he found himself appointed as the Pioneer Sergeant. The Pioneer Platoon was responsible for a variety of tasks. When in camp, all manner of maintenance and construction tasks were undertaken, sign writing, carpentry, plumbing and just about every other type of trade was required. Many of the Guardsmen who were charged with these tasks learnt their skills 'on the job' and had no formal qualification. As the Platoon Sergeant, Sid now found himself being called for, on a regular basis, to survey construction or repair tasks, some of them totally beyond the skills or resources available to him.

The Pioneers were an important part of the Battalion out of barracks too. It was their job to clear mines, explosives, and to construct defences when they were needed. They were equipped with three Bren Carriers and a 3-ton truck. So far they had not been called upon. Although there was a great deal of terrorist activity, the Battalion area of responsibility had been fairly quiet. They had trained with the rest of the Battalion on the search operations, and it was their job to clear the route into the village or search area.

Sid set about training his Platoon. He had experience of this from his time at Windsor and he soon found that the Guardsmen were keen to learn. They had not

Training with flame thrower, Palestine

received very much instruction on explosives, and he was able to use his SAS experience to the full in this area. He taught them how to make up and dismantle charges, how booby traps were constructed, avoided and, ultimately, how to dismantle them. His Pioneers were also responsible for the Battalion flame throwers, an unpopular collection of pipes and tanks full of petrol, carried on the back of an unfortunate pioneer. His platoon commander was a pleasant young officer, Lieutenant Lord Robin Bahniel, who was pleased to have such an experienced man as his Platoon Sergeant.

Sid soon attracted the attention of officers outside his platoon and was asked to teach his booby trap lessons to a wider audience. He was also tasked to assist in the preparation of the camp defences. Trenches were dug all around the perimeter for emergency use, and his expertise at explosive digging was in great demand. The ground was rock hard, but by drilling small holes into the ground and placing explosives into them, by means of a hollow pole, the earth could be loosened so that the trenches could be dug more easily.

Word spread of the Pioneers labour saving talents. One young officer asked if Sid could blow a hole for him six feet deep and three feet wide! The technique was explained to the officer patiently, so that that he understood that explosives couldn't produce square holes to exact dimensions. Sid wondered if he thought that the spoil blown from the hole would land in neat piles too. The Pioneer Platoon seemed to be happy and he was satisfied that they were competent in all aspects of their trade.

He had amassed some leave entitlement and decided that he would use this to visit South Africa. He had made friends in Durban and had fallen in love with the city the last time he was there. The visit was short but very enjoyable. Once again, he was made to feel very welcome by his South African hosts, and it was with great reluctance that he returned to Palestine.

Late January and early February saw the Battalion involved in a number of civil disturbances. These were mainly land disputes between Arabs and Jews, brought about by the Jews attempting to establish new settlements. The Grenadiers were called upon to 'cordon and search' a number of villages, and to mount regular patrols and road blocks in support of the Palestine Police. There had been a good number of bombings and other attacks, in and around Haifa, and as these were on the increase, it was felt that the 'Irgun' would soon find their way north. In April, the terrorists attempted to blow up a number of bridges quite near to the camp and tension increased.

A couple of nights later a Grenadier patrol came under fire. They quickly went to ground and fired back at their attackers. Assistance was sent for, and only when a similar request was received from the police, did officers realise what had happened. The policemen were temporary constables who were nervous after the recent attacks on the bridges. They had mistaken the Grenadier patrol for terrorists and opened fire. One of the constables was shot in the leg but fortunately there were no further casualties. There was however a more serious incident. Sergeant Clarkson was accidentally killed during a scheme.

In spite of the security situation, drill parades were held, and the Guardsmen's hopes were dashed when 'spring drills' went ahead as though the Stern Gang didn't exist. A good number of men were demobbed at this time, as their 'numbers had come up'. Some of those leaving were 'war men', but most were national service-men who were pleased to get away from Palestine when they had done their time. Due to the terrorist threat, a considerable number of men were required to guard the camp at night. They were usually visited by the officers and Warrant Officers on duty, to ensure that they were alert. Sometimes the Drill Sergeant or Sergeant Major would attempt to catch out the sentries by sneaking up on them. This prac-tice was most unpopular with the guardsmen and some of the pioneers complained to Sid. He was clearly in no position to do anything about it. He merely said, 'It's amazing the effect that a sliding bolt can have at two in the morning'. A few days later he heard that the Sergeant Major had been stopped in his tracks when a pio-neer had operated the bolt on his rifle. There had apparently been a rapid shout of identification from a fairly rattled voice in the darkness. Sid hoped that his comments wouldn't be discovered.

As the summer approached and the terrorist outrages continued, there was a good deal of frustration, and a feeling that more could be done to counter the 'Irgun'. There were plenty of search operations being done, and the pioneers were always involved, carefully checking the roads for mines. They also cleared a few bombs from railway tracks. Sid was sometimes asked to check for booby traps when weapons were discovered during searches. The search operations were at times quite unpleasant. The civilian population were often rounded up so that the searches could be carried out without interference. Women and children were sometimes herded into enclosures and the Guardsmen had to endure verbal abuse and shouts of 'Nazi'. Some of the veterans of Italy were enraged. They had lost friends fighting the Nazis. Many of the men were very uncomfortable having to stand with fixed bayonets over protesting civilians. They knew however, that the terrorists were to blame and that the military authorities had little choice. The anti British press condemned the army in the strongest possible terms and this too made the men very angry.

During one operation, Sid was summoned to a large truck parked at a small village which was being searched. The civilian inhabitants had been particularly uncooperative and the atmosphere was quite tense. One of the guardsmen had dis-covered a suitcase on the passenger seat of the truck and no one in the village would offer any information on its owner or the contents. The guardsman was under-standably reluctant to risk his life by opening the suitcase, so the problem was passed to Sid.

There were some nervous looking faces among the men but he had the answer in an instant. He handed the case to one of his pioneers telling him to move into the centre of the group of civilians and then to open the case. As the pioneer pushed his way into the sitting crowd there were nervous glances and murmurs which grew to loud protests. The village head-man was surrounded by protesting Jews who shouted in Hebrew. Sid imagined that they were looking for assurances that the case would not explode among them. The old man was seen to shake his head and to issue verbal assurances to the concerned villagers. This was exactly what Sid had suspected. The old man had known what was in the case all the time and was being deliberately obstructive. The guardsmen thought that this had been a brilliant tac-tic and that they had got one over on the civilians. There were however more senior people who felt that this simply wasn't cricket, and the civilians could have been placed at risk. Sid was more concerned about the risk to his pioneers, and he decided that if necessary he would do it again.

Early in June, three trains were blown up south of Haifa and a series of refugee ships were intercepted by the Navy. Incidents were now becoming more frequent and more serious. Around midnight on the evening of 16th June, Sid was summoned to Battalion Headquarters where he reported to the Commanding Officer. There was a great commotion. Apparently terrorists had attacked a nearby bridge at Al Zib. There had been a major fire-fight and a large explosion. The situation was very confused. He was told to take two Bren carriers, and clear the road across the bridge and on to the Lebanese frontier. He was to be accompanied by Palestine Police officers. He quickly organised his Platoon, who had by now got wind that something was going on, and after a very quick briefing they mounted up and headed for Al Zib. On the way to the scene, Sid learned more of the incident from the police. Apparently some local Arabs had spotted a large group of terrorists heading for the bridge and the nearby police post. They quickly warned the police who opened fire on the Irgun, some of whom had disguised themselves as British soldiers. A major gun battle had followed, but explosives carried by the terrorists had detonated prematurely, causing a very large explosion and effectively ending the battle. Several terrorists were believed dead and more injured.

The pioneers cautiously drove down the road and Sid peered into the darkness for any sign of activity. After some time, he spotted an object in the middle of the road. He couldn't identify it in the poor light, but it looked out of place and would need further investigation. The little convoy was halted and he sent a small party off to a flank, moving parallel to the road to check for any sign of activity. He allowed his little patrol a few minutes to get sufficiently far ahead, and then walked

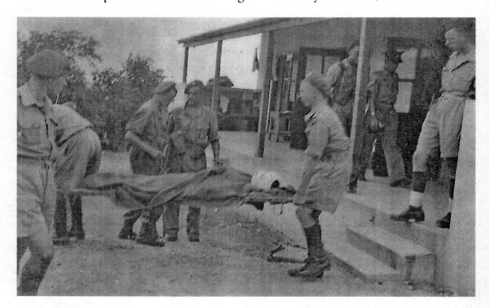

A wounded terrorist is arrested after the search of a settlement following the raid on the bridge at Al Zib, 17th June 1946

alone down the road toward the object. As he drew near he was able to identify an apparently discarded British Army Big Pack. It was an odd place for a piece of equipment to be lost and he became more cautious. As he approached, wires could be seen leading away from the pack and into the undergrowth, he was now certain that this was a terrorist bomb. He hoped that the flank party he had sent out would be sufficient to discourage any terrorist waiting at a firing point. Having considered the safest approach, he decided to use a small grappling hook to pull the bomb from a safe distance. When the rope was yanked, the pack moved several feet but there was no explosion. He returned to the bomb and taking out a small pair of pliers, he cut the electric cables leading into the pack. This done, he was able to carefully open the pack and remove the detonator from the explosives, rendering the device safe. There were several pounds of explosive packed into the small webbing container. There was more than enough to blow the Bren carriers off the road. Sid suddenly realised that he was dripping with sweat.

There was no time to spare. The pioneers mounted up once again and the carriers trundled off toward their destination. The bridge at Al Zib had taken a hammering. The explosion had caused a fair bit of damage but the structure was still intact. There were a number of armed policemen at the scene and there was evidence of the recent battle all around. The Grenadiers could see debris in the road and what looked like bodies scattered around. He received a briefing from the police and carried out a quick appreciation of the situation before carefully moving toward the bridge. There could still be explosives intact, or worse, concealed terrorists waiting to take on anyone moving onto the bridge. As he drew closer, he could make out various pieces of discarded equipment including weapons. There was a fair bit of twisted metal on the road. He imagined that this must have come from a part of the structure, although in the dark it was impossible tell where from. He also noticed what he thought were bundles of rags, but as his eyes focused he realised that these were the bodies of dead Irgun terrorists, or more accurately what was left of them. There were clearly several bodies on the bridge, but the blast had been so strong that it was difficult to tell exactly how many. There was a lot of blood about and what appeared to be a blood trail. There must have been several wounded men who were carried away.

Once Sid was satisfied that the coast was clear, he tasked his pioneers to search the bridge for explosives. They rapidly dispersed all over the structure, and guardsmen could be seen leaning over the sides, and scanning the bridge from underneath. A small amount of explosives was discovered, and he decided that the safest thing to do would be to blow them where they were. Once he had rigged up a small charge to initiate the terrorist bomb, he prepared to fire the charge electrically. At the critical moment, a party of curious Arabs walked into the danger area and had to be chased off. This was repeated several times, as the locals were keen to see the dead Jewish raiders. Eventually, the danger of the situation was conveyed to the Arabs by the Palestine police, and he was able to destroy the terrorist device. By now more Grenadiers had arrived at the scene and a follow up operation was getting under way. It was believed to be likely that the wounded terrorists were being sheltered by sympathetic Jews, and a major cordon and search operation was planned for the next morning.

The Pioneers once more mounted their carriers and drove across the bridge to complete the second part of their mission. They were not far from the frontier and Sid found that he knew the area well. It was close to where his Arab friend had hosted him for those pleasant weekends. The journey took some time and was fairly tense. There were several halts to inspect objects at the side of the road but all of these proved to be false alarms. There was no sign of the Irgun, they had long since melted into the countryside. But the guardsmen were pleased that the enemy would be going home a few men short. It was estimated that at least five terrorists had died that night. There was no sympathy for the opposition. They were regarded with contempt because of their cowardly tactics and willingness to commit atrocities.

The Pioneers eventually returned to their camp the next morning, tired but buoyed by a successful mission completed. Later that day, they learned that the follow up operation had been a success too. A wounded terrorist had been found in a nearby village and a number of arrests had been made. The terrorist was badly wounded and was taken into custody on a stretcher. He was well treated and received immediate medical attention. Many of the men speculated that if the Irgun had captured them under similar circumstances, they could not have expected the same treatment.

In the following weeks, the pioneers took part in many clearance operations. Roads and bridges were regularly checked, and safe approach routes were cleared for the rifle company men to enter villages. Several small devices were found and many weapons were recovered. On one occasion, Sid was tasked to assist with a problem at the entrance to the village of Hanuta. He had been told that a booby

The listing *San Dimitrio*, Haifa 1946

trap had been found, but when he approached he was surprised by what he saw. A very large wasp nest had been positioned on a stone post at the entrance to the village. A piece of string had been tied to it which trailed off into the village, where it disappeared out of sight. At first he found this amusing but then realised that thousands of angry wasps could be a real problem. An alternate route was found to the end of the string and the wasps were duly removed. It was a talking point and the source of some amusement, but the fact was that it had been an effective delaying tactic. On another occasion two cavalry men were killed nearby when terrorists exploded a roadside bomb. It had been disguised as a post by the use of plaster. Grenadiers fired at the firing point but the Irgun escaped.

At the end of 1945, Sir Allan Cunningham had replaced Lord Gort as the High Commissioner. He was now under pressure to take drastic action against the terrorists. On 28th June 1946, 'operation Agatha' was mounted. 17,000 troops moved into Jerusalem and the surrounding area, to carry out a massive cordon and search operation. Many arrests were made, and some weapons were found, including several at the headquarters of the Jewish Agency which was immediately shut down. The operation was declared a success and a large number of weapons were recovered. The Grenadiers too were involved in their own area of operations, but with limited success. The busy routine continued, and it seemed as though the Irgun were becoming more and more daring. The troops were now spending longer in the camp. Jewish cafes were out of bounds and operations were more frequent.

In mid July, RSM Baker left the Battalion. There were farewell drinks in the Sergeants' mess, but these were fairly low key because of the security situation. Sid learned that Baker was to be succeeded by RSM Harold Wood DCM, who had apparently taken over the training Battalion from 'old Snapper'. Wood wasn't due to arrive for some time, so there was no opportunity for the newer Sergeants to 'size him up', although he was well known to the old hands. Wood had served in the 3rd Battalion before the war and had won the DCM with them in 1940. He had served in Italy too and was well regarded. It was no surprise to learn that he was known as 'Timber'. The new Sergeant Major was among the first to congratulate Sid when he was awarded the British Empire Medal. The award came as a complete shock. He had absolutely no idea that he had been recommended for a medal, but his considerable contribution to the Battalion's operations had been noted. He regarded the medal as an award for all of his pioneers and their hard work. But he was quite proud to have been recognised. There was plenty of beer drunk in the Sergeants' Mess to celebrate.

The change over of Sergeant Majors was soon forgotten, as on the morning of 22nd July, the terrorists committed what would be remembered as one of the worst atrocities of the Palestinian emergency. The King David Hotel in Jerusalem housed the Secretariat of the Government of Palestine and the Headquarters of the British Forces. The terrorists took advantage of poor security to position a large quantity of explosives in the basement. After a short gun battle, the bomb was detonated, causing the wing housing the headquarters to collapse. There was chaos, as attempts were made to rescue survivors over the following days. Eventually 91 bodies were recovered, including civilians, fifteen of which were Jewish.

There was outrage amongst the British troops. When word filtered down to the guardsmen there was a great deal of anger. The men heard how the Jews had set up road blocks and had hindered the progress of the Royal Engineers as they moved to the scene with their lifting equipment. There was frustration that the troops were not allowed to be more aggressive toward the Irgun and many of the men felt that their hands were unfairly tied.

The terrorist attacks seemed to be less intense as the autumn approached, although Sid and his pioneers were regularly required to clear explosives from the roads and railway lines. In early November, the Battalion was tasked to cordon off Haifa docks, so that Jewish illegal immigrants could be disembarked from their ship. The San Dimitrio had a thirty degree list to starboard. Sid was amazed at how the ship had stayed afloat. Well over a thousand Jews walked down the gangplank. They were a pathetic sight and some of the guardsmen spoke of how they felt it was wrong to send those poor people back to a detention camp in Cyprus.

Things were even more difficult later that month as 'Operation London' was mounted. The Battalion once again cordoned the docks, but this time a much larger ship was involved. The occupants, numbering several thousand, were determined to resist deportation. An attempt was made by the Royal Artillery to board the ship, but they were driven back. Grenadiers took their place and assaulted the ship with the help of tear gas and a powerful hose. The Jews put up a fierce fight and several men were injured. Later the assault party would talk of being bombarded with corned beef tins!

At the end of 1946 and early 1947, the Battalion moved once again, this time to a camp in the Lydda district. Things here were rather busier and a series of operations were once again mounted. The Pioneers were usually heavily involved in one capacity or another and were by now very experienced. The Third Battalion became involved in mounting vehicle checkpoints and in guarding key points which were still being targeted by the IZL. Until then, the Battalion had managed to continue with its training, when it was not engaged on anti terrorist operations. But the situation had deteriorated so much that virtually no training was taking place. All available man power was required to guard key points, or was deployed on some sort of operation. Illegal immigrants continued to arrive, and the Battalion was frequently tasked to assist with escorting them in one direction or other. During one operation an armoured car hit a large mine. The vehicle was blown into the air and landed on top of Guardsman Roberts who was killed. There was once again a great deal of anger at the loss of a comrade in such circumstances. The Battalion had been relatively fortunate so far. Their casualties due to enemy action had been light, although Lieutenant D Charlesworth and Lance Corporal Billinghurst had both died in accidents. At the end of June, the Battalion changed its location once more, this time to the town of Nathanya.

A large number of terrorists had by now been captured and the Palestine government was under pressure to ensure that their outrages were severely punished. After a trial, a number of them were sentenced to death. One of these was Dov Gruner, a notorious criminal whose planned execution caused outrage amongst large sections of the Jewish community. A huge security operation was put in place to deal with the anticipated unrest that the execution would ignite. The Grenadiers, including Sid's pioneers, were positioned at various checkpoints all over the area. Gruner and three other terrorists were duly hanged in Acre Gaol on April 16th. They became the first 'martyrs'of the Irgun. The Army was able to contain the reaction, but there were yet to be repercussions from this and other executions.

On 4th May, in an audacious attack, the Irgun blew a hole in the wall of Acre Gaol. 255 prisoners were able to escape into the surrounding countryside. Ironically most of the escapees were Arabs. Inevitably search operations were mounted to catch the fugitives and the Grenadiers were heavily involved. In June, three Jews who had participated in the attack were subsequently tried and sentenced to death. Tension in the region was once again raised, as the army fully expected some sort of retaliation from the IZL. In July, two British Field Security NCOs, Sergeants Paice and Martin were abducted by Jewish terrorists from Nathanya in the Grenadier area of responsibility. The Irgun sent a clear message, if the death sentence was carried out on the Jews, then the British Sergeants would also hang.

The British authorities initially issued warnings and appealed for information regarding the two missing NCOs. When no information was received, the Brigade commander launched a massive operation to find the missing men. 'Operation Tiger' swung into action and a massive cordon was drawn around the town. A curfew was imposed on the civilian population. Entry and exit was tightly controlled via checkpoints. Special permits were issued to those who needed to leave the town on business. Once the cordon was in place, the town was divided into sectors and a huge search operation commenced. Military vehicles fitted with loud speakers drove around the streets appealing for information. The Grenadier Pioneer Platoon was required along with every other able bodied man in the Battalion. It was no easy task to search a town with a population of fifteen thousand people, and some said that it was like searching for a needle in a haystack. The pioneers checked every conceivable hiding place that was considered large enough to conceal a human being. On one occasion a cellar was deemed to be suspicious and the searchers were convinced that there was a false floor in place. The pioneers along with other members of the Battalion spent all night digging beneath the house. In the end nothing was found.

Operation Tiger continued for the best part of two weeks. It was always unlikely that the searchers would be able to locate the missing men, but it was hoped that the restrictions imposed on the population might generate some intelligence on their whereabouts. Many weapons were recovered, and more than a few wanted men were picked up, but there was no sign of the two sergeants. Few people doubted that the Irgun were ruthless enough to carry out their threat. The fate of the two sergeants was at the front of everyone's mind. At the end of the month the British authorities refused to bow to blackmail and the death sentence was carried out on the three Jews.

On 1st August, it was reported that the two sergeants had been murdered in retaliation, and the location of their bodies was made known to the authorities. The Grenadiers were quickly tasked to verify if the information was correct. The two bodies were found after a short search, in a Eucalyptus wood. Sid and the pioneers arrived shortly after. There was a strong suspicion that the area was mined, or booby-trapped, so a great deal of caution had to be exercised. The two young NCOs had been hanged. Their lifeless bodies hung by ropes from the branch of a

Grenadiers remove Jewish protesters, Palestine

tree. Because of the two week build up to the situation, there was a great deal of interest from the press and predictably they soon arrived at the site. The pioneers assisted the Royal Engineers in clearing the immediate area for mines, and a safe route was cleared to the bodies. Sid could see that each body had a large sheet of card pinned to its chest which appeared to have typed print on it. The press were clamouring for photographs of the scene and the whole affair was quite horrific for those involved.

The officer in charge of the Royal Engineers detachment decided that the bodies should have some dignity. He set about cutting the ropes which suspended the two murdered men. As the first body dropped to the ground there was an almighty explosion. Sid threw himself to the ground. Earth and rock whistled through the air. The immediate area was temporarily obscured by smoke and dust. It took a moment for the group to gather themselves and to realise what had happened. The bodies had been booby trapped by the Irgun. As the first body fell to the ground it had detonated a concealed mine. Miraculously, the Royal Engineer officer was not seriously injured, although he was badly shaken. The area was cleared more thoroughly this time and the young officer was led away for medical attention. As Sid and his pioneers combed the area for more surprises, they came across the badly disfigured remains of the second body. The first had completely gone, although there was evidence of its existence scattered around the little wood.

Some of the young men were given the grisly task of recovering the remains. The typed sheets that had been pinned to the chests of the two sergeants were also recovered. They were written in Hebrew, but Sid later learned that they contained an announcement that the two sergeants had been tried as spies. A series of charges had been listed including murder, torture and cruelty. The so called court had found the two guilty and had sentenced them to death. It went on to say that 'the request of the condemned men for clemency has been rejected'. The statement also claimed that this act had not been carried out in retaliation 'for the murder of Hebrew prisoners of war' but as an ordinary legal action of the 'court of the underground'. The men were angry and frustrated at this act of cold-blooded murder and when news of the note spread there was fury. This was a black day that would live with all those present for many years.

The terrorist war continued with no solution in sight. The Arabs too, attacked the British, and the troops became more and more frustrated. The Guardsmen were sometimes disgusted at the heavy handedness of certain other regiments, but they understood why they behaved this way. Many soldiers had been killed and some units had suffered quite heavy casualties. The manner of the murders further fuelled the anger of the troops. The terrorists often struck when the soldiers were least prepared to defend themselves, and the enemy showed little mercy. The Grenadiers were as frustrated as anyone else but they managed to maintain their discipline. There were no incidents of serious heavy handedness, even in the face of serious provocation.

The British government had become more and more weary of the Palestinian problem. There was no obvious solution and it was subsequently announced that Britain would give up the Palestine mandate, which it had held since 1920. The United Nations became heavily involved in the troubled region. In the autumn it was announced that Great Britain would withdraw. The country would be partitioned into two separate states, despite the fact that the Jews were still in a minority. The killing continued, as Jews and Arabs attacked each other in an effort to satisfy their mutual hatred.

In December 1947, the Battalion were told that they would be going home in the spring of the following year. Sid was delighted, as were the remainder of the Battalion. They were sick of being stuck between the warring factions. Trying hard to remain impartial and to protect the innocents, had worn them all down. There was clearly no solution to this. The best thing they could do, was to get out, and leave them all to it. Early in the New Year, companies of the First Battalion started to arrive in Palestine. They were to relieve their comrades in the Third but over a period of months so that they gained sufficient experience of the difficult situation. There were many familiar faces that Sid remembered from his time at Windsor. He had served with some of the seniors in France.

It was around this time that the Sergeant Major imposed a 'total swearing ban'. An observation had been made that the Battalion's language had deteriorated to an unacceptable level. They would soon be returning to civilisation and would be expected to behave correctly. No one was sure where this idea had originated but they all had their own theory, blaming everyone from the Padre to the Commanding Officer. The origins of the ban were irrelevant. The Sergeant Major enforced it ruthlessly. His Warrant Officers were instructed to stamp out all forms of profanity which they tried hard to do. Unfortunately, the ban didn't come easily to the seniors either and several CSMs were heard to shout 'Stop F***** swearing you'! or words to that effect. Naturally, the ban had little impact, and many became tired of enforcing it, returning to the ranks of the cursing majority.

The last few months dragged on with the security situation deteriorating rapidly. The Jews felt that they had won and were keen to occupy their new home. The

Arabs now felt betrayed, and hated the British almost as much as the Jews. Both sides stepped up their efforts to seize ground, or to consolidate what they held. The British were frequently caught between the two sides. Unfortunately, neither side regarded the British as neutral and they were treated as legitimate targets.

There was great relief when April came around. On the 4th, the Battalion was transported to the docks at Haifa. A major security operation was required to clear their route in, and to secure the docks. Things were infinitely worse now, than they had been when they arrived at the end of 1945. No one was sorry to leave Palestine and morale was high once the Battalion was aboard the M.V. Franconia. She sailed from Haifa, and finally docked at Liverpool ten days later. As always the troops crowded on deck to see the Mersey lights. Once disembarked, the evening was spent travelling to Windsor by train. Victoria Barracks was to be the new home of the Third Battalion and Sid was very happy with that.

Chapter 19

Home Again

Victoria Barracks was just as he remembered it, hardly anything had changed apart from the number of men within its high brick walls. The Training Battalion was gone now. Recruits were sent to Pirbright from Caterham instead. It was a little strange. He was used to squads of men drilling, and weapon training being conducted all over the barracks, but there was none of that now. The Third Battalion was about to be sent on a very hard earned leave, but there was plenty of work to be done first. The pioneers were kept busy. There were crates to unpack, signs to be put up and of course the Commanding Officer inspected every part of the barracks. They were back in battledress now and there were no terrorists to distract them. The Battalion parades were re-established very quickly and the Sergeants in Waiting could be seen hurrying across barracks in answer to any unexpected bugle calls. It was a frustrating time, the men just wanted to get away on leave, so it was a great relief when they were finally released.

Sid and Pat had written to each other nearly every day, during his time in Palestine, and they had both longed to be together again. He wasted no time on his return to Windsor, and the two were soon reunited. It was wonderful for them both, and he was amazed at how David and Brian had grown. This was a happy time. He would be in Windsor indefinitely, and they would be able to see each other on a regular basis. Pat and the boys went with him to Poole. Most of his leave was spent at his mother's home, where they were made very welcome. It was great to see all of

White cliffs on south coast

At home with Pat

the family again. His brother had survived incarceration at the hands of the Japanese, and had been repatriated to Australia at the end of the war. Sid learned that he had recovered well in the following years, and was now settled on the other side of the world. There was comfort too in the knowledge that he would be able to visit his family regularly, for the first time in many years, and that Pat would be able to accompany him.

It was a great leave, but as always it soon came to an end. He wasn't bothered, Pat was nearby, and he would be able to see her nearly every day. He could often be found at her father's house, or playing darts in his old haunts. There were fewer troops around now, and the yanks had all gone home, so Windsor was a much more pleasant place. He was able to take up football again and he represented the Battalion on an almost weekly basis. His love for the beautiful game was unaffected by his years overseas and he often took Pat, David and Brian into London to see the Arsenal play. Pat was not a great fan herself, but the boys were always enthusiastic about these trips.

The Battalion soon settled back into the London district routine. The expected drill parades were held, to get the men back up to the standards required to carry out public duties. The Guardsmen were expecting to be issued their tunics and bearskin caps but this was not to be. To their surprise, they learned that the Guards were still mounting guard in khaki. There was disappointment in some quarters, most of the men had never worn home service clothing and they had been looking forward to the experience. The war had been over for some time but budgetary constraints did not yet allow for the Brigade of Guards to don their traditional uniforms. Mounting guard in Windsor would be a real experience. It had been over a decade since Sid had been on a proper ceremonial parade. There was hardly anyone who had done the job in his current rank. Most of the men had never done any form of public duties. The learning curve would be a steep one.

Hour after hour was spent on the parade square as the Sergeant Major and Drill Sergeants knocked the Battalion into shape, using the well tested and familiar formula that had been in use as long as anyone could remember. Before long the desired results had been achieved and the first company was ready to mount Guard. On 22nd May, the Third Battalion Grenadier Guards mounted guard at Windsor Castle. To the relief of all concerned, the parade went smoothly and in the following weeks a steady routine was established. Sid rarely took part in these routine activities. His role as the Pioneer Sergeant meant that he was a member of the 'Battalion Staff' and as such was only required to attend the more prestigious occasions. He was on parade on 31st May when Princess Elizabeth once again inspected the Battalion, this time at Victoria Barracks. Wet weather meant that the parade had to be changed, but the troops were delighted to see their colonel once again. The young princess was always popular with the troops and they were honoured by her presence.

Preparation for the King's Birthday parade was now under way. This was to be only the second proper Trooping of the Colour parade since 1939. The Battalion was to find 150 street liners for the parade, and they could be seen practising around barracks daily. Much to everyone's surprise it had been decided that the parade would be held in full dress, so there was much to be done. The fitting of tunics and the grooming of bearskins became a major priority. When the great day finally arrived all of their rehearsals were in vain. The parade was cancelled due to wet weather. It was the first time, with the exception of the war years, that a birthday parade had been cancelled since the general strike of 1926.

Industrial action was to touch the Battalion in a different way that month. The country's economy was struggling to recover from the war years and rationing was still in place. There was a good deal of discontent and industrial unrest which resulted in a number of strikes being called. Most significant was the bitter strike action taken by dockers. The government decided to use troops to break the strike and the Third Battalion were ordered to provide 200 men for this task. The troops who were detailed were rapidly transported to London docks. They were made responsible for unloading stores from the cargo holds of a variety of merchant ships. Large rope nets were lowered into the holds. The Guardsmen filled them with perishable goods and meat which were then lifted onto the dockside. Non Commissioned Officers were detailed as 'Tellers' while the Guardsmen did most of the lifting and carrying. Occasionally there were breakages and goods spilled out. These were unofficially considered as 'perks'. Their employment as dock workers was mercifully short and the Grenadiers soon returned to Windsor. This was as well because the task rapidly became unpopular.

The situation in Palestine still dominated the news at this time. Sid learned that the First Battalion had been among the last troops to leave the troubled region. They had extracted themselves with some difficulty, as the Jews and Arabs fought for control of the key areas. His old friends in that Battalion were now safe in Tri-

Sid Dowland

poli. In August, the Third Battalion welcomed a new Commanding Officer, Lt Colonel TFC Winnington and a new Sergeant Major, RSM 'Reg' Butler. No one knew it at the time but they were to lead the Third Battalion on another adventure.

In June 1948, communist insurgent forces commenced a guerrilla war which was designed to end British rule in Malaya. Chinese veterans of the fight against the Japanese were motivated to now turn their hatred against the British. Weapon caches which had been concealed deep in the jungle were unearthed, and distributed to the fighters of the 'Malayan Peoples Anti British Army' (MPABA) or later the 'Malayan Races Liberation Army' (MRLA). There was widespread intimidation and murder of Chinese, Malay and Indian workers employed by British or European owned enterprises. The situation continued to worsen as the authorities struggled to contain the insurgents. On 16th June, three European managers were murdered and the high commissioner was forced to declare a state of emergency. On 14th August, the Battalion received mobilisation orders for 'Operation Visor'. They were to deploy to Malaya as part of 2 Guards Brigade with the 2nd Coldstream and 2nd Scots Guards.

The pace of life naturally quickened once again and a good deal of training was carried out in the Great Park, or at other local training areas. Many of the men found it hard to believe that they were to deploy overseas again after such a brief period at home. Sid had to break the news gently to Pat. The situation wasn't helped by the fact that no one could say for how long they would be overseas. He once again found himself in demand.

The Pioneers would be needed in the jungle and not for fixing broken windows. Many reserves and reinforcements joined the Battalion at Windsor. Some of the national servicemen who were due to be discharged in the coming months were informed that their service was to be extended. A large number of recruits joined from the Training Battalion at Pirbright. They were accompanied by their training staff and had not completed their basic training. The presence of so many raw Guardsmen in the barracks became the subject of some discussion by the more experienced men.

The training regime continued right up to the day of departure. The Third Battalion once again marched out of barracks, behind the Corps of Drums, to the railway station. Large crowds were there to see them off and there were, as always, many tears shed. The train transported the troops to Liverpool from where they finally sailed on 10th September 1948, aboard the SS Staffordshire. The voyage was predictably cramped and some of the newest national servicemen had difficulty with their hammocks. Many were sick and unsurprisingly the ship smelt badly below decks. It was always a welcome relief to get on deck and breathe the fresh sea air. At Malta the troops were allowed ashore for a few hours before they embarked once again for the voyage to Tripoli where they dropped anchor once more. The heavy seas made it impossible for the ship to dock and there was a great deal of difficulty in ferrying a large draft of men from the 1st Battalion out to the Staffordshire. When the troops were eventually taken on board, they were a very welcome addition. These were largely senior Guardsmen and experienced Non Commissioned Officers who would complement some of the younger Third Battalion men.

Next, the troopship sailed down the Suez Canal, allowing the men a view of the Sinai Desert on the port side. The Egyptian land to starboard was more fertile, and Sid saw many familiar sights from his previous service in this area. As they entered the Red Sea, he was reminded of the uncomfortable time he had spent here with the Sixth Battalion travelling in the opposite direction. Classical music was played over the ship's loud speaker system by the Orderly Room Sergeant, who had a woefully inadequate selection of music. The troops rapidly tired of listening to the same record over and over. Some said that it was some form of brainwashing technique and others jokingly threatened mutiny if it didn't stop.

Mercifully, the Staffordshire put into Colombo in Ceylon and the troops were once again allowed ashore. It was a welcome break after being confined aboard their iron prison for so long. This was new ground for Sid and he was eager to explore the city. There was terrible poverty in many areas, quite unlike anything that most of the men had seen before. It was possible to be seated inside a luxury hotel by travelling just a very short distance. The first of many 'Tiger' Beers were supped in these hotels, before returning to the Staffordshire and the voyage across the Indian Ocean to Singapore. Eventually on 7th October, after almost four weeks on board the troop ship, they docked at the Far Eastern Port.

Chapter 20

Malaya

Very few members of the Battalion had served in the Far East before. Some of the Officers had visited the region but there was virtually no experience of the jungle environment that they would soon be operating in. The humidity was overwhelming for the young national servicemen, most of whom had never been out of the UK before. Jungle green uniforms had been issued to the men. They had been wearing them for some time, and everyone seemed to have black sweat marks down their backs and under their arms. They couldn't wait to disembark from the ship in the hope that the temperature on land would be cooler than aboard the Staffordshire.

Sid knew a little about Singapore, it was here that his brother had been captured during the war. It had been a British naval base since 1867, and had become an important strategic and commercial centre. He had heard it referred to as 'Gibraltar in the Far East'. The Island of Singapore lay at the southern end of the Malay peninsula. It was there, in February 1942, that the Japanese had overwhelmed the British and Commonwealth defenders after a rapid advance down Malaya. The fall of Singapore was probably the worst British defeat of the war. 100,000 men had been captured by a much smaller Japanese force. Many of the prisoners had been held in the infamous Changi Prison and others had been sent to work on the Burma railway. As he looked out across the harbour he wondered how his brother must have felt, six years earlier, as he had been forced to surrender. His thoughts turned to the present, as Guardsmen made their way down the gang plank, rifles slung over their shoulders.

A military band was playing on the quayside and there was much hustle and bustle. Military fatigue parties transported boxes and bundles, and others supervised parties of native dock workers. There was a group of senior officers looking on and Ghurkha soldiers mixed with Malay Police Officers. There were unfamiliar sights, sounds and smells, it was all quite exciting. But Sid was in no doubt that there would be some difficult work ahead of them in the coming months. The Battalion was to spend the next couple of days organising itself at a large transit camp on the outskirts of Singapore. But his Pioneers were required to move up country and to organise their new home.

The advance party boarded an old steam train destined for the troubled Selangor province, over 200 miles to the north. As they crossed the causeway, which linked the island of Singapore to the Malay Peninsula, there was a feeling that they were crossing into a more dangerous area. Some called it 'bandit country' and it was certainly true that bandits had been very active in recent months. Convoys and trains had been attacked by the communists, so the Grenadiers trundled further north with their feelings of security starting to desert them. In many places the jungle came right down to the railway tracks. Sid noted how easy it would be to mount an ambush on their vulnerable transport. Troops had been stationed on the roofs of the carriages, in small enclosures surrounded by sandbags. Each of them was equipped with a Bren gun, and they surveyed the jungle nervously.

Sungei Besi Camp, Malaya

The heat and humidity was unrelenting, although it was possible to catch the breeze if you sat in the right place. The simple wooden benches were very uncomfortable and holes in the floor at the end of the carriages provided the only toilet facilities. It was a nervous and uncomfortable journey, so there was some relief when the train finally came to a halt, after many hours of puffing through the dense green scenery. To his surprise he found that there was no station, just a grass clearing, deserted except for a few locals selling bananas. He was however pleased to see a couple of 3-ton trucks and a well armed escort of Ghurkhas. No one was keen to hang around. The advance party, complete with their baggage and stores, was soon loaded onto the trucks for another nervous journey, this time by road, to their final destination where they hoped to be more secure.

The road trip through the thick jungle was thankfully short. The highlight was when they passed through a huge tin mine which they later learned was the largest in the world. When they arrived at their destination Sid was appalled. Sungei Besi camp was not a camp at all, at least not yet. The Ghurkhas had cleared a huge expanse of undergrowth and there were scores of piles of 'tentage' dumped around the clearing. But there were no buildings, no standing tents and no perimeter fence. He soon realised that they would need to get stuck in quickly, if they were to have any tents erected in which to sleep that night. The little party tried to make sense of the heaped canvass and began erecting the heavy green structures.

Suddenly, the grey skies produced the most terrific downpour, rain the like of which none of them had seen before. There was no shelter and everyone was soaked to the skin in seconds. The heavy rain hammered into the tents making it impossible to continue. The ground quickly turned to slush and visibility was obscured by the sheer volume of falling water. As they sheltered under the dripping, and now seriously sagging tents, Sid wondered how they would manage.

The rain storm was mercifully short and subsided after about half an hour. They were to learn that this was an almost daily routine, at this time of year, in this part of the country. They were able to erect a few tents before it got dark. There was just about enough time to put their few belongings inside, and to mount a guard before the light went completely. There were no beds yet, just a blanket and a mosquito net. The troops had been warned about malaria and the importance of taking their daily Paludrine tablets. Sid was quick to remind them about how serious the disease could be. He knew all about that. The guardsmen took turns patrolling the little camp in pairs throughout the night. The lead man carried a Sten gun and his partner followed a discreet distance behind armed with a rifle. It was a very nervous night and they felt vulnerable. The bandits could be anywhere around them, waiting to strike at any moment. The Englishmen were unused to the sounds of the jungle at night, and were very wary of the vicious insects, spiders and snakes that they imagined all around them. Fortunately, they survived the night without serious incident, and were able to watch the sun come up over the steaming jungle the following day.

Sgt Dowland, Malaya, 1948

They started work where they had left off and managed to restore the dripping canvass to something resembling accommodation. More green and brown structures joined those that had already been erected, and they were positioned according to a carefully thought out plan. Experience told them that monsoon ditches would also need to be dug around the tents. It was important to prioritise so that the key structures were in place before the rest of the Battalion arrived. Most important was the Orderly Room complex. It would house the Commanding Officer and the key personnel in Battalion Headquarters, not least of whom was the Sergeant Major. It took eight tents to house the headquarters before the advance party were able to move on. They worked all day, but it seemed that the tents would never be erected. There were still hundreds of canvass piles lying out in the jungle clearing.

The Battalion main party soon arrived at Sungei Besi. They had come by train via Kuala Lumpur, the capital city of Malaya, which was only about seven miles from the camp site. Some of the seniors were rather disappointed at what they found, and were less than complimentary about the work rate of the advance party. In the late afternoon Sid's little group had the last laugh. The heavens opened once again, soaking the new arrivals, who suddenly began to realise what the advance party had been up against. The soggy and steaming men walked about the camp area wondering what on earth they had let themselves in for.

Over the next few days the camp took shape. The Commanding Officer was keen to get the men properly trained for the job that lay ahead. A route march was organised which the troops found extremely difficult in the humidity. A small party of officers and NCOs had been sent to learn about jungle warfare, but the rest of the Battalion was alarmingly young and inexperienced which was a great concern. Soon they would commence operations proper. The Battalion had to support the police in the southern half of Selangor province, which included Kuala Lumpur. The country seemed massive. The men wondered how they would restrict the activities of the communist bandits who lived deep in the jungle, and who seemed to operate with impunity.

The bandits had been very active in Selangor, and had killed a large number of soldiers already. Sungei Besi seemed like an attractive target and security was stepped up. Training continued daily. Companies and platoons marched out into the surrounding countryside so that they could learn the skills that they would need to operate effectively. No shower facilities were yet in place. It soon became common practice for the men to strip off during the afternoon downpour, and to soap themselves while the monsoon lasted. It was resourcefulness at its best, but not a pretty sight!

The Pioneers were in great demand as there was a huge amount of work to be done around the camp. As the weeks passed, the pioneers started to build some more permanent structures from bamboo and other materials. The Sergeant Major was keen for the sergeants' mess to be rather grander than the canvass construction that they had hitherto become used to. A rather splendid 'Basha' rose from the ground. There were showers and water storage tanks to be built, together with fences and signs. The whole platoon was kept very busy in Sungei Besi. Once the men became accustomed to the extreme weather conditions, life at the camp was bearable. The pleasant green hills and wild jungle were strangely beautiful, provided that you were not patrolling through them.

Grenadiers in action with a 2 inch mortar, Malaya, 1948

Second Guards Brigade soon became fully operational, and the inexperienced men of the Third Battalion quickly learned their trade in the jungle. The guardsmen experienced how difficult it was to hack their way through dense thickets of saplings, festoons of creepers and large clumps of bamboo. There were massive tree trunks with huge roots that patrols had to clamber over. They often encountered fast flowing rivers which were extremely dangerous to cross. Deep sticky swamps were full of insects, all of which seemed intent on eating them. They learned to overcome their initial fear of the deadly snakes and other poisonous creatures. They also became expert at removing the bloated and blood filled leeches that clung to their bodies. They got used to being permanently wet, and became accustomed to the light canvass jungle boots that they had been issued. The eerie sounds of the jungle at night, and the constant buzzing of mosquitoes became routine. They had to adjust to the painfully slow rate of advance, when on the move during the day.

The Brigade had adopted a new insignia, a bayonet crossed over a Kukri on a background of blue red blue. It was displayed on the Battalion's vehicles, another task for Sid's busy sign writers. The rifle company men were now undertaking patrols into the jungle for several days at a time. They were carrying out search or arrest operations with the police. The pioneers were not used on many of these early operations, as they were fully occupied at Sungei Besi. Sid's Platoon had been reorganised. Some of his old hands from Palestine had been discharged and replaced by others, some very recently.

Lance Sergeants 'Jigger' Hall and 'Smudge' Smith were his right hand men in the Platoon. Both were fairly easy going and hardly archetypal Grenadier Non

Commissioned Officers. There were two Corporals, Ken Robinson and Dave Sheldon. Ken was a huge man, standing fully 6'6". He had a tremendous sense of humour and together with Dave, played the harmonica extremely well. There was little to do in the camp during the long evenings. The Pioneers would often be found crowded into a tent, singing along to the accompaniment of the two musical corporals. Guardsman Tom Parker was older than most of the others and sported a huge beer belly. He was pals with Peter Youdale, another real character, and one of the Platoon sign writers. Then there was Waldron, a Norfolk man who reminded everyone of an old farmer, and Dave Skeltcher, another of the Platoon jokers. His personality was the opposite to that of Guardsman Schofield, a rather introverted character. He kept himself to himself. Bernard Porter was a little man from Birmingham who wore a perpetual smile. Nothing got him down and he was a popular member of the team. Somehow all of these different characters managed to gel, and the pioneers were a very happy group. Sid looked after his men, but was quick to put them right if they went off the rails.

There were a great many characters outside the Platoon too. CSM 'Daddy' Cullen was responsible for Headquarter Company, and was a popular and entertaining Warrant Officer. His personality was in stark contrast to the 'Scorpion', another of the Battalion's CSMs, who was reviled by most of the guardsmen. He was a strict disciplinarian and the men did their best to avoid him, although this proved to be difficult. The 'Scorp' was the scourge of Sungei Besi. The Battalion post NCO was none other than Wally Durant. Sid's old pal had decided that after two years as a civilian, the army was more to his liking. Wally had reenlisted earlier in the year. The two old friends were able to sink many 'Tigers' together, to the accompaniment of Wally's legendary and dubious musical talents.

Living on the edge of the jungle in a tented camp, with the constant threat of attack by bandits, meant that life was not quite the same as being 'in barracks'. NCOs who made themselves unpopular could suddenly find themselves the victim

of revenge pranks. A number of Drummers managed to throw the rifle of one of their NCOs into the latrine. Unfortunately for them they were discovered, and were made to recover the missing item with grappling hooks, as the Battalion's CSMs stood over them. The guilty men were then made to clean the stinking weapon and were reported for the offence. It was hardly a worthwhile venture.

As the companies became more proficient in jungle operations, the length of time spent under the dense canopy increased. The troops often carried out patrols in the Kajang area to the south of Kuala Lumpur, or 'KL' as it was known. Kajang had a reputation as a dangerous area and the police had invested a great deal of time and energy in intelligence gathering. There were a bewildering number of locals involved in the fight against the communists. Interpreters, trackers and Chinese policemen were all to be found accompanying Grenadier patrols. The aboriginal people who lived in the jungle areas were courted by the authorities for their local knowledge. Unfortunately, they were also wooed by the communists, and the troops rarely trusted them fully. They could often be seen walking around semi clothed, clutching shotguns or even blow pipes. Iban trackers were often attached to patrols. They wore all manner of clothes, from scrounged jungle shirts to simple loin cloths, until they were properly equipped by the Quartermaster. They were invariably covered in tribal tattoos and had their ear lobes pierced and stretched. There were many stories about their blood-thirsty nature, but their skill in the jungle was never in question.

As well as having to learn new tactics to cope in the jungle environment, there were different weapons too. The No 5 Lee Enfield rifle replaced their normal No 4s and the Battalion was issued with the Australian made Owen Gun. This was a similar weapon to the Sten but was regarded as being more reliable and soon became popular. Sid also noted that the American M1 carbine was still in use in the jungle. He wasn't surprised and still rated the weapon highly.

Pioneers were now required to accompany patrols on certain tasks. If there were any suspected booby traps, Sid or members of his platoon, would be required to make them safe. Sometimes when a village abandoned by bandits was discovered, he would lay his own booby traps in the hope of catching a communist terrorist off guard. Operations were stepped up and there were some notable successes, with a steady number of suspects being arrested. During December and January contact was made on several occasions with CTs, ie Communist Terrorists, as they were now starting to be known. The rules of engagement seemed to be simpler than in Palestine and several CTs were killed. Settlements were burned, to deny shelter and to discourage Chinese squatters. The squatters were moved on by the police and the army. This made it more difficult for the MRLA to sustain themselves in the jungle. The government strategy was to isolate the terrorists from any form of support, and to hunt them down, wherever they chose to hide.

Back at Sungei Besi, sport as always was organised. Sid made himself available to play cricket, and of course his beloved football, which helped to break up the monotony of life in Malaya. When they were off duty, the troops had taken to swimming at the large tin mine. There were two huge holes in the ground, one of which had become a pleasant looking lake and the men wasted no time in using it for recreation. Unfortunately, a number of serious ear infections resulted and the troops became more cautious.

A cricket match Malaya. Note the Owen Gun nearby.

The Battalion was fortunate to be close to Kuala Lumpur and the troops were often permitted to take leave there. These trips were a popular escape from the green of Sungei Besi. There was civilisation in KL, hardly London town, but welcome none the less. There were cinemas, bars, restaurants, and of course the usual establishments of ill repute. The guardsmen were by now more than used to Tiger Beer, and the regular trips into KL were used to increase their familiarity with the Asian brew. Before they knew it Christmas had arrived, although there wasn't much of a festive feel about the place. It was still incredibly humid and the temperature was often above 100 degrees.

The pioneers were tasked to decorate the various messes as best they could. There were now permanent bashas that had been built for the men to eat in. The officers and sergeants had smaller but grander versions. Sid's men manufactured whatever decorations that they could from any materials that could be begged, borrowed or stolen. It was amazing what could be knocked up with some wood and a lick of paint. The sign writers produced some life sized painted guardsmen as a reminder of life in England. Christmas dinner passed off successfully, and the Battalion hierarchy seemed pleased with the pioneers' efforts.

Because of the long period of time spent overseas with the third Battalion, a good number of the more senior guardsmen and Non Commissioned Officers qualified to be sent home early. Sid found that he fell into this category, but decided to remain in Malaya with his Battalion. As a result he discovered that he was entitled to a substantial period of leave which he opted to take while he could. A popular leave centre had been established at Penang to the north, which the troops travelled to by train. The camp there had one of the best beaches in the country and was very popular. Hong Kong was an alternative for those who wanted to leave Malaya and he considered the option for a while.

Then he realised that he was unlikely to be so close to Australia again and thought about visiting his brother there. He applied to take leave in Australia and to his surprise his application was granted. Sid now set about organising his travel arrangements. He would need to draw a substantial amount of money to finance his passage, and he arranged for a transfer of some savings from his account in the UK. Unfortunately the cash didn't arrive before his departure date, but he was able to arrange a loan through the Quartermaster. Soon after he set off for Singapore where he would board the liner for Australia.

Several interesting and relaxing days were spent in Singapore. There was time to see the city that he had found so fascinating a few months before. He had been issued a banker's draft and was desperate to change it for cash. He visited several banks in the city, but none of them were keen to give the considerable sum of £100 to a Non Commissioned man. Sid was very frustrated as he entered yet another marble floored bank. He decided to take a different approach with the Chinese bank clerk. He explained why he needed the cash, and told the civilian how difficult it was to obtain any credit unless you were an officer. The Bank Clerk looked at him suspiciously, and then asked what regiment he belonged to. Sid replied that he was in the Grenadier Guards and the clerk immediately altered his attitude. He was very happy to change the draft and quickly handed over the money. The Third Battalion Pioneer Sergeant left the building very happy, and more than a little grateful that he had chosen to join a regiment with such a good reputation.

His liner duly arrived in port and he was able to board the ship, bound for Australia as a second class passenger. He was required to share a cabin during the voyage and soon met his travelling companions. There was a young Malayan, who was bound for university in Sydney where he intended to become a Doctor. He was a pleasant and well-mannered young man who Sid soon learned to like. The others were less agreeable. One was an Irishman who had just been released from prison. He had served a short sentence for fighting aboard another ship. The other was being deported for some heinous crime or other. Sid decided to keep an eye on his personal possessions during the voyage. The ship had a very good bar and there were plenty of activities to be enjoyed as they crossed the ocean.

The liner eventually made port in Australia where he was met by his brother. They were both delighted to see each other. They had not met since well before the war and there was so much that had happened in the years since. They were able to compare notes on their war service, in two different armies fighting for the same empire. There were many differences between their POW camps. Sid was appalled to hear from his brother how the allied prisoners had been mistreated by the Japanese. He had heard many stories, but to hear an eye witness account from his own brother was dreadful. It had taken Walter a long time to recover from his time in captivity, but he now seemed fine. He had been an upholsterer before the war and had decided to set up his own business.

Sid was able to use his woodworking skills, by helping to build a workshop for his brother from which to practise his trade. The two spent many happy hours together. They talked endlessly of their childhood experiences and of their other family members and friends. In all, he spent a month in Australia, and was grateful that he had been able to see Walter again. But as always, time ran out and he was forced to say his farewells and board ship back to Singapore.

Little had changed during his absence. The rain still fell heavily in the afternoon and the tiger beer was still consumed over card games in the evenings. He had been away for six weeks and some of his friends were surprised to see him. They thought he had been posted back to England. There were lots of enquiries about how he had managed to wangle such a long leave. But nobody really minded, his war service was well known, and people knew that he always did his bit.

March 1949 proved to be a busy and rather tragic month for the Battalion. Until then there had been a number of successes. Quite a few bandits had been accounted for and several enemy camps had been destroyed. Fortunately there had been no serious casualties as a result of enemy action, but that was about to change. Early in the month, during a patrol deep in the jungle, a Grenadier Platoon commanded by Lt John Farrar settled down to camp for the night. The Platoon Commander decided to check the alertness of his sentries. He was tragically shot and killed in the process. The sentry responsible for the shooting was an old hand from the years spent in Italy who had not been prepared to take chances when there were bandits about. There was a long trek to bring the dead officer's body out of the jungle and the Platoon was understandably mortified at his death. In the subsequent investigation, the guardsman who had fired the fatal shot was found to have acted correctly. But it was a terrible blow to all concerned, and a tragic waste of a young life.

On 12th March, another Platoon was tasked to carry out a patrol in the Sungei Jeloh valley near Kajang. The patrol of about twenty men was mounted in three 15cwt truck. They were due to be dropped off on a foot patrol into the dense jungle. As the trucks slowly made their way along the winding tracks, the lead vehicle suddenly found the road ahead blocked. As the vehicle slowed to a halt, the calm was suddenly shattered by the sound of gunfire. A party of around 15 terrorists had mounted a well planned ambush. A number of men were hit. Those who managed to dismount from the vehicles had great difficulty in finding and identifying the enemy. Grenades were rolled down the slope by the attackers which caused more confusion. Captain DW Hargreaves, together with three other men, mounted a counter attack up the hillside. He was quickly hit and wounded, along with several other members of the Platoon. The bandits were able to make good their escape, leaving the badly mauled Platoon to tend to their dead and dying.

News of the ambush reached Sungei Besi shortly afterwards. Like the rest of the Battalion, Sid's pioneers waited for news of the casualties. Five men had been killed, or died of their wounds shortly afterwards. Another two had been wounded along with Captain Hargreaves. Among the dead was Cpl Chriscoli. He was a well known veteran of the North African and Italian campaigns, and holder of the Military Medal. Everyone knew at least one of the dead men, and there was a great deal of anger in the camp. Guardsman Youdale, the sign writer, had been a Trained Soldier at the Depot, and had looked after Guardsmen Hall, Herrett and Martin when they were recruits. All three were now dead, along with Guardsman Ryan. The Pioneers were subsequently ordered to make the crosses to mark their graves. It was Youdale who painted the names of his former charges on the crosses. March was a black month for the 3rd Battalion and a solemn atmosphere fell over Sungei Besi for some days.

Sgt Dowland dismantles a booby trap, Batu caves 1949

Operations against the bandits had to continue regardless of the recent losses and the pioneers were warned for another task. Sid and most of his platoon would be required on this job, so they set about drawing the stores and equipment that would be required. The operation was to take place at the Batu Caves, a massive complex of underground caverns and tunnels. Reputedly it stretched for some 50 miles below the surface. Intelligence suggested that the MRLA had been using the vast network of caves for concealment and for transit around the region. Some reports suggested that a headquarters was sited there. It was clearly impossible to mount a search operation on the whole complex, so it was decided that some of the main cave entrances would be cleared. The opportunity would also be taken to booby trap the huge caverns, to deny their use to the bandits.

This was clearly a job for Sid's expertise and he was quite excited at the prospect. He knew that his men were well trained on the explosives that they would be using. The chances of encountering a communist patrol were higher than normal. He considered how he would go about the task. There would be plenty of places for the bandits to hide and they would be quite vulnerable at the cave entrances. Grenades were the answer. A few Mills Bombs lobbed around the corners would be enough to see off any terrorist. He sent a couple of men off to draw as many 36 Grenades as they could. He also thought about the quantity of explosives they would need and the other materials to assemble the deadly booby traps.

Once preparations were complete, all the troops involved in the operation mounted their transport and headed off toward Kuala Lumpur. The weather was dreadful and dense, heavy rain soaked everyone to the skin. The Commanding Officer and the Adjutant had decided to come on the operation too. They travelled in a separate vehicle. The pioneers and their supporting troops dismounted some distance from their objective, which would be approached on foot by means of a jungle trail. There was a very long march through the thick jungle. They moved towards the vast wall of rock that somewhere concealed miles of tunnels. The rain continued to fall and progress was very slow. Each of the pioneers was heavily laden with ammunition and explosives including a bag containing eight Mills bombs per man. The leading troops were very cautious. The rain would mask the sound of their approach, but there could be bandits anywhere near the caves.

The long snake of green clad soldiers eventually wound their way through the dramatic landscape. Huge granite towers covered in thick green undergrowth towered above them. They made their way towards a massive cavern that could be clearly seen from some distance. Sid had been told to clear the first half mile of the cave. Then they would lay booby traps to deny the caves as a transit route for the CTs. The Grenadiers arrived at the entrance and he conveyed the plan to the remainder of the pioneers. They were to keep spread out with their Sten guns ready to fire. He would lead them into the cave and would use grenades to clear round any corners. He peered round the rocky outcrop which formed the cave entrance.

Seeing that it was clear he cautiously stepped into the cavern, his Sten pressed against his shoulder ready for action. He could see fairly clearly for about a hundred yards. There was no sign of any human activity. As he moved deeper inside the ancient formation, the light started to dim. The sound of the heavy rain behind him receded, to be replaced by a hollow echo as rocks fell away from his feet. Torches were switched on to aid their advance. After a few minutes, he reached the point where the cave bent sharply away to the right. Sid hugged the rock wall and pulled a grenade from his ammunition pouch. If there were any bandits lying in wait this would soon sort them out. He signalled his intent to the man following him. After a short delay he pulled the pin and gently lobbed the grenade around the corner. All of the following pioneers clutched their weapons, in case the imminent explosion forced any desperate communists out of their hiding place.

The Mills bomb detonated with a massive roar, amplified ten fold by the rock walls of the cave. Everyone was temporarily deafened. The noise from the explosion was much greater than they had expected. Now there was something else, a high pitched screaming and a very loud flapping noise. Bats! millions of them. The grenade had disturbed a huge colony which had previously gone unnoticed above their heads. The frightened creatures now swarmed around the cave in panic. Their screeching was ear piercing. The Grenadiers were forced to squat, with their hands over their heads for protection, as the bats dive bombed them. There were so many that it was impossible to move. The little group endured the onslaught for about five minutes until Sid decided to beat a retreat to the cave entrance. It was impossible to continue until the bats had settled back into their resting places on the cavern roof.

It took some time for the colony to settle itself back into its original position. The Commanding Officer decided that it would be best not to use any more grenades inside the cave. If they had been there at all, any bandits would be long gone by now. Sid was able to set a few booby traps, before moving on to another cavern which would hopefully be bat free. He posted a rear sentry who was detailed to watch over the jungle trail that they had approached on. The sentry had climbed into a tree where he was able to observe the trail. His Sergeant had given instructions that no friendly forces were expected to approach along the trail, so if there was any movement it would most likely be bandits.

The young pioneer settled onto his perch and listened to the pouring rain as it struck the undergrowth. It was occasionally interrupted by the distant report from the Mills grenades inside the caves. He suddenly became aware of a rustling noise. Someone was approaching up the track. Alert now, he cocked the Sten gun and prepared to open fire on the approaching bandits. He took careful aim and waited for the first communist to appear. As the figure emerged from the jungle he shifted his aim and started to depress the trigger. He then noticed that this was a European. Although he was soaking wet, he soon saw that it was a Grenadier officer. The safety catch applied, Guardsman Youdale breathed a sigh of relief. The young Captain had arrived unannounced and had decided to join his Commanding Officer. He had almost joined his maker.

The operation at Batu Caves took all day and was very tiring. No bandits were encountered and there was little evidence of human activity. Sid did locate a cooking pot and this was duly booby trapped but without success. Some days later the pioneers returned to dismantle their lethal explosives. No one wanted to kill or injure the local aboriginal people who might inadvertently trigger the devices. The operation to dismantle the booby traps took almost as long as the one to set them.

Back at Sungei Besi the pioneers settled back into the routine. There was always plenty to do in camp, as well as out in the jungle. The Battalion continued its seemingly endless patrol programme against the communists. Contact was rarely made with the enemy and the guardsmen found the patrols rather frustrating. What the young National Servicemen failed to appreciate was that the constant presence of the army in the jungle made movement very difficult for the communists. Undoubtedly their operations were hindered. Such patrols were being conducted all over the country. Occasional contact was made by most units, who invariably claimed to have killed the odd bandit here and there. The attrition rate was such that the MRLA were forced to withdraw ever deeper into the jungle in order to regroup. Their operations became fewer during the summer of 1949. Even so the Third Battalion still managed to account for a considerable number of bandits.

The Grenadiers were informed that they were to return home in July 1949. The troops were delighted to hear the news. They desperately wanted to see their loved ones again, especially those who had served in Palestine, and who had only been in England for a few short months since the end of the war. Days passed into weeks. The advance party from the Suffolk Regiment arrived, and began the takeover in Sungei Besi. The Guardsmen were excited and eager to get away. But they took the time to pass on their hard earned experience to the newly arrived Suffolks, before finally exchanging their familiar No5 rifles and Owen guns.

The Emergency had been contained. The war was far from over, but the Third Battalion felt that they had played an important part in the campaign. They were praised by the Brigade Commander and by the High Commissioner. As they boarded the troopship for England there was immense pride at a job well done. The conflict in Malaya was to continue, until finally declared over in 1960. Over 100,000 British troops were to serve there during the emergency, but the Third Battalion Grenadier Guards had seen the last of the green Malayan Jungles.

Chapter 21

Epilogue

The 3rd Battalion disembarked at Southampton and were moved by train to Waterloo station. It was no surprise when they were met by the Regimental Band. It was all rather reminiscent of their return from Palestine. They marched along the Embankment and down Birdcage Walk, passing Wellington Barracks, where the 1st Battalion Welsh Guards turned out to give three cheers. Then on to Chelsea, Sid's first posting from the Depot, thirteen years earlier. Not much had changed in the old Barracks. It was pretty much as he remembered, with its old accommodation blocks.

Shortly after their arrival he was promoted to the rank of Colour Sergeant, and appointed as Company Quartermaster Sergeant of Number Three Company. He was now known as 'Pay Sergeant', a term unique to the Grenadiers and internally abbreviated to 'Paybloke'. Life was now very different; there was less freedom than in his appointment as Pioneer Sergeant. He was required to carry out routine public duties. He now had a whole Company to administer with all the associated problems, but he soon became accustomed to his new job.

His disembarkation leave was spent mainly with Pat and the boys. She was now getting very used to his disappearing acts. Pat's father wondered if Sid would

Csgt Dowland on public duties, London 1950

193

ever 'pop the question'. They were able to see each other fairly regularly, as Windsor was easily reached by train. The boys again became accustomed to their regular football matches. Sid found himself mounting the Kings Guard on a regular basis. This was far from routine for him as he had not mounted guard since before the war, and had never done so as an NCO, much less as a Senior. It was a steep learning curve as he memorised the sequence of the guard mounting ceremony and the commands that he was required to give at various points.

He often encountered faces from the past. On one occasion, whilst on guard, he noticed a distinguished looking gentleman in plain clothes. It was none other than General 'Boy' Browning, his old commanding officer. Sid was well aware that Browning's ascent had been rapid during the war years, and that he had commanded the Airborne Forces. He called his little detachment to attention and delivered a smart salute, asking, 'Leave to carry on sir, please'. Browning was impressed that he had been recognised in plain clothes and he thanked the unknown Grenadier Pay Sergeant.

Sid often wondered where his old pals were. He had served with so many characters over the years. Most of them had been discharged from the Army and he sometimes bumped into them at regimental gatherings. His old pals from the SAS were rarely seen, but he was able to piece together what had happened to most of them. SSM Feebury had predictably rejoined the SAS and had won the DCM in 1944. Dougie Wright recovered from his illness and went on to take part in many operations in the Mediterranean and Yugoslavia. He was awarded the MM. Kosbab left the army after the war. He had been unable to alter his character and there were doubtless a few people who were glad to see the back of him. He often

The Sergeants Mess of the Third Battalion Grenadier Guards with HM the Queen

turned up at regimental events where he sometimes encountered his close circle of friends from the war years.

The men who died in Sardinia were buried on the island, and were eventually interred in the Cagliari Communal cemetery. Much later, Sid learned that George Cass had no known grave, but that he was commemorated on the Cassino memorial. Noriega had thankfully managed to recover from his illness and he survived the war. He was unable to discover whether the Italian American traitor was ever apprehended. There was however, a very comprehensive file on the circumstances of the Sardinian raid which would remain open sixty years on.

As always Sid mastered his employment and a steady routine was established in London. The Third Battalion was on parade for the King's Birthday Parade in 1950. On 7th June 1951, they trooped their own colour on Horseguards Parade. The King was ill. For the very first time the salute was taken by Princess Elizabeth, their Colonel. CQMS Dowland was not on that parade as he had been posted to HQ 1st Guards Brigade.

The Brigade was based in Tripoli, but spent much of its time in the Egyptian Canal Zone, where it was required to protect British interests. He enjoyed being in North Africa. Some of the men hated the heat and the lack of home comforts, but he was so used to serving in the desert that it was second nature to him. However, the country had changed. The British army was concentrated in the Canal Zone and there was a good deal of unrest. The Egyptian population was becoming increasingly anti British, and there were fears that the situation could turn ugly at very short notice. The end of the Second World War had not brought the stability that everyone expected.

Tension between east and west, an upsurge in nationalism, and the spread of communism dictated that the army was in great demand. The conflict in Malaya was ongoing and the French were fighting in Indo China. The war in Korea, which had commenced in June 1950, was raging, threatening to spark another global conflict. The tide of nationalism was sweeping across North Africa. The state of Israel was still hugely resented by its neighbours, after the war of 1949. The British were seen as an unwelcome imperial power in the region, and many held the British responsible for the situation in Palestine.

Sid's latest post was as the Quartermaster Sergeant of the Brigade. He felt quite at home in Tripoli and was required to make frequent trips to Egypt with the rest of the Brigade. He knew Egypt so well now that he was able to find his way across the vast country with ease. The First Battalion were still in the 1st Guards Brigade when he arrived, and he was able to spend a good deal of time with old friends. At the end of June, the Third Battalion once again arrived in the Middle East for a tour of duty. Their spell at home had been a brief one and they now set about the process of acclimatisation and familiarisation.

The last of the First Battalion men returned to England in September 1951. The Battalions consisted largely of National Servicemen, but Sid noticed that they were treated in the same way as the 'regulars'. He was pleased by this. Some of the regiments he had dealt with seemed to make a distinction between the two, and treated the National servicemen as second class citizens. He now found that many of his 3rd Battalion pals turned up, especially when a favour was needed. Many items found their way from his stores to the Grenadier lines, which may not have been completely legitimate.

Sid finally proposed to Pat. He returned home in 1952 to marry his long suffering fiancé. Pat's father was convinced that he was only marrying her for her pension! The two were finally wed near his home in Poole. They had been courting on and off for eleven long years. Pat had put up with frequent and extended periods of separation. Most of his family were there for the wedding and Pat's relatives made the journey to Dorset. The 'newly weds' decided that Pat would travel to Tripoli with the boys, and that they would move into a married quarter.

The whole family was excited at the prospect, but their hopes of an early move were dashed when Sid was told that no quarters would be available for some time. He returned alone to Libya, and spent almost another year between Tripoli and the Canal Zone, before a married quarter became available. Meanwhile, Pat returned to Windsor to commence her life as an Army wife, but it seemed that little had changed. Her husband was still thousands of miles away in the desert, whilst she went about her business in England.

In 1953 the Dowland family were reunited when Pat and the boys flew to Libya from Stanstead airport. It was very exciting, none of them had ever been out of England before and here they were flying off to a new life in North Africa. Pat had decided to make the most of the experience. At least she would see more of her husband. There was a brief stop over on the island of Malta and they took in the sights eagerly. The weather was gorgeous and they hoped that Tripoli would be the same. When they arrived in North Africa, Sid was waiting. He took them to their new home, a flat in a block of six, at Azzizia on the outskirts of Tripoli.

Pat felt immediately at home in the little flat. It was quite comfortable and big enough for the boys, who had grown into healthy teenagers. Sid had been granted a couple of weeks leave so that the family would not be abandoned in a foreign country. They were able to explore the Libyan capital together. The boys enjoyed the beach and the warm Mediterranean sea. It was a great adventure for them. Pat learned where to shop and more importantly where not to. She very quickly became accustomed to the way of life. Predictably, Sid's leave soon came to an end and he disappeared back to Egypt.

Pat found it a little unnerving, suddenly being alone and knowing that her husband was a very long way away. However, the three of them made the most of the situation and quickly adapted to their circumstances. The boys enjoyed the experience immensely. They were able to frequent the beach and to visit the many sights in and around Tripoli. Before long Brian had set himself up with a little business, cleaning the windows of the married quarters. David was working as a mechanic at a nearby American airbase. The family acquired a new member, when they were joined by 'Bruce', the Alsatian dog. He proved himself to be most effective when it came to deterring local thieves. Some of the Arabs were notorious for their ability to steal anything from right under your nose. But Bruce seemed determined to keep them away.

Although the family were very settled in Tripoli, they saw hardly anything of Sid. Like the other married men he only made it back to Libya on rare leave periods. The Empire gained a new sovereign in that year when Princess Elizabeth was crowned Queen. But there was little chance of celebration for Sid, or any of the men in Egypt. The security situation had deteriorated badly and there were many incidents of terrorism. It meant that the Brigade remained on alert whatever they were doing. Agitators stirred up the locals and there were several casualties in the Third Battalion.

By coincidence, Sid's posting with the 1st Guards Brigade came to an end at almost the same time as the 3rd Battalion's tour of duty.

Both returned to England, the Battalion back to Chelsea, and Sid to another CQMS post, this time at the Guards Depot, Caterham. He had come full circle. It was nineteen years since he had first walked through the fearsome barrack gates. There were many changes. The war years and the introduction of National Service had made this inevitable. The old barrack blocks were still there with their familiar names, even the Coldstream Block had survived in spite of Kosbab's best efforts. The damage caused by a German 'Buzz Bomb' had long since been repaired, but the scars were still visible. The uniforms were different now, no longer the long khaki puttees, no more folded greatcoats, battledress was worn instead. The sentry still stood at the gate and the old Depot was still a hive of activity. The recruits seemed to be just as hard worked as he had been and he found this reassuring.

Most of the instructors were 'war men' and there were some very experienced veterans around. The recruits were now mainly National Servicemen, and it seemed to Sid that they always seemed unhappy. He often compared their 'lot' to his own, all those years earlier. He reasoned that they should have had more time available for fun. They had less kit to prepare now but he noticed that after lights out, the recruits often continued their shining by candle light. This was something that he had never found necessary. His enduring memory was of Wally dancing around the barrack room, but it seemed that the National Servicemen had little time for such antics.

It was no surprise, to anyone who knew him, when Sid was selected to play in the Depot football team. His advancing years had not yet caught up with him on the pitch. Experience was as important as enthusiasm on the football field and he had plenty of both. He also played cricket regularly, and he captained the team on

Still playing football, 1954

some occasions, even though it was dominated by talented young officers. He was also able to qualify as a football referee and his talents were in great demand. This was the first time that the family had been united for any significant period of time since their marriage.

Thomas Avenue in Caterham was a pleasant place to live and two happy years were spent there. Tripoli had been fun, but there was more security here and they were able to see their relatives too. David was called up for National Service which was no surprise, but he opted to join the RAF which appalled Sid, or so he said. There was a great deal of leg pulling about the teenager's choice of service, but Sid was secretly very proud of him. There was a brief flurry of activity during the Suez crisis of 1956 but this was short lived. Sid was told that his next posting was to be to the Guards Training Battalion at Pirbright. That would take him to the end of his service.

He knew Pirbright well. Many hours had been spent there on the ranges or on one training scheme or other. He was still a CQMS, and there was little difference to his job now that he was in Pirbright. He made sure that the recruits in his company were well looked after, and that the Squad Instructors didn't neglect their administrative duties. Pat soon got a job working in the NAAFI and the family once again settled into their new surroundings. The role of the Training Battalion was much the same as the Grenadier Training Battalion had been in Windsor. Squads of men rushed around and were taught their trade by experienced instructors, using much the same methods that he had employed in Windsor. Sid's last two years passed rapidly.

On 30th October 1958, he was officially discharged from the army. It was a strange feeling, to stand in front of the Commanding Officer for the very last time. Standing there, listening to the Colonel, he could see through the window squads of recruits marching across the square. As he was finishing, they were just starting and he wondered what might be in store for them. For the last 23 years he had attended the Commanding Officer's Memoranda every time that he had changed units or employment. But this time it was different. The Colonel shook his hand and wished him luck, as did many other members of the Depot Staff. He was well known and respected by everyone and they all knew that his services would be missed. He had decided to settle close by and he suspected that he would see many of these people again in the future.

At the time, it was customary for serving Grenadiers to join the Old Comrades Association. Sid was no exception. He was affiliated to the Surrey Branch which held regular meetings nearby, and he attended most of them. He found a surprising number of old acquaintances in the Surrey area, and was able to reminisce over a pint on regular occasions. Through the Association he maintained a link with friends who were still serving and became convinced that it was a very worthwhile organisation.

The Dowlands purchased a house in Cove, near Farnborough and Sid was able to get a job with a local firm. The company manufactured electrical instruments and he trained as an estimator. Initially he found this rather difficult. It took a long time for him to master the skill and to readjust to the slightly slower way of doing things in civilian life. David had by now completed his National service and was also employed with the firm, as was Pat. It was now Brian's turn to be called up and to Sid's horror he enlisted in the Devon and Dorsets. There were many discussions on the merits of this great county regiment, but not involving Sid, as far as he was concerned this was heresy. Brian endured even worse leg pulling than his brother, but he knew Sid was joking and was proud that he too was serving his country

He was now attending regular meetings of the Grenadier Guards Association. He was well known and became respected by many of the more senior members. A vacancy came up for the job of Branch Secretary. It never even occurred to Sid that he might be considered for the post, besides he was busy enough. His resourcefulness had not been overlooked and he was approached about the job. He was reluctant to become over involved because of his other commitments, but some of the committee members could be very persuasive. Before he knew what was happening he had been voted in as branch secretary.

Much of his time was now taken up with branch business. There were functions to be organised, minutes to be taken, letters to be written and so on. The Association was not just about social events. Its primary function was to look after the welfare of Grenadiers young and old. There were many men who fell on hard times through illness or bad luck, and the Association was often able to lend a helping hand. The widows of Grenadiers who had been killed on active service, or had died through illness since leaving, were also helped. Sid maintained a register of these ladies and they were never forgotten when regimental or Association events were organised.

As the years progressed he became more and more involved with the Association. His commitment was recognised outside the branch. He was invited to become the southern area representative, and then to join the executive committee. He soon found his way on to the finance committee too. In the meantime he was made redundant from his job in Frimley. He found another position with a company in Maidenhead. Although his own circumstances were difficult during the transition, he always found time to meet his association commitments. Most important were the 'welfare visits'. Invariably he made these in person, making reports on the needs of individuals, and their families, to the General Secretary in London. As always his attention to detail was meticulous. It was simply not acceptable to forget something as simple as a Christmas card. He understood the importance of such small gestures to lonely and vulnerable people.

Up and down the land, there were many retired officers who possessed large country properties. Many of them were quite happy to have parties of Grenadiers descend upon them for tea. Sid was never slow to exploit such an opportunity. Together with other stalwart members of the branch, he arranged weekend trips and holidays. These events became more and more ambitious in their scale. As word of their success spread, they became extremely popular. The Surrey Branch even chartered its own aircraft for overseas trips. The visits and vacations always went smoothly because of his flawless attention to detail.

Trips were arranged to Germany, France, Italy, Belgium, Holland, Austria, Yugoslavia, Libya and Tunisia. During the Tunisian holiday some of the branch members were able to visit the site of the 6th Battalion's action at the Battle of the Horseshoe. Sid was able to visit the Sfax Military Cemetery to the south of Tunisia. Here he was able to locate the graves of many 6th Battalion men who had perished on that fateful day in 1943. There was a poignant moment when he found the grave of Captain Geoffrey Gwyer.

Sid Dowland at the grave of Captain Geoffrey Gwyer, Sfax Military cemetery, Tunisia

When the Dowland family took a private summer break in Sardinia, he took Pat to the island of Maddelena where he had been held all those years earlier. He could hardly recognise anything, but it was strange to see the place in different circumstances. Most importantly he located the final resting place of his friend Tommo. The Italians had been as good as their word. After the war the Commonwealth War Graves Commission had ensured that those who had died on the island were appropriately commemorated. The little cemetery was immaculately kept and Sid left the island reassured that his comrade would not be forgotten.

Later, during an Association battlefield tour at Cassino, he found the name of George Cass on the memorial. He watched as others found the names of other fallen Grenadier comrades. He realised how important these moments were to the men who had given much of their youth to fighting for freedom. Some would be able to make the journey only once. But they would return home pleased to have been able to see the place again, in a more peaceful setting.

There were Garden parties and dinners, holidays and welfare visits, the list was never ending. Being a key figure in the Regimental Association, he received regular invitations to events in the Battalions. Years after his own service had ended, boxing remained popular and he was usually to be found with a ringside seat. As the years progressed, the last men that he had served with left the regiment, but his links with the serving Grenadiers remained as strong as ever. New faces replaced the old and key appointments changed, to be filled by fresher faced men. The veterans of the Second World War became fewer as middle age passed. Rock and roll

'In pensioner' Dougie Wright M.M. Grenadier Guards and SAS

gave way to the Beatles, the Americans followed the French out of Indo China, and the British army found new challenges in Northern Ireland.

The decades came and went but Sid's tireless devotion to his comrades and their families was unshakeable. He retired from work in 1981 but never even considered scaling down his Association activities. He still met with his old pals whenever he could but he rarely saw the survivors of Operation Hawthorn. Dougie Wright became an 'In Pensioner' at the Royal Hospital Chelsea, and they met from time to time. Sadly, Jim Kosbab died prematurely in 1958, but whenever his pals met, Kossie's antics were remembered.

The woodworking skills that he acquired from his time as Pioneer Sergeant served him well in later life. He spent a great deal of time sawing away in his workshop retreat. He managed to produce a popular line in home made bird tables, which soon turned into regimental decorations when he was let loose with a paint brush. Scores of these were purchased at regimental events and the profits were immediately ploughed back into Regimental charities.

Ill health eventually forced retirement from his position as branch secretary. But even when he found it hard to get about, he attended the monthly branch meetings. His experience and wisdom on regimental matters was much sought after. Sid was now the much respected 'old sage' of the branch. He may have retired, but he was quick to point out errors when they occurred, and to 'educate' committee members when he felt it necessary.

One of the major events in the branch calendar was the annual dinner. Sid and Pat hardly missed one of these during his many years with the Surrey Branch. At the 2001 dinner there was a surprise in store. His service was well known in the wider regiment. It had even reached the ears of the Regimental Colonel, HRH the Duke of Edinburgh. Sid was presented with a certificate, signed by the Colonel himself, in recognition of his long and devoted service to the regiment. This was a unique honour and nothing more than his 34 years as secretary deserved. He was delighted and greatly honoured by the award, as were the other branch members who were proud of their secretary.

It was extremely fitting that his service was recognised. Many said that he deserved to have been further decorated when he was still serving. His certificate was put in a frame and had pride of place in his home. Sadly his health continued to deteriorate. It became a struggle to attend the branch meetings, but it did not stop him.

Sid died suddenly in October 2002, at the age of 85. His passing sent shockwaves through the regimental community and he was terribly missed by everyone who knew him. Doubtless he was reunited with Tommo, George Cass, Kosbab and perhaps Captain Gwyer was waiting there for him too. One thing was certain, he would never be forgotten by the Grenadier Guards.

Glossary of Terms

1. Organisations

Grenadier Guards
> The First or Grenadier Regiment of Foot Guards. Formed in 1656 at Bruge in Flanders by the exiled King Charles II. The name 'Grenadier' was awarded to the regiment in 1815 by the king in commemoration of their having defeated the French Imperial Guard at Waterloo. It is the senior of the five regiments of Foot Guards.

Guards Brigade
> A formation consisting of two or more Guards Battalions commanded by a Guards Officer. Not the same as The Brigade of Guards which was until 1968 a term used to describe all Foot Guards units.

Guards Division
> A collective term used to describe all five regiments of the Foot Guards since 1968. Not the same as A Guards Division which is a war time organisation made up of two or more Guards Brigades.

Household Division
> A collective term used to describe the two Household Cavalry regiments and the five regiments of Foot Guards

Household Cavalry
> A collective term used to describe the two regiments of Household Cavalry; the Life Guards and the Blues and Royals.

Battalion
> Infantry unit normally made up of 500-800 men and commanded by a Lieutenant Colonel

Company
> Infantry unit normally made up of about 100 men and commanded by a Major.

The Kings Company
> The senior company of the Grenadier Guards. It is the Sovereign's personal company and has certain privileges and duties. Comprised of the tallest men in the regiment. The company commander is the sovereign.

Platoon
> Infantry unit normally made up of around 30 men commanded by a lieutenant or second lieutenant.

Corps of Drums
> Platoon sized unit who are trained to play drums, flutes and bugles. Each Battalion has a Corps of Drums, they should not be confused with the regimental band. Drummers remain with their Battalions during all operational deployments.

Guards Machine Gun Regiment
>Formed in 1918, comprised of five field and one training Battalion only one of these (4th) was made up from the Foot Guards, the others having been drawn from converted Household Cavalry units. Disbanded in April 1920.

2. Ranks and appointments

Commanding Officer
>The officer in command of a Battalion normally a Lieutenant Colonel. Never abbreviated to CO within the Household Division.

Commandant
>The officer in command of the Guards Depot normally a Lieutenant Colonel

Adjutant
>The Commanding Officers primary staff officer, normally a Captain. The Adjutant has specific responsibilities in relation to discipline and duty.

Subaltern
>A Lieutenant. Addressed as 'Mr'

Ensign
>A Second Lieutenant. Addressed as 'Mr'

RSM
>Regimental Sergeant Major. Known as 'the Sergeant. Major' in the Grenadier Guards. Never referred to as the RSM. The senior warrant officer in a Battalion.

Drill Sergeant
>A Warrant Officer primarily responsible for drill, discipline and duty. The Drill sergeants work directly to the Sergeant Major. There are normally two Drill Sergeants in a Battalion.

CSM
>Company Sergeant Major. Responsible for the Administration of a company. Junior to the Drill Sergeant.

Drum Major
>Senior Non Commssioned Officer in charge of the Corps of Drums. Appointed by Royal Warrant

Police Sergeant
>The sergeant in charge of the Regimental Police and charged with enforcing discipline. The Police Sergeant works directly to the Sergeant Major.

Pioneer Sergeant
>The Sergeant in charge of the Pioneer Platoon.

Superintending Sergeant
>A Platoon Sergeant serving at the Depot. He was responsible for supervising a number of squads that were administered by Lance Sergeants.

Lance Sergeant
An appointment senior to that of Corporal but junior to sergeant. Only Corporals of the right calibre were appointed Lance Sergeant.

Guardsman
A Private of the Guards Division (since 1918)

Drummer
A Guardsman in the Corps of Drums. Drummers were required to sound the various bugle calls daily.

Regimental Cook
Before the formation of the Army Catering Corps, cooks were found from the Battalion strength. The numbers of regimental cooks were scaled down and eventually phased out in the late 1970's.

Picquet Sentry
A Guardsman on duty for general tasks at the Guard Room

Officers Servant
Officers were traditionally allocated a soldier servant. This man was required to carry out all forms of administration for his officer, in return he was paid from the officers own pocket.

Battalion Staff
A term used to describe a small number of key personalities within a Guards Battalion. Due to their status they have certain privileges, such as not parading for officers junior to the Commanding Officer

In Pensioner
A retired soldier resident at the Royal Hospital Chelsea

3. Equipment

SMLE
Short Magazine Lee Enfield. Standard British Army rifle from 1903. Eventually phased out during the Second World War and replaced by the No 4 Rifle. A further lighter version, the No5 was introduced for jungle operations.

BREN Gun
British Army Light Machine Gun from 1936. Modified, adapted and eventually replaced in the 1960's.

BREN carrier
Light armoured tracked utility vehicle.

STEN Gun
British army sub machine gun introduced during the Second World War.

Lewis Gun
British army light machine gun introduced during the First World War, replaced by the BREN, although the Lewis was extensively used in WW2 also.

Vickers Gun
   British Army tripod mounted medium machine gun. Water cooled and served by at least two men.

Owen Gun
   Australian version of the STEN.

Mills Bomb
   Standard British Army hand Grenade from 1936.

Kukri
   Curved knife traditionally used by Ghurka soldiers.

Colours
   The Regiment's battle honours and symbols, embroidered onto silk cloth. Carried on a polished wooden pike. Each Infantry Battalion has two colours; the Queen's and Regimental. Additionally the three senior regiments of Foot Guards have a larger state ceremonial colour which is carried in the presence of the sovereign.

Home Service Clothing
   Term used to describe 'full' or ceremonial dress, in the case of the Foot Guards the Bearskin Cap and red tunic

Bearskin cap
   Headdress made from the pelt of the Canadian black bear. Awarded to the three senior regiments of Foot Guards in 1815 for their actions at Waterloo. Adopted by the Irish and Welsh Guards on their formation. Not to be confused with the Busby which is quite different and not worn by the Guards.

Tommy Cooker
   Improvised stove often made from an ammunition box and used with petrol.

Paludrine
   Anti malarial medicine

Buzz Bomb
   German V1 Rocket entered service in 1944 to devastating effect. So named because of the characteristic buzzing sound emitted by its engines.

U Boat
   German submarine – Unterseeboot

Stuka
   German Junkers 87b dive bomber, famous for the terrifying sound emitted from its air brakes when diving.

ME 109
   German Messerschmitt 109 figther. Known to its pilots as 'Emil'

Schmeisser
   German MP38 Machine Pistol. Usually known incorrectly as the Schmeisser because the weapons designer Hugo Schmeisser actually had nothing to do with its design. Over a million were produced during the war.

Respirator
    Gas Mask

4. Miscellaneous terms

Last Post
    Bugle call traditionally sounded to indicate that patrols had returned safely
    having reached the 'last post'. Now commonly played at funerals and at acts of
    remembrance.

Reveille
    Bugle call traditionally sounded to rouse the troops. Often played after the last
    post at acts of remembrance.

Grenadiers
    A Grenadier Guards slow March, traditionally played when returning to bar-
    racks.

Guards Depot
    The training establishment where recruits to the Household Division were
    trained.

Memoranda
    The process whereby soldiers would be formally seen by their Commanding
    Officer. This could be to make an 'application', they could be 'ordered to at-
    tend' for any one of a number of reasons or they may be 'in the report'. The
    process is more widely known outside of the Grenadier Guards as 'orders'.

Orderly Room
    The Room in which a Grenadier Guards Commanding Officer conducts his
    memoranda

Shining Parade
    A formal parade conducted in complete silence where Guardsmen were re-
    quired to clean their equipment whilst sitting astride their beds.

Detention
    A term meaning military imprisonment. All Guards Battalions had their own
    cells within the unit Guardroom. A Commanding Officer could award 28
    days detention without recourse to a higher authority. Sentences were super-
    vised by the Regimental Police.

King's Birthday Parade
    Formal parade held in June to celebrate the sovereign's birthday. In London
    this takes place on Horseguards Parade but it was celebrated all over the Em-
    pire. Also known as 'trooping the colour' and as the 'birthday parade'

Guard of Honour
    A body of soldiers normally about a hundred who parade in Honour of a per-
    son or event.

Public Duties
    State and ceremonial duties.

Scheme
A military term; from 'Scheme of Manoeuvre' both words were often used to describe a training exercise.

Concentration area
A designated area in which a military formation gathers or 'concentrates' before an operation

Blitzkrieg
German term meaning 'Lightning war' and use to describe their new rapid tactics during 1940.

Stand to
Military term meaning 'stand to arms' or simply prepare for action.

Shell scrape
Shallow trench constructed to give limited protection.

Luftwaffe
The German Air Force

Afrika Korps
Element of the German Army that fought under General Erwin Rommel in North Africa

Mention in despatches
Official recognition for an individuals actions during operations. Those receiving an MID are entitled to wear an oak leaf on their campaign medal.

Close Arrest
A soldier held under escort or in the cells pending trial. Not the same as detention.

Gestapo
German secret police – Geheimstadtspolizei

Regia Aeronautica
Italian Air Force

Wehrmacht
German regular Army

Advance to Contact
Military term meaning for a force to advance until it comes into contact with the enemy.

Cordon and Search
Miltary operation requiring a target area to be sealed off by means of a cordon and then searched by a second force.

Maginot Line
French defensive line comprised of forts and underground bunkers. It was constructed between the wars at huge expense and was designed to protect France's eastern frontier. In the event it proved utterly useless as the Germans simply went around it.

Stern Gang

Generally regarded as the most extreme group of Jewish terrorist operating in Palestine during the late forties. They were responsible for a number of atrocities.

Lord Haw Haw

Infamous Irishman William Joyce who broadcasted daily propaganda on behalf of the Nazis. At the end of the war he was captured, tried and hanged by the allies.

Turkish Crisis

In 1922 a large body of British troops was sent to Turkey in response to an uprising by the Turks angry at the presence of Greek troops on their soil. The Allies were determined to keep control of the Dardenelles. The crisis soon blew over and the Dardenelles were returned to Turkish control. 2nd Bn Grenadier Guards was sent out as a part of 1st Guards Brigade.

Siege of Tobruk

Tobruk had been under siege for much of 1941, it eventually fell in June 1942. 201 Guards Brigade was decimated in its defence and was later reformed.

Abbreviations

AWOL	Absent Without Leave
BEF	British Expeditionary Force
CB	Confined to Barracks
CQMS	Company Quartermaster Sergeant
CT	Communist Terrorist
DSO	Distinguished Service Order
DCM	Distinguished Conduct Medal
IZL	Irgun Zwei Lumi – Jewish terrorist organisation
KD	Khaki Drill
KL	Kuala Lumpur
MM	Miltary Medal
MP	Military Police
MSM	Meritorious Service Medal
MTB	Motor Torpedo Boat
NCO	Non Commissioned Officer
NAAFI	Navy Army and Air force Institute
RAMC	Royal Army Medical Corps
SAS	Special Air Service
SBS	Special Boat Squadron
SSM	Squadron Sergeant Major
VC	Victoria Cross

Related titles published by Helion & Company

Diary of a Red Devil:
By Glider to Arnhem with the 7th
King's Own Scottish Borderers
Albert Blockwell
208pp   Paperback
ISBN 978-1-906033-20-0

Striking Back: Britain's Airborne and
Commando Raids 1940–42
Niall Cherry
448pp   Hardback
ISBN 978-1-906033-25-5

A selection of forthcoming titles

The Silent General. Horne of the First Army: A Biography of
Haig's Trusted Great War Comrade-in-Arms
Don Farr   ISBN 978-1-90603347-7

Sniping in France. With Notes on the Scientific Training of Scouts, Observers and Snipers
Major H. Hesketh-Prichard DSO, MC   ISBN 978-1-90603349-1

A Journey to Hell and Back. A Photographic Record of 3 Para in Afghanistan, 2006
Jake Scott   ISBN 978-1-906033-35-4

HELION & COMPANY LIMITED
26 Willow Road, Solihull, West Midlands, B91 1UE, England
Tel 0121 705 3393   Fax 0121 711 4075
Website: http://www.helion.co.uk

Lightning Source UK Ltd.
Milton Keynes UK
UKOW02f0421201014

240308UK00002B/12/P